YOUTH POLITICS IN PUTIN'S RUSSIA

Youth Politics
IN PUTIN'S RUSSIA

Producing Patriots and Entrepreneurs

Julie Hemment

INDIANA UNIVERSITY PRESS

Bloomington & Indianapolis

This book is a publication of

INDIANA UNIVERSITY PRESS
Office of Scholarly Publishing
Herman B Wells Library 350
1320 East 10th Street
Bloomington, Indiana 47405 USA

iupress.indiana.edu

Manufactured in the
United States of America

Library of Congress
Cataloging-in-Publication Data

Hemment, Julie.
  Youth politics in Putin's Russia :
producing patriots and entrepreneurs /
Julie Hemment.
    pages cm
  Includes bibliographical references.
  ISBN 978-0-253-01772-7 (cl : alk.
paper) – ISBN 978-0-253-01779-6 (pb : alk.
paper) – ISBN 978-0-253-01781-9 (eb)
1. Youth – Political activity – Russia
(Federation) 2. Youth – Government
policy – Russia (Federation) 3. Youth –
Social conditions – Russia (Federation)
4. Post-communism – Social aspects –
Russia (Federation) 5. Putin, Vladimir
Vladimirovich, 1952- I. Title.
  HQ799.R9H46 2015
  305.2350947 – dc23

                              2015010639

1 2 3 4 5   17 16 15 14 13 12

For

VALENTINA AND HER STUDENTS

CONTENTS

· ACKNOWLEDGMENTS *ix*

· Introduction *1*

1 Collaborative Possibilities, New Cold War
   Constraints: Ethnography in the Putin Era *41*

2 Nashi in Ideology and Practice: The Social
   Life of Sovereign Democracy *70*

3 Seliger 2009: "Commodify Your Talent" *104*

4 From Komsomol'tsy-Dobrovol'tsy to Entrepreneurial
   Volunteers: Technologies of Kindness *141*

5 "Arousing" Patriotism: Satire, Sincerity,
   and Geopolitical Play *177*

· Conclusion *214*

· NOTES *223*

· BIBLIOGRAPHY *239*

· INDEX *253*

ACKNOWLEDGMENTS

I HAVE INCURRED NUMEROUS DEBTS OF GRATITUDE IN THE course of this book project.

I'd like to first express my deepest gratitude to my friends and colleagues in Tver' – Valentina Uspenskaya, Dmitry Borodin, and other colleagues associated with the Center for Women's History and Gender Studies at Tver' State University, and of course the members of the student research team. The opportunity to work with you so closely for this long has been so very enriching and inspiring. I am appreciative of the support of other administrators, faculty, and staff at Tver' State University, and to the local officials, activists, and young people who participated in our research and generously shared their time with us. Thanks to Grigory Uspensky and the rest of the Uspensky family for their hospitality and friendship over the years, and to Oktiabrina Cheremovskaia and family also.

I am lucky to have been supported by grants from a number of institutions. I am grateful to the Marion and Jasper Whiting Foundation and the Provost's Committee on Service Learning at the University of Massachusetts, which provided seed money to get this project started. A short-term fellowship at the Kennan Institute enabled me to begin library-based research on youth voluntarism during the summer of 2006. A National Research grant from the National Council for Eurasian and East European Research (NCEEER) and a short-term travel grant from the International Research and Exchanges Board (IREX) – both funded by the State Department through the Title VIII Program – supported the pilot study I undertook in the fall of 2006. Research between 2008 and 2011 was supported by a multiyear award from the National Science Foundation and IREX. A second NCEEER award enabled me to devote myself to writing.

This work has been intellectually nourished and sustained by the input of many friends and colleagues.

I would like to express my appreciation to my wonderful departmental colleagues for their support of this project – as well as for tolerating and supporting my absences. Thanks especially to Jackie Urla, Betsy Krause, Krista Harper, Elizabeth Chilton, Lynnette Sievert, Art Keene, Tom Leatherman, and Bob Paynter. A fellowship from the Center for Research on Families at UMass was a terrific boost at a crucial project-incubating moment. Thanks to Sally Powers and Wendy Varner for sharing their grant-writing expertise and for being the warmest and most generous of colleagues.

For their feedback at various stages of this project, including project conceptualization, seeking funds, and considering publishing strategies, I'd like to thank Michele Rivkin-Fish, Stephen Jones, Kristen Ghodsee, James Richter, David Ost, Olga Shevchenko, and Nancy Ries. The opportunity to workshop my chapters with my local writers' group friends was one of this project's greatest blessings: Barbara Yngvesson, Michelle Bigenho, Joshua Roth, and Beth Notar, thank you for your generosity, encouragement, and perceptive comments – and some great meals. For their thoughtful input on draft chapters, thanks to Suvi Salmenniemi, Ruth Mandel, Jussi Lassila, James Richter, and Jen Sandler. Special thanks are due to Michele Rivkin-Fish, for her support, friendship, and intellectual generosity through all stages of this project. Michele, I owe you so much, especially for your generous support in the latter phases of writing. Your questions, prompts, and insights on my writing have enriched this book immensely.

I am grateful for the many invitations I have received to present on this material.

The Kennan Institute Workshop "International Development Assistance in Post-Soviet Space," organized by Ruth Mandel, proved a fruitful site from which to launch this project. The month I spent in Helsinki as a visiting fellow at the Aleksanteri Institute for Russian Studies (July 2009) enabled me to share my preliminary findings at a crucial point in my research. Between 2009 and 2013 I made a number of presentations:

to the Seminar in Gender and Transitions at New York University, to the Five Colleges Seminar in Slavic Studies, and at Binghamton University, Glasgow University, Williams College, and the Havighurst Center for Russian and Post-Soviet Studies at Miami University, Ohio. Thanks to Chris Thornhill, Gulnaz Sharafutdinova, Janet Johnson, Sergey Glebov, Sidney Dement, and Olga Shevchenko for extending these invitations and putting me into dialogue with your wonderful colleagues. This interdisciplinary input greatly assisted me as I struggled to make sense of Russia's fast-changing political field and helped me craft my chapters.

The opportunity to discuss questions of ethics and the politics of representation with colleagues associated with the Laboratory for Transformative Practice at UMass in the latter phases of my research was very much valued. Thanks to Sonya Atalay, Jane Anderson, Jackie Urla, and other lab participants. My participation in the Mellon-LASA workshop "On Protest" pushed me to new insights and was tremendously intellectually stimulating. Thanks to Sonia Alvarez, Barbara Cruikshank, Millie Thayer, and other colleagues associated with this project for inviting me.

The highlight of the writing process was a book workshop dedicated to discussion of my draft manuscript, held in the summer of 2014. Tom Leatherman and Bob Paynter, thanks for encouraging and supporting this workshop strategy; Olga Shevchenko, Doug Rogers, and Barbara Yngvesson, I owe you eternal gratitude for participating in it. Your critical observations and perceptive comments, at the levels of both the big picture and the precise and meticulous, helped me tighten my analysis and bring the book to conclusion. Both your insights and your generosity – which extended to reading revised sections of my chapters over the summer – made a deep impression and remain with me.

I'm grateful as well to the students in my Europe after the Wall class, especially to those who participated in our Tver'–UMass Amherst Skype conference in the fall of 2010. Students in my graduate Anthropology after the Wall classes, who got to read first drafts, were terrific and insightful early responders to my chapters.

I've benefitted hugely from the research assistance of Alina Ryabovolova, Yulia Stone, Nyudlia Araeva, and especially Dana Johnson, whose careful eye and super professionalism whipped my chapters into shape and helped me meet my deadlines.

Portions of the material that appears in chapters 2 and 4 were included in articles published in *Slavic Review, Anthropological Quarterly,* and *Problems of Post-Communism.* I thank the editors of these journals – R. Richard Grinker, Bob Huber, and especially Mark Steinberg – and my external reviewers for their assistance in helping me develop my ideas. I'd also like to express my thanks to my editors at Indiana University Press, Rebecca Tolen and David Miller, and especially to my copyeditor, Eric Levy, whose support and careful attention helped me bring this book to completion.

Finally, I'd like to express my deepest thanks to my family and friends, whose love and friendship have nurtured me through the challenges of professional life and parenting over the years – and supported me when they came into collision. Thanks to Pamela Hemment, Peter Hemment, Drew Hemment, Emma Krasinska, Sam Walker, Katy Thompson, Jens Matthes, Naomi Diamond, Chris Wilkins, Susan Elderkin, Ella Berthoud, Cynthia Bond, Sondra Hausner, Lisa Echevarria, Seth Johnson, Katie Shults, and Ted White. My frequent trips to Russia were sustained by the generosity of my Moscow-based friends, faithful comrades who were so profoundly important in (quite inadvertently) setting me on the path I've followed: Katya Genieva, Slava Shishov and family, Aleksei Danilin, Elena Danilina, and Kirill Gopius. Gosha Han deserves special mention. He provided the logistical, domicidal, and social infrastructure for my Moscow visits and I couldn't have managed without him.

My immediate family members deserve special thanks for cheering me on in this project and tolerating my absences. Thanks to my children – my wonderful daughter Cleo and twins Ellie and Timo (who arrived mid-project to keep me on my toes and who granted me a whole new perspective on Russia's "I want three" pronatalism). Their playfulness and sweetness made my departures so hard, but my returns so delicious. My deepest gratitude goes to Frank, my husband and partner in parenting, who has stuck with me with good humor through all of the twists and turns of this academic life. In holding the fort and nurturing its occupants during my various absences (especially in the latter phases of writing), he has made this book possible. I owe you, I know (and the highly lucrative potboiler is next on the to-do list!).

YOUTH POLITICS IN PUTIN'S RUSSIA

INTRODUCTION

We climbed out of the car a little uncertainly, stiff after the three-hour drive from Tver'. Ahead of us we could see a checkpoint with a small tent and red flags. I could make out billboards and tents dotted through the trees. This then was Seliger 2009, the high-profile federal youth educational camp that brought thousands of young people to Tver' oblast from all over the Russian Federation. I confess to the excitement I felt in this moment; it was reading about the first youth camp at Seliger in 2005 four years previously that had piqued my interest in Russia's youth policies. Now I was there, with my Russian university teacher colleagues – an invited guest, or "VIP." It felt like an ethnographic coup. The earlier camps were controversial, organized by the newly founded pro-Kremlin youth organization Nashi (Ours), and attended by its participants. They drew a lot of critical attention from international media commentators and from liberal-oriented Russian journalists as well, both as a result of their Soviet-era resonance (their orchestrated activities and summer camps strongly resembled those of the Komsomol, the Communist Youth League), and because of the belligerent patriotism they articulated. I had tracked these camps via newspaper reports, drawn by the startling images of thousands of young people in red T-shirts doing mass calisthenics under posters of President Putin. Among Russian critics, images such as these had won the organization the moniker "Putin Iugend" (literally Putin Youth, recalling Hitler Youth), and its participants "nashisty" (a play on *fashisty,* or fascists). At a time of increased geopolitical tension between Russia and the West, Nashi and these camps appeared to offer confirmation of Russia's descent into authoritarianism. This year's camp – true to the more "civil" turn of the new (2008) Medvedev presidency – was different, distinct from its predecessors, or so its organizers claimed. Officially at least, it had nothing to do with Nashi, but was a federal event. Co-organized this year by the Federal Youth Affairs Agency and the Ministry of Sports, Tourism, and Youth Policy, it marked the climax of Russia's Year of Youth events. It was not restricted to Nashi members, but open to "talented" youth across the federation. It invited them to participate in sessions organized around a wide variety of themes, including leadership, entrepreneurism, and voluntarism.

We had been exuberant on the way, my colleagues cracking jokes about what we would find; now, in the face of the Russian flags and camo-clad security guards, we sobered up a little. Somewhat hesitantly, we made our way toward K P P #3 (*kontrolno-propusknoi punkt*), the entrance, or more accurately the checkpoint, that our contact Vitaly – a regional representative of the Federal Youth Affairs Agency – had directed us to.[1] The security guard looked at us skeptically, five less-than-youthful people: my colleagues Valentina and Maria, their husbands Grigory and Alexei, and myself. In that moment, the thrill of transgression subsided and I felt suddenly conspicuously foreign and anxious, too. I was sure how this would end – we would be thrown out, turned away, like previous critical interlopers at prior Nashi camps. But in a few minutes, the confusion was resolved; our contacts materialized and the guard handed us visitor tags, signaling that we could pass. To my surprise, I recognized one of the faces in the group tasked with showing us around; it was Olga, a student in the Sociology Department who had attended one of our team research presentations in May. In fact, all of our guides that day were students at Tver' State University where my colleagues taught.

As we walked, we split into two groups. Anton, a third-year political science student who was an organizer at Seliger attached himself to me, the foreign researcher, providing a clear and informative commentary, while my colleagues fell behind, lingering to take photographs and chat with some of the students they had recognized. Anton explained that the

0.1. Seliger 2009 camp. "Together we will win!"

camp, which ran for six weeks, was organized into eight themed sessions (*smeny*), each attended by five thousand participants ("Fifty thousand talented young people from eighty-four regions of Russia in one place!" as one glossy promotional brochure put it), who could attend one or more of these themed sessions, as they wished. This session, Programma Territoriia, invited those who were interested in developing tourism-related business projects. We walked along a boardwalk past large tents; Anton explained that this was where lectures took place, and where participants could meet with experts who could advise them on their projects, as well as with potential sponsors. I spotted posters and logos of participating Russian companies – the cosmetics company Faberlic, and a sports equipment business. We passed various art installations, then went on to the campsite itself. There were many things of note, including the "Bank of Ideas," a drop box where, Anton explained, people could deposit brief descriptions of projects, to be read and reviewed by "experts"

0.2. The Bank of Ideas, Seliger 2009.

0.3. Two tandems: Putin-Medvedev, Valentina and I, at Seliger 2009.

at the camp; and an art installation of a twenty-foot-high oil derrick and oil pipeline that offered critical commentary about the West (a skull and crossbones signaled that foreigners should keep out).

As we neared the campsite, signs of political ideology loomed large. We passed giant-sized posters depicting Prime Minister Putin and President Medvedev. As we continued, we saw large red banners with patriotic slogans and quotations from Putin, Medvedev, and other prominent politicians strung between trees punctuating our path ("Russia Forward!" one announced; one portrayed Putin and Medvedev side by side with the 2008 presidential election slogan, "Together we will win!"). We passed another installation that honored World War II: two young men in Soviet army uniforms standing solemnly on guard next to a flame, marking the grave of the unknown soldier. However, there was evidence of fun and relaxation, too. By the shore of the lake we saw a group of kayakers preparing to set off. Anton explained that while there were some mandatory activities and educational events, participants could choose from a menu of other activities to engage in: from themed workshops and internet surfing to sports (as well as kayakers, we saw kids mountain biking and rock climbing) and traditional crafts (weaving and ceramics, taught by older women wearing brightly colored, traditional woven dresses).

After our tour, Anton took us to the site he was in charge of: a cluster of tents where the group of twenty youth participants he supervised resided (they lived in residence-based encampments, many of which bore the names of the towns where they lived). This *dvadtsatka* (group of twenty) was immaculate. The students – all from Tver' – had claimed this space as their own. Like groups from other towns, they had made a nice little fence out of reeds and installed it around the perimeter. The cozy interior was a hive of activity: while young women tended the wood fire, a couple of young men cut large pieces of wood into manageable chunks with axes and electric saws. We sat, content and relaxed among our own, eating the sandwiches and fruit that this group had kindly prepared for us. While my colleagues drank tea and chatted with their students, I interviewed a few participants.

At the end of the day when we had taken leave of our hosts, my colleagues and I conferred over our picnic on a grassy patch between the camp and the nearby monastery. Despite our considerable skepticism going in, we agreed that we had been favorably impressed. Maybe because it was the last day of the camp – and because we were attending the tourism session, probably the least "ideological" one – the mood had been light and friendly. It was impossible not to be affected by our meeting with the students and by this easy camaraderie. Valentina was well known here; she was a beloved teacher to some of these young people and it had not been a meeting of "ideologues" versus "critical outsiders." We were seduced too by the simple pleasure of being outside and enjoying the beauty of Seliger. It was a special place. The wooded banks were redolent with the smell of firs; the sunlight shone with a silvery twinkle on the lake. My colleagues may have had fond memories of the place itself – Lake Seliger had been a popular destination for hikers, picnickers, and those engaging in "tourism" as it was configured during the Soviet Union; it was a top location for informal gatherings and the simple, unofficial pleasures of hiking, singing around campfires, gathering berries and mushrooms. Valentina subsequently told me she had spent time there on an archaeology dig as a student. Maria remarked how strongly it recalled the Komsomol camps she had enthusiastically attended in her youth, and here remembered them warmly as opportunities to be outdoors with other young people and to be active. "What's not to like?" said Valentina, who had done her best to evade the Komsomol during her own youth and remembered it less fondly. "Fresh air, guitars, the chance to relax with other young people!"

In Russia, youth are the new subjects of state policy. In the Putin era (1999–), the state has channeled substantial funds toward youth via a national project of patriotic education, devoting significant energy and "administrative resources" to set up new pro-Kremlin youth organizations and to make events like Seliger 2009 happen.[2] These projects seek to energize and activate young people and encourage them into diverse forms of civic activity. The Putin-era youth camps and the state-run organizations that propelled them have been highly controversial. Critical commentators in Russia and the United States alike tend to view them as quintessentially Russian, or as Bolshevik throwbacks, part of an ideological campaign to produce loyal and politically docile youth – "the Putin Generation."[3] Dominant media and scholarly accounts depict Russia's state-run youth organizations as false projects that seek to dupe innocent young people and divert their energies away from "real" and independent forms of civic engagement and activism, as the cynical output of political technologists in the Kremlin's pay, and as evidence of Russia's authoritarian turn and rejection of liberal democracy (Wilson 2005; Baker and Glasser 2005). These critical accounts encode a set of problematic assumptions about (post-)Soviet society, which Alexei Yurchak (2006, 4) has called "binary socialism" – a construction that rests on oppositions such as oppression/resistance, truth/lie, and authentic/inauthentic, and that assumes Russia's status as exceptional. This trend has increased in recent years, as relations between Russia and the West became steadily more strained.

However, the Russian state's preoccupations are hardly unique. Both its anxieties about youth and the tactics it adopts are widely shared. In organizing events like Seliger 2009, the Russian state is on trend with empowerment talk and reconfigurations of governance taking place globally. Indeed, in the first two decades of the twenty-first century, the dangers and promise of youth and their occupation(s) have become familiar global themes.

Discourses of "failed" or dangerous youth proliferate in the post–Cold War and post-Fordist context (Comaroff and Comaroff 2006). From Italy and Serbia to Japan and Uttar Pradesh, young people are the source of a wide range of anxieties. Unemployed youth – especially males – with their idleness and lack of formal occupation, are imagined as "threats" to the state and civil society (Jeffrey 2010). European policymakers wring their hands over the phenomenon of "NEETs" (young people not in employment, education, or training).[4] In the aftermath of the 2008 economic crisis, this concern has extended even to highly educated youth – the graduates of colleges and universities who find themselves unable to find formal economic occupation. Youth unemployment exceeds 50 percent in some EU countries, and young people now make up a substantial portion of a global "precariat" (Standing 2011). In 2013 European leaders warned that youth unemployment could lead to a continent-wide catastrophe and widespread social unrest aimed at member state governments;[5] indeed, these discussions refer to unemployed youth as a "ticking time bomb" (borrowing the metaphor originally coined by IMF director Christine Lagarde in 2011, after the Arab Spring), one that might blow in concerning directions.[6]

These discussions play out across diverse global locations, from liberal democratic "advanced" democracies to newly independent postsocialist states and "emerging" economies, as anthropologists have tracked. They intersect with a wide range of anxieties, including alarm about demographics (aging national populations in Europe, low birthrates), immigration, and national security. Anne Allison (2013) traces how the youth of Japan are blamed for precarity and Japan's lack of productivity. Craig Jeffrey (2010) traces anxieties around highly educated Indian newly urban youth – the children of rural farmers who now cluster unemployed in urban centers, seeking work and engaging in forms of "timepass." Andrea Muehlebach (2012) traces the generational implications of neoliberal welfare reform in Italy as well as the moralizing projects young people are subject to. This is a generation that's simultaneously castigated and admired. Purportedly apolitical, apathetic, cynical, and vulnerable to political manipulation, but tech-savvy and innovative as well ("the Facebook generation"), Millennials are considered to share core characteristics and suffer a similar plight globally. Above all, they can be threatening to the status quo.

There are many undesirable directions that unoccupied, idle youth might take – antistate, antiglobalist, radical, foreign sponsored, xenophobic, and far right. Indeed, in Europe young people have taken the lead in far-right and popular nationalist movements. They were at the forefront of the global uprisings that began in the late 1990s and that have accelerated in the aftermath of the 2008 economic crisis and austerity policies it gave rise to as well – the antiglobalist, anticorporate forms of activity that emerged as a response to neoliberalism and the tight relations between economic and political elites. Sidestepping electoral politics, they have spawned an innovative repertoire of rebellion and protest – occupying plazas, streets, and banks.

In response to this purported crisis, youth have become the new subjects of a reenergized set of global policies in the twenty-first century. National and international bodies and agencies – such as the European Union, UNESCO, and USAID – have devised projects and created technologies to "empower" and "activate" young people and – when necessary – to "reintegrate" them into society (Eliasoph 2011; Muehlebach 2012). These global "empowerment projects," as sociologist Nina Eliasoph refers to them, make bold claims about the transformative effects they can accomplish, both within youth participants themselves and within the societies they live in.[7] Animated by a liberal vision that sees youth as a force of modernity and innovation (Amar 2014, 37), these global projects posit youth participation as a necessary ingredient for democratic renewal and an antidote for authoritarianism (Greenberg 2014).

Critics, or those influenced by dominant accounts of Russia, would likely home in on certain aspects of what I have described at Seliger – the Putin posters and political slogans that dotted the landscape and hung between trees. I want to draw attention to other aspects of what I saw there and suggest a different frame. The young people I encountered were animated by a diverse range of concerns. Many of the participants I spoke to were anxious about jobs; they were drawn to Seliger by the promise of the skills-development workshops and the sponsorship and networking opportunities it offered. While some, as Valentina observed, came to relax with other young people, others were passionate about the diverse projects they had brought and wished to develop. One young man spoke to me with passion about the "ethnotourism" project he was working on, a project of historical preservation and economic regeneration he wished to undertake in the rural, depopulated village he came from. Other participants had an urgent sense of social mission and came to Seliger to develop projects to assist orphans, veterans, and the needy. The young people I spoke to largely ignored the Putin posters; as one young woman put it to me with a smile, "We came only because it was not a *nashisty* [Nashi activists'] forum."

This suggests that the Russian experience is best understood not in isolation – as most mainstream accounts prefer – but as part of a broad renegotiation of the contract between state, civil society, and individual citizens. Rather than mere Soviet throwbacks, Russia's state-run projects are forged at the crucible of shifting relations between states, society, and capital that are taking place globally. While they draw on Soviet forms and logics, they respond to twenty-first-century disenchantments that are widely shared: cycles of economic crisis, disillusion about political liberalism, and the ever-widening gap between the affluent and the precarious under globalizing neoliberalism.

YOUTH, NEOLIBERALISM, AND COLLABORATIVE ETHNOGRAPHY

This book traces some of the youth projects the Russian state crafted during the Putin era, projects that sought to occupy the participants' time and harness their (political, productive, and reproductive) energies – at a time of considerable global upheaval. Drawing on a collaborative research project that engaged provincial youth in the process of inquiry, this book interrogates Russia's state-run youth projects ethnographically and considers their implications for the redrawing of state power and citizenship. What kind of citizens did the Russian state seek to foster? Which young people did these campaigns engage and what sense did they make of the projects they were enticed into? The book traces the arc of Russian youth policies from 2001, when the state began to pay serious attention to youth, to 2011, the year of political protests when the state youth project began to unravel. It focuses specifically on the youth organizations and projects that regional and federal politicians and state agencies set up, and the kinds of activities they engaged in.

Analytically, I am interested in both the governing intention of these projects and their reception by those they engaged. I examine the play of logics that took place within them, attentive to both continuities and discontinuities with Russian and Soviet forms, and their resemblance to and divergence from global forms as well. While Seliger 2009 certainly retained the patriotic-nationalist flavor that aroused controversy (and dished up elements of the Soviet past), it also offered an eclectic mix of projects. Here, the entrepreneurial logic was striking: it invited young people to innovate while improving themselves and doing good under the slogan "Commodify Your Talent!" (*Prevrati tvoi talant v tovar!*).[8] Resembling global empowerment projects everywhere, these projects bore the contradictory hallmark of the neoliberal moment they responded to: letting the state off the hook as they "empowered" people to seek individualized solutions, inculcating hierarchies as they claimed to equalize (Eliasoph 2011). They manifested the psychological turn associated with the neoliberal moment as well – the self-work and the technologies neoliberal governmentality entails (Cruikshank 1999; Hyatt 2001a; Matza 2009; Zigon 2011). At the same time, these projects bore specific inflection, the result of Russia's unique positioning within the global processes I have invoked and of its recent history: the dislocations of the USSR's demise and the international democratizing interventions that it enabled.

I examine Putin-era state-run youth projects as a creation of the last Soviet generation,[9] designed for the first post-Soviet generations. While their architects came of age in the 1970s and 1980s and witnessed socialism's demise,[10] the youth these state-run projects target were born in or around 1990 – one year after the fall of the Berlin Wall and one year before the USSR's dissolution. How did those who have no lived experience of socialism respond to the Soviet-era images and values that were offered them? How did these globally linked and tech-savvy Millennials make sense of nationalist-oriented state-run campaigns, and what motivated their architects to create them? My ethnographic chapters grapple with these questions, tracing young people through their engagement in a number of state-run projects: the pro-Kremlin youth movement Nashi, the federal youth educational forum Seliger, state initiatives to promote youth voluntarism, sexualized political campaigns, and state-sponsored pronatalism.

My first task in this book is to account for these state-run youth projects and the policies that propel them. I do so by locating them as a response to the painful dislocations of the postsocialist period, the result of market-oriented and liberalizing reforms. The nineties were a decade of democratization – international agencies and NGOs brought models of civil society, decentralized governance, and community participation to postsocialist states. Many Russians today criticize these interventions and the neoliberal paradigm on which they rested.

Russia's state-run youth projects can be interpreted as a retort to this; they were born in a time of backlash, a moment when the Russian people were broadly united in bitter resistance to neoliberal economic policy – the controversial economic "shock therapy" that, it is commonly maintained, brought the country to its knees – and to the international "democratizing" interventions that legitimized it. They emerged at a time when Russia was struggling to forcibly reassert itself on the global stage under the newly elected president Vladimir Putin, to advance a distinctively nationalist set of goals and articulate a "national idea." Fueled by Russia's oil-and-gas prosperity in the 2000s, they have been part of a bold project to "rebrand" Russia.

At the same time that state-run youth projects advanced a trenchant critique of nineties-era interventions and the models and paradigms that guided neoliberal democratization, they also drew on them. "Modernization" (of the economy and society) has been an important theme of the Putin-era project of national renewal (particularly pronounced in the Putin-Medvedev period). I have been struck throughout by the complex tumble of symbols, images, and governing logics that were manifest in the projects state actors have crafted. Throughout I show how these youth campaigns rather surprisingly married late capitalist preoccupations with innovation and talent to Soviet-era and nationalist discourses (Blum 2006).

A central theme of the book is the tracing of the paradoxical kinship between Putin-era state-run projects and the nineties-era interventions that preceded them. Russia's political technologists are globally aware, borrowing both from the neoliberal toolkit of international democracy promotion and from the diverse repertoires of protest it stimulated. I join those who examine the complex afterlife of nineties-era democracy promotion (Fournier 2012; Greenberg 2014; Manning 2007; Razsa and Kurnik 2012; Kurtovic 2012) to consider the work of the political technologists serving the Russian state.[11] In dialogue with these scholars, I am interested in the complex transformations that take shape as democracy-promoting technologies circulate and hit the ground. My ethnographic research shows that the same techniques and strategies which entered the repertoire of celebrated democratic oppositional waves – from the color revolutions in former Soviet contexts to the Arab Spring – can be equally effectively deployed (or "rebranded") for pro-regime purposes (c.f. Manning 2007).[12] In tracking them from their inception in 2005 to the Putin-Medvedev era, I consider the play of logics and technologies within these campaigns and examine their complex fusions.

Contra dominant accounts, my research revealed the instabilities of Putin-era social engineering. While the governing intent was very pronounced in Russia's youth projects and announced itself very explicitly – as one banner slung between trees at Seliger 2009 put it, quoting then-President Putin, "The development of the person [*razvitie cheloveka*] is the main goal and an essential condition for the progress of contemporary society; it's absolutely a national priority" – I discovered that the technologies the Russian state devised were frequently ignored – both by the agents of the state responsible for their dissemination and by the youth who received them. Moreover, these projects were chaotic and unstable, part of a diffuse and uncertain project of governing that did not emanate exclusively from a unified state. They were the creations of diversely positioned actors (Ong and Collier 2005; Ong 2006) propelled by the animus, complex sense of nostalgia, and disappointment and disaffectation – with liberalism, with the West – their authors experienced. They reveal both continuities and discontinuities – not just with official Soviet-era technologies and models, but also with the informal logics of late socialism – including repertoires of satire and mischief. One such repertoire was *stiob,* a mode of parody or ironic aesthetic that was widespread in the USSR – Alexei Yurchak (1999, 92) refers to it as a "late socialist cultural disposition" – and which was originally turned against the Soviet state and its ossified logics; here these projects' architects deployed it against liberal logics and discourses and pieties (liberalism, feminism, civil society), as well as the subjects who espoused them.[13]

Engaging recent scholarship in the anthropology of neoliberalism and postsocialism, my chapters examine the complex play of logics that took place within state-run youth projects and campaigns and the forms of citizenship and subjectivity they beckoned forth. I show that – like neoliberalism itself – Russia's state-run youth projects were flexible and multivalent (Ong and Collier 2005; Ong 2006). Moreover, they had un-certain and unintended effects. The campaigns I examine – Nashi, proj-ects to commodify youth at Seliger, voluntarism-promoting projects, and sexualized political campaigns – articulated complex fusions that combined elements of neoliberal rationality with other cultural forms (socialist, Orthodox, nationalist). Unmoored from their original pro-grams, these conceptions took on new meaning in these projects, which contained niches of unpredictability, allowing alternative forms of so-ciality to flourish.

At the same time that I consider the ways the recent past shaped these campaigns, I am attentive to these campaigns' use of the Soviet past as well – the strategic and selective ways Russia's political technolo-gists drew on it. State-run youth campaigns frequently invoked Russia's imperial and Soviet legacies to bolster Russia's contemporary geopoliti-cal role. As we saw at Seliger, the Great Patriotic War (as World War II is referred to), the Soviet Union's most sacred symbol (Tumarkin 1994), loomed large. Significantly, this was a neoliberal imagining, where So-viet heroes (not only soldiers, but also cosmonauts and inventors) were respun as innovators and entrepreneurs. Once again, this historical re-visioning engaged multiple actors. The revival of the Soviet past in the present is a tactic of Russia's political elites, part of a state-led project to synthesize a "national idea" (Smith 2002), yet it coexists with a veritable nostalgia industry that has pop-cultural elements and popular roots (Cassiday and Johnson 2010; Ivanova 1999; Yurchak 2008). The "branding" of what some refer to as the "New Russian Patriotism" is undertaken by diverse cultural producers in a dizzyingly commodified terrain (Goscilo and Strukov 2011b; Menzel 2008; Norris 2012); it is commercially driven, as well as state supported – indeed, the state/nonstate distinction becomes increasingly hard to maintain. I draw on recent anthropological scholarship on memory and nostalgia and works in Russian cultural and performance studies to explore the ways state-run youth projects were crafted and their reception by the young people they engaged, attentive to the contemporary cultural forms – film, literature, social media – that state projects coexisted with.

My second task in this book is to communicate a thick description of youth participation in these projects. The book is structured around an account of the collaborative research project I undertook between 2006 and 2011 with Russian scholars and youth in the provincial city of Tver' – Valentina Uspenskaya, Dmitry Borodin, and the other colleagues with whom I traveled to Seliger and their students.[14] This methodology afforded me the insights of young people who are differently positioned within this terrain: ardent activists of various state projects; occasional participants – those who enjoyed the freedoms and perks participation has afforded; and the unengaged young people who remained determinedly aloof. As the host of the annual youth camp at Seliger, Tver' oblast served as something of a hub for state-sponsored youth projects. In the course of our project, increasing numbers of local youth became involved in them. In 2009, Russia's Year of Youth when federal attention peaked, our research team comprised students who were actively engaged in Seliger 2009. Some were drawn to our project because they were disenchanted and motivated to critique the state-run projects they had participated in. For them, our project became a site where they could puzzle and make sense of their prior engagements. Others became involved in these structures for the first time as a result of our project – for example, interning at the offices of the regional youth committee, the state organ tasked with organizing Year of Youth 2009 events in Tver', as a means of data collection.

In presenting this complex data I explore the multiple forces that propelled, inspired, and animated these projects as well as young people's diverse reasons for participating in them. In Russia, because of the

Soviet legacy of officially mandated political participation, attitudes toward politics and political authority are complex and defy the simple binary pro/anti-state. As Alexei Yurchak (2006, 9) has shown, during the late socialist period peoples' participation in official structures and events was agentive and individualized. The Komsomol insiders he profiles did not take official pronouncements at face value, yet they took part in Komsomol activities enthusiastically and found them meaningful (in ways that did not always correspond with the goals of the state). Caroline Humphrey (2002, 14) pointed to this complexity in a prescient remark she made about Russia's resurgent authoritarianism in 2001: "The way this is experienced internally," she wrote, meaning within Russia, "is [likely to be] very different from the face put on it externally, for the benefit of international relations." Indeed, this research yielded rich insights into a terrain that was blurry, and less stark than most Western accounts of Russian youth politics suggest. The collaborative method got me to something different on the topics of youth, neoliberalism, the state, and subjectivity. It propelled me into proximities and entanglements that not only enabled me to gain insight into the ways the state youth project was "experienced internally," but also revealed to me young people's responses to the "face" it assumed, that is, the subtle ways they apprehended state political performances. Above all, it was a research process that was peopled with diversely positioned actors, who brought competing analytic frames to the processes in motion, exposing me to multiple vantage points and enabling me to realize the slipperiness of political identification within them. The chapters that follow are thick with voices, as I show how student team members jostled to interpret, satirize, and make sense of the projects they engaged in. Drawing inspiration from anthropological accounts of social movements, I argue that just as we need "thickness" to complicate romantic notions about "resistance" – accounts that emphasize heterogeneity of perspectives among the activists we might sympathize with and favor, and the internal tensions and politics within movements – we need it to unsettle our ideas about pro-regime movements as well (Ortner 1995; Urla and Helepololei 2014).[15]

The following chapters trace the trajectory of some of the youth who were swept up in these projects between 2004 and 2011, highlighting their debates and sense-making about politics, power, and citizenship. I focus on the forms of incitement young people encountered – how they were persuaded, moved, and challenged to engage in the projects offered to them – and draw attention to the meaning and very real sense of satisfaction they derived from participation in those projects. As I saw that day at Seliger, the young people at the camp casually disregarded the overbearing images of state power. Beneath the red banners and giant Putin-Medvedev posters they were relatively free; within the confines of the wholesome regimen (no smoking, no drinking, early curfew), they were able to run their own affairs and make their own choices, picking from an enticing menu of leisure options as well as educational programs. Our expectation of encountering Otherness was defied by the comforting experience of the familiar.

This book's final task is to make a methodological-ethical intervention by making the case for collaboration in ethnographic projects. It can be read as a meditation on what it means to do ethnography in the Putin years and as a manifesto for collaboration across geopolitics. For this collaboration was a sequel; it grew out of my earlier work with Valentina and her scholar-activist colleagues (1995–1998). I lay out the contrasts and continuities of our two collaborations, undertaken eight years apart under strikingly different political conditions, and theorize the form of collaboration this project represented: a "second-generation East-West feminist exchange" that was shaped by and responded to a much less hospitable political climate.

We designed this second project to consciously intervene in the discourse and politics of new Cold War binarisms. After a brief moment of post-9/11 accord and mutual recognition as Bush famously glimpsed Putin's soul at their first summit in Slovenia ("I looked the man in the eye. I found him to be very straightforward and trustworthy and we had a very good dialogue. . . . I was able to get a sense of his soul"), Russia-US relations steadily deteriorated. Putin's nationalist reassertion met with alarm in US and Western European policy circles, and talk of a "new Cold War" rumbled (Cohen 2006). This hostile rhetoric sharply escalated in the mid-2000s, both in Russia and in the United States. In the West, much of this rhetoric was directed at the person of Putin himself (Cohen 2012). As components of the Putin-era patriotic

rebranding project, the state-run youth projects we examined were centrally embroiled. Valentina and I conceptualized our research process
as a project of discursive destabilization that would intervene in this
climate by enacting international collaboration and exploring points of
commonality between Russia and the United States. Our project was
prompted by the recognition of similarity and common processes: the
repoliticization of youth under neoliberalism, and schemes to responsi-
bilize and "empower" youth. As educators in state universities we were
on the front line of these processes and both experienced the pains of
university corporatization and educational reform.

Based as it was on the long-term relationship between Valentina and
me, this research enacted and modeled a kind of international collaboration that was becoming increasingly difficult to achieve in Russia. Our
project both interrogated and intervened in these processes by engaging
young people in the process of inquiry, creating a conversation between
differently positioned youth and across the professor-student divide. In
so doing, it created new spaces for dialogue and facilitated a critical comparative discussion about power, social responsibility, and citizenship.
In detailing our project I show that beyond the rich insights it generates
(c.f. Humphrey 2002; Lassiter 2005), collaborative research encodes a
space of connection and possibility. Against the certainties and cold
assumptions of this increasingly hostile geopolitical terrain I argue that
we need this method more than ever.

RECRUITING PATRIOTS

To provide evidence of the tensions that animate these youth projects
and the play of logics that interests me, I offer a couple of snapshots
dating from May 2009, when I visited Tver' and the student research
team shortly before the summer camp at Seliger. The first occurred during a presentation I was making to a class of undergraduate sociology
students. My colleague Valentina had asked me to speak to them about
cultural anthropology and the earlier collaborative projects she and I had
engaged in. When I mentioned our research topic of youth and noted
that the Seliger 2009 camp appeared to mark a sea change in state youth

policy, Andrei, a master's student and a member of the research team who was employed by the regional youth committee and who happened to be sitting in on the class, leapt to his feet. To my surprise, he took my characterization as an invitation and began to issue a recruitment speech. "Yes," he said, signaling his agreement with my statement, "it's a really historic event. It's unprecedented! Go to the Year of Youth site," he urged the group. "You can either register your own idea, as it were, or join one of the projects that's already established within the themes." Andrei continued, eagerly, "The goal of this camp isn't just to teach young people to write cool projects and launch them – it's also to enable them to earn money from them. It usually goes like this: we have a terrific project, but we can't enact it, because we don't have any money for it. But at Seliger, the government is prepared to give you money to realize these projects. There's going to be a huge number of VIPs [*veepy*], more than you ever dreamed of, from the president of the Russian Federation and Zhirinovsky,[16] to Valentina Ivanovna." (He nodded toward Valentina, who had indeed received an invitation to attend as a VIP guest. She bowed, with mock solemnity, prompting general laughter.) "Right now, all the participants of Youth Year are drawing up a list of the VIPs they'd like to see . . ." Looking around the room and realizing with some exasperation that the assembled first-year students looked unmoved, he raised his voice slightly, his eyes shining, "It's a really serious event, which will help you not only realize your projects and find good contacts, but it will help you to find work in the future, to find yourself a good employer."

A few days later in the same room, I witnessed another recruitment device. This time, the event was our results-sharing miniconference where student team members delivered short papers on their research. The agent was an unexpected guest, Vitaly, the Tver' representative of the Moscow-based Federal Youth Affairs Agency (Rosmolodezh) – a new structure set up under the auspices of the federal Ministry of Sports, Tourism, and Youth Policy – and a Nashi *komissar,* or leader, active since 2005. He had learned about our conference from some of the student researchers who interned at the offices of the regional youth committee where he was based, and he had pledged to attend. As promised, he had brought promotional and recruitment materials for Seliger 2009: glossy brochures, flyers, and a couple of video commercials (*roliki*) to screen after the student research presentations. After giving his recruitment spiel, very similar to Andrei's, and showing us a couple of upbeat commercials, he inserted a final DVD into his laptop. "This is the forbidden one," he explained. "It's not officially endorsed by Rosmolodezh, but you can get it on the internet or YouTube." Mildly perplexed, I sat to watch this contraband unfold.

Unlike the other materials he had shared, with their can-do tone, this commercial was bleak and forbidding and used scare tactics to compel participation. It underscored the negative consequences if young people failed to heed the call. It began positively enough, as text scrolled to a lilting melody: "The time has come, a time for change, your time." As classic icons of Soviet-era accomplishments drifted across the screen (cosmonauts, civil engineering, weapons), the text itemized Russia's strengths: "The biggest country on earth. The richest country on earth. The best country on earth." Then, as the soundtrack speeded up, accompanied by an ominous pounding bass, it swiftly moved to condemnation and alarm. Startling text flashed by: "But your country won't exist. . . . You don't do anything; you just exploit it [on-screen were two pairs of feet, amorously entangled in bed]. School is your profession and it is useless to the nation. You work for some random guy. You drink. You smoke. You get high. You will die between the ages of fifty-five and sixty-five. Kids? – not in your plans. A family? – not in your plans. Joining the army? – not in your plans." The high-adrenaline pounding continued: "Everything is about you [on-screen, a young man ate a Big Mac]. . . . All you'll leave behind is a tablet and sixteen digits." At this, the screen depicted a picture of a headstone with the caption "Was," and the dates of "your" birth – 1990 – and death.

Reeling a little from this sensory assault, I took a look around the room at the students assembled. These sociology and political science students were mostly sophomores and juniors; many of them, I imagined, were in fact born in 1990 or even later. What did they make of this? The textual barrage continued, accompanied by the urgent pounding of the bass: "You're a consumer, a battery, in a huge, foreign machine. What do you consider valuable? Money? Your phone? Hip clothes? Your car?

Parties? All of these are worth nothing." As more images of Soviet-era accomplishments flashed on the screen (smelting, Soviet soccer teams, Mishka the bear, the mascot of the 1980 Soviet Olympics), the video insisted that this was all past tense. "Those who preceded you fought, built, innovated, fell, picked themselves up and carried on so that you would live. They built a great nation. And you? Are you an ungrateful brute, or one who could change the world? A nobody or a hero? The last or the first? Choose for yourself, but know this. . . . There is no one except you. No one else can live your life for you. There are two options for our nation: rebirth or oblivion. Find answers at www.gomol.ru [the federal Year of Youth site]."

I was stunned by what I had seen, struck both by the way the video portrayed Russia and by the severity of its address to youth. The Russia it invoked was a once great but now mortally damaged nation, hemorrhaging under constant attack by hostile forces. It addressed young people as Russia's potential saviors, yet those it portrayed were materialistic, cynical, and morally degenerate, in thrall to empty Western promises and devoid of any sense of civic duty. Riveted by what I had seen and heard and scrambling to make sense of it, I looked around the room. I could not detect any particular reaction. The students sat, idly fiddling with their pens and their phones and talking among themselves; they appeared entirely unfazed, as they had through Andrei's recruitment speech a few days earlier. As I later learned, they had heard it all before.[17] "I understand this isn't for you and that this is a meeting of the best students," Vitaly assured us seriously as he began to pack up his materials, "but 90 percent of students in the country don't understand why they are getting an education. Having heard your research presentations, I know you are different."

I begin with these two vignettes – events that played out within days of each other – to evoke some of the central tensions of these youth projects. As we can see, they are shot through with contradictory logics. On the one hand, these projects are upbeat and forward-looking and seek to appeal to youth by offering them concrete, material, and very contemporary rewards (jobs, skills, mobility, connections). On the other, they are frequently belligerent and defensive. They hearken back to Soviet times to locate images of Russia's greatness and to index the complex and ambivalent positioning of youth within it: Russia's best hope and its greatest weakness as well.

The two sales techniques I have portrayed illuminate the play of themes this book investigates – the deployment of the Soviet past and its neoliberal retrofitting. They also reveal competing elements that have animated state-run youth projects since 2001 and which uneasily coexist: a bold and optimistic insistence on Russia's path toward modernization, its determination to become more competitive in the global economy (by training a new cadre of entrepreneurial leaders, encouraging "talent" and "innovation"), and a defensive and belligerent xenophobia that is deeply suspicious of external, foreign forces and the consumption, markets, and liberalism they represent. For it is in the name of this future that Russia's Soviet past makes an insistent – and highly selective – resurgence.

The "forbidden" commercial exhibited this logic well. Beyond what was visible to me in the moment, the commercial contained rich intertextual elements, that is, it drew upon concepts and meanings from diverse interpretive repertoires (Hall 1996). Indeed, I subsequently discovered that the melody on the soundtrack was "Prekrasnoe daleko" (Beautiful distance), the theme song from a late Soviet-era children's TV miniseries, *Guest from the Future* (1985). This film, extremely popular at the time and well loved today for its retro charm – we can locate it as part of a nostalgic revival of the pop-cultural artifacts and images of the late Soviet period (see Yurchak 2008)[18] – is about a sixth grader, Kolya, who discovers a time machine and is transported to the twenty-first century. Together with his twenty-first-century peer, Alisa, Kolya undertakes a variety of adventures to save the world from intergalactic pirates. The film represents many things: the futurism, optimism and idealism of the late Soviet period (Yurchak 2008), and an idealized depiction of Soviet childhood. To the young people assembled that day who were not yet born in 1985, it would have conjured fond, retro-chic images of the brave, red tie-clad pioneers, working together to build a better future. The song's title, "Beautiful Distance," evokes the "radiant future" of Soviet propaganda posters and billboards at the same time that it alludes to the romance of Soviet achievements: cosmos, exploration, Soviet cosmonaut Yuri Gagarin (Yurchak 2008). The juxtaposition of this song with the images of dissolute, actually existing twenty-first-century youth is an extremely dissonant one. The lyrics underscore the challenge the video lays down: "I hear a voice from the beautiful distance / It's calling me to wonderful places / I hear the voice and it's asking me strictly / What have I done today for tomorrow?"

Drawing on the rich data our collaborative project produced, I trace the ways that young people make sense of this call to engagement and these appeals to the Soviet past, exploring the extent to which and the ways in which they heed them. For although they appeared skeptical of Vitaly's and Andrei's state-sanctioned message and subsequently reported their disdain for the promotional materials they deployed (one team member referred to the commercial as "that deadly video" to me), many of them signed up to attend Seliger 2009.

YOUTH IN HISTORICAL CONTEXT: RUSSIA'S PATH TO THE BEAUTIFUL DISTANCE

Putin-era youth projects had a historical precursor: the Komsomol (Communist Youth League) that was founded in 1918 at another historical peak of anxiety about youth.[19] During the Soviet period, young people embodied both the hopes and the fears about the new society; they were simultaneously viewed as the vanguard of the construction of communism and as bearers of vestiges of the old, bourgeois order, as particularly susceptible to Western (bourgeois) influence (Pilkington 1994, 54). As such, they became targets of state policy.

The Komsomol kept young people fully occupied; it managed their time, organized their activities, undertook their moral education, and guaranteed career paths as well. During the 1920s young Komsomol activists were actively deployed, sent to the country to enlighten and teach; they were on the front line of the antifaith campaign, for example, spreading in the hundreds across the country in a "quasi-missionary Crusade against the faith" (Stites 1989, 107). They took the lead in ideological and moralizing work, holding seminars and study groups, working to instill Communist values and culture in young people, to dissuade them from counterrevolutionary behavior. Komsomol activists were also on the front line of experimental creative projects. During the Cultural

Revolution (1928–1932) they engaged in the commune movement, and in radical art movements.

Founded as an independent youth group that would closely support the Bolsheviks, by the end of the civil war the Komsomol had become an organ of the party state. By 1936 when Stalin declared socialism accomplished, the Komsomol became more involved in social control; experimentation and debates ceased and it became "a single, unified and ideologically motivated organization" (Pilkington 1994, 31).

The Komsomol as remembered by members of the last Soviet generation was a quasi-mandatory organization.[20] It engaged young people in a variety of educational and "voluntary" projects – construction, agricultural work – through the institution of the *subbotnik* (voluntary day's labor). Komsomols undertook socially oriented work such as visiting with veterans, orphans, or the elderly. Belonging – if not quite mandatory – was strongly advised, and the few who opted out generally fared poorly (Komsomol membership as well as party membership was a requirement for most jobs). By the late Soviet period, all that had been radical, experimental, political, was long gone. Indeed, "activists" – those who actually read Marxist-Leninist texts and took them literally – were regarded with wry amusement by their peers (Yurchak 2006, 104) and pragmatism reigned. This is not to say that Komsomol work was not meaningful; it was a site of a different kind of agency and meaning making than Communist rhetoric announced. Komsomol insiders' positionality granted them a kind of ironic detachment vis-à-vis the workings of Soviet power and a specifically agentive way of operating within it. They were able to skillfully navigate this realm and to distinguish between what was meaningful and what was pro forma as they pursued their own creative projects (Yurchak 2006).

These projects unraveled in 1991. Russia saw out the twentieth century with a bang, and the collapse of the Soviet Union that year came as a shock to its citizens. Its demise, Russia's integration in the global economy, and the process optimistically referred to in the West as "transition" entailed cosmological upheavals no less intense and strange than the intergalactic events experienced by Kolya and his friends in *Guest from the Future*. It too brought "foreign" elements to Russian soil – capitalism, market relations, democratic discourse, forms of governance, and norms. It brought new conceptions of gender, identity, and ethnicity, and a distinctive model of subjectivity, too: the Western individuated "self" (Lerner 2011). If not quite as "epochal" as many suggested at the time – recent scholarship prompts us to see "East" and "West" as intimately related and mutually constituting (Buck-Morss 2002; Bockman 2011; Gal and Kligman 2000; Collier 2011);[21] images of the West permeated the imaginary during the Soviet period and entrepreneurial logics were prevalent in late socialism as well – the collision was still very intense. In post-Soviet Russia, the most "salvific" or utopian elements of what Comaroff and Comaroff (2001) have called "millennial capitalism" were pronounced. The capitalism that was brought to Russia in the early nineties promised the earth: the prospect of freedom and opulence, a form of salvation; crucially, a way to correct the deviation that was Communism. The explicitness of this promise and the enthusiastic ways people responded to it – particularly the ways in which they conceptualized the need to change themselves – was what hooked me initially and prompted me to begin studying postsocialist processes of cultural change.

During the Soviet period, self-work and moral education had taken place under the auspices of the Komsomol. This project sought to instill collective values and forge a distinctively socialist subject. During the early nineties, commercially produced (mostly foreign-emanating) manuals on self-management and self-transformation flew off the shelves, as people sought ways to convert themselves from *Homo sovieticus* into *Homo economicus*. People threw themselves enthusiastically into diverse forms of self-fashioning, as many anthropologists have explored. While some fruitfully brought a governmentality lens to the topic, in order to analyze the processes and practices via which the neoliberal subject gets imagined, promoted, and created, others focused on how (and why) this self-work was so enthusiastically embraced (Rivkin-Fish 2004; Yurchak 2003; Zigon 2010). Counterintuitively, the answer often lay in the resonance and resemblance between neoliberal logics and the socialist forms they ostensibly displaced.

As an English-language teacher in one of Moscow's first business schools in 1990, I had an excellent vantage point from which to view this project – the desires and needs that drove it, and its gendered characteristics as well. I found these self-help texts' bold injunctions and the enthusiasm with which so many Russian people responded to them quite perplexing. Most startlingly, these discourses involved a set of inversions. What was previously coded socialist and good was inverted, while that which was disparaged under socialism became *de rigueur,* as in the term "careerist" itself. Under state socialism, the term connoted someone with selfish, narrow, individuated goals, contrary to those of the party and state. In the nineties, these very qualities were elevated.[22] Magazines and journals vividly depicted the new men and new women and the qualities they should embody – creativity, mobility, flexibility (Dunn 2004; Yurchak 2003).

By the end of the 1990s, this enthusiastic project had largely run its course. Market relations were both well established and the source of deep ambivalence. Although consumerism was widely embraced, many had a sense of disappointment with the actually existing market economy. Rather than bringing general prosperity, reform had enabled crony capitalism and the rise of a narrow, super-rich class of oligarchs. However enthusiastic about reform they may initially have been, most Russian people were disenchanted by the lived reality in which they experienced desperate uncertainty, losses of social protection, and a pervasive vulnerability, particularly in the aftermath of the economic crisis of 1998. Indeed, the introduction of neoliberal logics in the former Eastern bloc had unanticipated results; it led to the revival of socialist-era practices (for example, personal network–based strategies and workplace-based collectivities) and forms of personhood (Dunn 2004) and deep nostalgia for socialist-era cultural forms, as well as the forms of idealism and sociality that socialism purportedly allowed (Berdahl 1999; Nadkarni and Shevchenko 2004; Oushakine 2009; Yurchak 2008).

By the time Vladimir Putin took over the reins of power from an ailing Boris Yeltsin in 1999 and unexpectedly found himself at the helm of the Russian state, "liberalism" was broadly discredited. Serguei Oushakine (2009, 35) notes that youth slang played on the term "liberal values," where "*la-ve,*" an abbreviation of that term, became slang for "cash"; Eltsinism (the rule of President Boris Yeltsin) became "Elt-cynism" – the purported cynicism and self-interested pursuit of political elites (Oushakine 2009, 112), and *demokratiia* (democracy) became *dermokratiia* (shitocracy). Those who did not benefit from this turbulent period – the majority – were sick of such inversions and felt betrayed, resentful of inequalities and fearful of their vulnerability. People who came of age during this time experienced this acutely; young people, especially those provincially located, felt "discursively disenfranchised" from the marketizing and consumerist forms of cultural production I have described, and enraged by the "lies" liberals sold them about the prosperity, stability, and transparency the new market order would deliver (Oushakine 2009, 34). This paved the way for a nationalist reassertion.

Recognizing the need to distance itself from the foreign-identified neoliberal interventions of the nineties, the Putin administration reversed many policies. Notably, it broke with the International Monetary Fund and renationalized key industries (oil and gas). It took a stand against other forms of "foreign meddling" too – taking steps to contain the actions of international democracy promoters as well. Domestic nongovernmental organizations (NGOs) – the independent associations and advocacy groups (human rights, ecology, women's issues) that had been the darlings of international democracy promotion – now found themselves marked and newly targeted, especially during Putin's second term (2004–2008).[23] Putin's moves won him the reputation of an anti-Western crusader (as well as an "authoritarian" reviver of Bolshevik practices among commentators and politicians in the United States and Western Europe). His image was that of a resolute leader who stood firm against internationally mandated neoliberal norms and made amends for the national humiliation these policies had given rise to. Yet at the same time, in keeping with his project of "modernization" and somewhat under the radar, the Putin administration advanced other, market-oriented reforms, especially in the realm of social welfare (Collier 2011; Cook 2007; Hemment 2009; Wengle and Rasell 2008).

"Sovereign democracy" – the term coined in 2005 by Putin's deputy chief of staff and chief political technologist Vladislav Surkov, the man who is not insignificantly credited as Nashi's ideological creator – tellingly names the ambiguities of this complex liberal assemblage, a mélange where political liberalism is discredited while economic liberal policies are partially pursued. This is a "neoliberalism without liberals," in Tomas Matza's (2009, 494) fortuitous phrasing.[24]

If during the early post-Soviet period, then, people looked to undertake a moral reckoning of accounts with socialism (Borneman 1998; Dunn 2004; Verdery 1996), in the mid-2000s the calculations became more complex. With the passage of time, the decade of the nineties – the decade of "democratization," or "transition" – became an identifiable epoch. Its legacy and significance is highly contested in Russia. While for some, including my liberal democracy/Western–oriented feminist Russian colleagues, the first decade after socialism's demise represents the moment of liberation from the political constraints of state socialism, for many others it represents a time of crisis, an identifiable trauma (Oushakine 2009; Shevchenko 2009). In some circles, the Yeltsin era is remembered as a shameful free-for-all, where neoliberal reforms resulted in the pillaging of the country and the emergence of an oligarchical class. "The nineties" has become synonymous with the term *bespredel,* literally boundlessness – a lamentable and unwelcome chaos that signals Russia's losses and the inversion of her greatness (Borenstein 2005; Oushakine 2009, 7).[25] Even among the relatively prosperous, it often signals inchoate disenchantments and the loss of a (Western) ideal (Nadkarni and Shevchenko 2004). Serguei Oushakine (2009) offers us a name for this phenomenon. What he calls the "patriotism of despair" is an amalgam of negatively structured forms of patriotic attachment that emerged in response to the state's withdrawal in the immediate post-Soviet period and which was profoundly productive.

By the end of the nineties, when Putin assumed the presidency, anxiety about youth was at its peak. Public discussions – invoking public-opinion polls – portrayed the generation as apathetic, apolitical, problematically self-interested, and embodying the negative elements of transition to a capitalist economy. These discussions overlapped with demographic alarm about low birthrates and deeply felt concerns about the "death" of the nation (Rivkin-Fish 2005). The main policy documents of this period – the Conception and the Strategy,[26] formulated in response to a draft program worked out by the Ministry of Education and Science in 2005 – articulated a specific set of anxieties. The "problems" of youth they identified include ethnic intolerance, unemployment, the low numbers of marriages, the housing crisis, and the demographic situation. They noted as well the danger of apoliticism (*apolitichnost'*), which leaves young people vulnerable to political manipulation.

Beginning in the mid-2000s, the Putin administration used its petrodollar-fueled prosperity to embark upon a bold cultural project designed to turn things around. Reversing a decade of youth neglect in 2001, it launched the State Patriotic Education Program, which engaged several ministries in a project to increase patriotic feeling among young people,[27] and founded the first pro-Kremlin youth group, Moving Together (*Idushchiye Vmeste*). It channeled funds to the Russian movie industry to produce nationalist "historical blockbusters," a new genre of films which applied Hollywood techniques to themes drawn from Russian history, portraying images of Russian greatness and offering up diverse heroes from Russia's past (Norris 2012).[28] The (commercially driven and state-nurtured) "New Russian Patriotism" that took shape, and which the Putin team presided over, was expressive of both a desire for prosperity and a "post-traumatic nostalgia for the grandeur of the imperial Russian past" (Menzel 2008, 4). It was militarized (Sperling 2009), but also highly commodified. Glamour (*glamur*) was its central tactic, an ideology of money, success, entertainment, and conspicuous consumption which became a matter of "national pride" and was promoted by political elites accordingly (Menzel 2008; Rudova 2008). In this petrodollar-saturated milieu, "spectacle became the order of the day" (Goscilo 2013b, 2), and Putin's public persona was a central element. Indeed, images of Putin (often shirtless, engaged in macho pursuits) flooded the media.[29] The New Russian Patriotism did not displace the anxieties I have described, but reframed them, elevating this newly branded nationalist sense of superiority and antagonism toward the West. Indeed, glamour and the patriotic performances associated with it – like Russian capitalism more broadly – has borne the logic of an "arms race" (Klingseis 2011, 108); it comprises bold acts of determined self-assertion expressive of "a stylized performance of post-Soviet Russian-ness, as disobedient, disdainfully proud and infinitely powerful in this state" (Heller 2007, 204). Simultaneously, state-sanctioned cultural products and media discussions invoked the decade of the nineties as a time of national instability analogous to periods of foreign occupation or state collapse.

These oil-funded glamorous cultural spectacles bolstered national pride and contributed to constructing an image of the Russian state as a powerful unified actor (Rogers 2015),[30] however, the oil-and-gas economy did not improve employment prospects for youth; it grew by circulating wealth rather than by creating new jobs or transforming production. The New Russian Patriotism – or what liberals derisively refer to as oil-and-gas glamour (*neftegazovy glamur*) – was a "simulacrum" of social mobility, which emerged at a time when the Putin-era state structure was ossifying and most people's opportunities for advancement were dwindling (Klingseis 2011, 91, drawing on Mikhailova 2008). Indeed, the young people I spoke with during 2005–2011 were all anxious about their futures. While they may have been captivated by glamour and celebrity culture and participated in the "arms race," they knew it was not an even playing field; they were only too aware of the limitations on social mobility they would encounter (Trubina 2012).[31] This was a time, then, of considerable volatility. The state-run youth projects this book examines were situated here.

PRODUCING PATRIOTS: FROM NASHI
TO "NEW YOUTH POLICIES"

Nashi (Ours) was founded in the spring of 2005. Building on its precursor Moving Together, it started out as a patriotic movement to provide ideological support for the Kremlin. Between 2005 and 2008, the movement grew; at its peak, during the 2007–2008 election cycle, it claimed several tens of thousands of members (and many more supporters) and had approximately fifty regional branches across the Russian Federation. Nashi's hallmark activity was the high-profile mass event – pro-Kremlin campaigns that brought tens of thousands of young people onto Moscow's streets and plazas. Nashi summer educational camps – held at the popular resort Lake Seliger – also attracted tens of thousands of participants, and were attended by high-ranking politicians and Kremlin aides. At the local level, Nashi activists engaged in a wide range of activities that received less media coverage. They organized events for orphans and programs for local veterans, and ran sessions on cultural tolerance and friendship with international students. Nashi ran socially oriented public awareness campaigns as well, campaigning against littering, graffiti, and the sale of cigarettes and alcohol to minors. Like the Komsomol, Nashi had a reward structure and promised forms of social mobility for its participants. Nashi activists took classes and seminars in Moscow as well as at Lake Seliger. Active komissars were rewarded with the opportunity to study at Nashi's own Moscow-based higher-education institute – the Natsionalnyi Institut Vyshaia Shkola Upravleniia.

The year 2008 was a turbulent one for Nashi; the presidential administration distanced itself from the organization, following a number of controversial campaigns, and it was restructured after the federal elections, resulting in the closing of the majority of the regional branches. However, it reemerged as a number of "directions" (*napravleniia* – themed projects or suborganizations) later that year. Nashi komissars (and Nashi founder Vasily Yakemenko) continued to spawn diverse youth projects until 2012.

In the Putin-Medvedev era, or "tandemocracy" as Russian pundits dubbed it (2008–2012), youth projects morphed. The "new youth policies" espoused by the newly founded Federal Youth Affairs Agency had a different flavor. Here, "modernization" rhetoric was prominent and the entrepreneurial dimension more pronounced. This tendency culminated during 2009, Russia's Year of Youth, and was especially manifest in its flagship event, the educational youth camp Seliger 2009. This camp ran eight themed sessions – leadership, entrepreneurship (two sessions), tolerance, voluntarism, tourism, public relations, and art – each of which was attended by thousands of young people and lasted two weeks. Theoretically at least, participation was competitive; applicants were invited to submit social and business project proposals via the internet. At the camp, they attended lectures and "master classes" in which they learned skills and developed their projects and had the opportunity to network with potential sponsors – business representatives and state officials. Beyond these high-profile national youth projects, there were regional and municipal state-run youth projects too, as mayors and governors took this lead.

Amid their diversity, these state-run projects shared certain characteristics. They targeted educated but economically marginal young people who may have had talent and ambition, but whose futures (and future electoral contributions) were uncertain: the students of provincial high schools and higher-education institutions.[32] Many were dwellers in the outskirts, first-generation urbanites who had a precarious toehold in the provincial cities where they resided. These were youth who did not have wealthy parents, or access to the elite educational establishments of Moscow or St. Petersburg, and for whom Seliger 2009 offered a rare chance at vacation (they would otherwise be working for money, or helping their parents at the *dacha,* or country house) and a strategy for upward mobility, or "social lift," as state youth projects referred to it. As Valentina put it, this was not for the *zolotoaia molodezh',* or golden youth, the privileged children of the super wealthy. Neither was it for working-class or marginal youth. Like the Komsomol, contemporary state-run youth projects offered a place where sincerity and commitment would be rewarded. They promised a vanguardist role for those who actively participated in them, seeking and encouraging certain qualities: talent, goal orientation, and industry (*aktivnost'*).

Unmistakably creatures of the Putin era, these New Russian Patriotic projects urged young people to overcome the dysfunctions of the nineties and the transition era. Materials summoned forth "talented, innovative" youth who would distinguish themselves from the purported apoliticism, cynicism, or "indifference" of those who preceded them (such as the the degenerate beer-swilling consumer the forbidden commercial portrayed, who was not prepared to do anything for himself or for his country).[33] This was a gendered process, too. Against the specter of demographic decline ("crisis," the "death of the nation"), low rates of marriage, and catastrophic levels of emigration, these state-run projects encouraged young people to stay, procreate, and serve the nation.

RETURNS: SECOND-GENERATION RESEARCH

In undertaking to write about Russia's state-run youth projects, I have taken on an ethnographic object that is controversial both in Russia and in the West. In 2010, the centrist oppositional party Yabloko issued a press release announcing the following: "The Russian state has engaged in a discriminatory policy toward young people, and has given up on its social obligation to them. At the same time, the government is not interested in the civil development of young people, as it sees them as a threat to the existing authoritarian-bureaucratic regime." The document denounces "oil-and-gas glamour" (*neftegazovy glamur*) as a Kremlin project, one that specifically seeks to produce docile subjects, to anesthetize or "debilitate" youth and ensure their political loyalty.[34]

These views are widely shared by the liberal intelligentsia and many youth scholars (Omel'chenko 2006), as well as by my Russian colleagues. Although many people I spoke with shared deep concerns about higher education and jobs and agreed that reform and modernization were necessary, they did not find this "projectifying" mode of enactment (with its bling and show) sufficient. Against the tide of binary socialism, I have chosen to tell a different story about state-run youth projects, one that locates them within broader flows (c.f. Gal and Kligman 2000). The play of continuity and discontinuity, similarity and difference – with the Soviet past, with global movements and other circulating forms – within Russia's state-run youth organizations is a central theme of this book.

Anthropology has a reflexive imperative, meaning it insists we attend to our own location (that is, where we are positioned in relationship to the set of issues we examine), and how this affects our analytic concerns. This reflexive commitment is especially important when working in the politicized context of postsocialist states. My preoccupation with these topics – continuity, similarity, and difference – stems from my own uneasy positioning. As a critic of nineties-era democracy promotion interventions, I am aware of the uncanny sense of commonality between Putin-era civil-society projects and the nineties liberal interventions they denounced and displaced. My earlier research (1995–1998) examined the international democracy promotion project that took form in the immediate aftermath of the Soviet Union's demise, and the neoliberal vision of development, or "New Policy Agenda" (Robinson 1994) that undergirded it. This was neoliberalism's "high noon" (Hyatt 2011, 105); the Washington consensus was intact and reformers in Eastern Europe and Russia enthusiastically embraced it. I was part of a generation of anthropologists who sought to displace and challenge the prevailing wisdom about "Transitology" and interrogate its triumphalist and hubristic assumptions.[35]

Intrigued and baffled by the hopes, expectations, and yearnings of the immediate postsocialist period, I located myself among some of neoliberal democratization's most perceptive critics: feminist-oriented scholars and activists associated with the Independent Russian Women's Movement (Valentina and her scholar-activist colleagues in Tver'). I witnessed the fact that democracy-promoting projects did not deliver what they promised – the version of "democracy" that agencies promoted post-1989 was highly particular and historically contingent; it was narrow, thinned out (Coles 2007; Nugent 2008). The emancipatory tools and technologies that were offered Russian citizens – civil society, empowerment – worked in concert with neoliberal structural changes.

My early work contributed to a robust critical scholarship that interrogated the civil-society agenda and the project of transnational governmentality it brought into effect. This scholarship has explored how "democracy," "civil society," and "empowerment" were compromised categories. During the nineties, democracy became "a vehicle with many other passengers," in Kimberley Coles's (2007, 8) felicitous phrasing. It was the vehicle via which neoliberal rationalities and technologies arrived in postsocialist space; the economic policy – shock therapy – that accompanied it led to major social dislocation and the impoverishment of most Russian people. The "Civil Society Agenda" (Alvarez 2008) "demobilized" and depoliticized social movements by professionalizing them – all while claiming to do good in their name (Alvarez, Dagnino, and Escobar 1998; Sampson 1996). In short, this scholarship has explored international democracy promotion's role in an emerging system of transnational governmentality, that is, a neoliberal system of governance in the Cold War era (Coles 2007; Ferguson 2002). In these studies, "democracy is viewed not as utopian dream following authoritarian or totalitarian regimes but rather as an exercise of power in its own right" (Paley 2001, 1), one which is at times more effective in enacting control over populations than the regimes it displaces.

During 1997–1998 I witnessed democracy promotion's complex and ambiguous effects. The international agency staffers who arrived in Russia in the nineties (with the Ford Foundation, IREX, the MacArthur Foundation, and George Soros's Open Society Institute) certainly aimed to empower the people. They sought out local associations and groups as part of their work to support democratic institution–building, using the civil-society concept to put forth appealing ideas of citizen participation and energized associational life. However, constrained by the New Policy Agenda framework, they authorized very limited forms of organization and agendas. Despite their claims to be "grassroots," the NGOs that agencies sponsored were often narrow, professional, bureaucratic affairs (Hemment 2004b; Richter 2002; Wedel 1998). They existed as a series of projects (*proekty*): temporary, short-lived enterprises that had less to do with local issues than with the concerns of the elites who designed them. Suspicious of the state apparatus, these NGOs focused on pushing for reforms that would make it more accountable to global norms, for example in the areas of human rights, gender equality, and the environment (Richter 2009a). However important, these issues seemed distant and irrelevant to most Russian people. At a time of increasing unemployment and an eroded safety net, when public health indicators plummeted and mortality rates went up, campaigns for abstract "rights" were easily dismissed as insubstantial, elite, and disconnected from the urgent crises facing the population. Furthermore, they appeared suspiciously internationalist in orientation, to be subordinating Russian national goals to international norms and values. The ironies of feminist-oriented campaigns were especially acute. Projects to "empower" postsocialist women were part and parcel of a neoliberal restructuring process that dismantled the forms of social protection that had sustained women during the socialist period (such as workplace-based kindergartens and paid maternity leave). Indeed, Belarusian feminist scholar Elena Gapova (2009b) notes that many people in the former Soviet Union came to associate the "new feminist agenda" with the new forms of inequality that took form in the postsocialist period.

In all, while the civil-society concept continued to have salience for some in the region, such as my Tver'-based civic activist colleagues, the concept and work undertaken by NGOs failed to gain broad legitimacy. In the context of dramatic economic dislocation and impoverishment, the broader public regarded NGOs cynically, as vehicles for self-interest and elite advancement (Hemment 2004b, 2007a; Ishkanian 2003; Richter 2002; Wedel 1998).

As I left Russia to write up our collaboration, the civil-society concept continued to morph. In the face of resurgent forms of authoritarianism in the region (notably the Milošević regime in Serbia), US policymakers respun civil society as a mode of "soft intervention" that could accomplish regime change, and aid was channeled to pro-democracy activists accordingly (Carothers 2004; Greenberg 2014, 14). In the post-9/11 era, civil society's content shifted further still, as democratization aid militarized under the Bush "Freedom Agenda."

My reflexive awareness of the slipperiness of the civil-society concept and the problems of democracy promotion meant that I had an ambiguous relationship to the Putin-era civil-society projects that took form in its wake. I was both uncomfortably aware of the proximities and skeptical of the NGO forms that have continued to mutate – the global formations Nina Eliasoph (2011) calls empowerment projects, which I have earlier alluded to, and which Putin-era youth projects compete with and in many ways resemble.

My Russian colleagues and I were differently invested in the topic of state-run youth organizations. As a result, there were moments of friction as our different expectations and interpretations of what we encountered became evident. Their response to this state-run project was clear: they viewed it as a troubling return to Soviet-era chauvinism and nationalism. As educators, they were concerned about the way young people were implicated in these top-down projects. Their work in the university meant that they confronted youth policies on a daily basis. Their university classrooms were polarized, the site of heated discussion as students made sense of these youth-oriented initiatives and programs. They were deeply concerned too by what these programs displaced. My colleagues had been beneficiaries of the international interventions and civil society–promoting project that Putin-era youth and civil-society projects disparaged. Valentina was one of the pioneers of the feminist scholarly and activist exchanges of the immediate postsocialist period. As founder of the feminist-oriented women's group Zhenskii Svet (Women's Light), she participated in many of the early activities associated with the Russian independent women's movement. While not uncritical of the processes I have noted (my own analysis draws on her sharp insights), she worked in productive collaboration with some of the foreign foundations which arrived in Russia in the mid-nineties. Her Center for Women's History and Gender Studies, founded in 1999, was funded between 2000 and 2004 by the Ford Foundation; it consciously embraces and enacts a progressive-liberal internationalism (Hemment 2007a; Salmenniemi 2008).

Our different positioning meant that we brought different priorities to the project. Based in the United States I had distinctive concerns. The pace and rhythm of this research methodology, together with the background I brought to it, made me unusually preoccupied with the politics of representation. Atypically for ethnographers, more of it took place from afar than up close. Short and intense periods of ethnography (wherein I attended events and spoke with and interviewed members of the team) were interspersed with long periods of apprehending Russia through the pages of the *New York Times* and through the eyes of my own students (whose sense of Russia's menace is as acute as the anti-Americanism of Tver' students). In a context where Cold War tropes prevail, how to represent Russia's state-run youth projects? What would a feminist politics of representation on this topic look like? I have been aware that accounts that do not consciously resist these binarized modes of representation have the unintended result of reinforcing liberal triumphalist discourses, becoming entangled in critiques of Russia as neoauthoritarian.[36]

While – steeped in the anthropology of postsocialism – I was concerned with accounting for the cultural material these projects draw on, Valentina and her colleagues were impatient with the "patriotism of despair" and the political technologists (grown-ups) who encouraged and spun it (they are "producers," she muttered; they are making a "show"). It was the cynical and utilitarian attitude toward youth that she objected to – a mode of operation she associated with the Komsomol (in which she had participated only very marginally). Valentina spoke frequently about how it was a project of former Komsomol activists: "There's always a forty-something-aged man in the background, pulling the strings!" she complained.

We had different analytic coordinates as well. While I was drawn to note points of similarity and continuity with broader global processes, my colleagues were more likely to focus on the uniquely Russian elements (the state was doing it wrong, doing it crudely, missing the mark of a Euro norm, corrupt in its intent). They were less likely to invoke "neoliberalism" or refer to global neoliberal shifts, since, despite the disappointments they had experienced, they remained deeply invested in the NGO/foreign interventions of the 1990s. Moreover, in post-Soviet Russia there are numerous impediments to anticapitalist critique. Not only is it compromised by its proximity to the discredited Marxist-Leninist dogma of the past, but it also brings one uncomfortably close to the positions of the nationalist right wing; nativist antiglobalization rhetoric is prevalent in Russia as in other postsocialist contexts (Kalb 2009). As liberal intellectuals invested in maintaining a dignified, middle-class subjectivity of which a sense of global, pan-European citizenship was part, my colleagues were understandably less likely than I to raise this analytic, even as they were deeply concerned about social inequalities (Rivkin-Fish 2009; Salmenniemi 2012a).

Our collaboration placed us in productive debate in and around these issues. Wrestling with this play of similarity and difference within our project and contemplating the "situatedness" (Haraway 1991) of our analytic orientations pushed me to new conclusions and led to new entanglements also. In detailing our divergent responses and some of the moments of friction between us, I consider these themes, using our relationship as a kind of diagnostic.

The chapters that follow examine some of the projects the Russian state crafted to occupy young people between 2005 and 2011, each revealing different angles of the negotiations between state and society that take place. They introduce the diverse technologies the Russian state devised and trace them at two levels: that of governing intent and of reception.

Chapter 2 focuses on Nashi, the Kremlin's most controversial youth organization. This early project was forged at the intersection of nineties-era democratization aid and the militarization of democracy assistance under the first Bush administration. An explicit retort to Ukraine's Orange Revolution, this project was pitched as a counterinsurgency operation to prevent similar foreign occupations from taking place in Russia. It offered young people distinctive technologies (themselves borrowed from oppositional movements both domestic and foreign: the radical oppositional National Bolshevik Party, the "Orange" technologies deployed in the Ukraine) to occupy or take control of the streets. Drawing on interviews with Nashi activists, I show how this political technology project was not static, but was adapted and negotiated by its participants, just as nineties-era civil-society projects had been. Like their NGO activist predecessors, Nashi komissars used the form presented by the state to pursue a variety of agendas, which may or may not have overlapped with those ideally imagined by these projects' architects.

Chapter 3 traces the more civil face of Putin-Medvedev tandemocracy, focusing on Russia's Year of Youth events and the state-run encampment Seliger 2009. Developed in the aftermath of the 2008 global economic crisis, Seliger 2009 addressed the problem of youth mobility and employment. While the early Seliger camps (2005–2008) were associated with Nashi and served as venues for a nationalist-oriented patriotic education, Seliger 2009 resembled a giant job fair. Once again, this state-run campaign offered a distinctive blend of logics. In contradistinction to the fusty formal institutions of higher education, Seliger cast itself as an alternative cutting-edge venue for twenty-first-century education; it offered a repatriated, "socially responsible" form of entrepreneurship to young people and encouraged them to develop a specific kind of "talent" for the nation. The chapter examines the shifts in subjectivity these commodifying logics entailed, and examines the uncertain ways youth responded to them.

Chapter 4 explores the Russian state's activation of youth via voluntarism projects. Again, in keeping with global tendencies, this state project constructed voluntarism as a form of ethical labor by which young people could prove and redeem themselves as worthy and productive citizens (c.f. Muehlebach 2012). However, it bore specific inflection as well, invoking the Soviet-era *Komsomol'tsy-Dobrovol'tsy* (volunteers) who preceded them.

Chapter 5 turns to the topic of sex and gender, examining some of the provocative, sexualized patriotic performances associated with state-run youth projects. Locating them as quintessential products of Russia's oil-

and-gas (corporate-neoliberal) state form, I account for them by tracing the complex gendered shifts of the postsocialist period. During the Cold War gender relations were part of a "Cold War shadow boxing" (Gal and Kligman 2000, 9), and discourses and policies about families and reproduction in Western Europe and socialist states mirrored each other in curious ways. In the Putin era, this mirroring has escalated, infused with the mischief and energy of the transformed stiob that is part and parcel of Russia's nationalist reassertion. The chapter examines these campaigns as "geopolitical performances" that speak back to the liberal governing project in a provocative and troubling way. As I consider the campaigns, I consider the challenges of representation, too, tracing how as a Western feminist observer I found myself entangled and strangely implicated. This chapter reveals more indeterminacies as well, for these projects had unintended results – spiraling off into irony and critique of the state. Here, as in other chapters, I show how youth responded to state-emanating technologies in unexpected ways. While engagement in state-run projects did entail shifts in subjectivity, the process did not take place as it was intended. Indeed, young people frequently ended up more critical than docile.

Before we get there, it is necessary to excavate the contours of the collaboration that produced this knowledge. The next chapter introduces my colleagues, their concerns, and the provincial university they were situated in, and lays out the relationships within which our research project was embedded.

ONE

COLLABORATIVE POSSIBILITIES, NEW COLD WAR CONSTRAINTS

Ethnography in the Putin Era

DECEMBER 2006, TVER'

Flushed with success, I scuttled toward the familiar apartment. The city streets were crowded, full of shoppers on their way home at the end of the day. Young people clustered around the kiosks and benches, drinking beer and crowding the paths. As I pressed the button and waited to be buzzed in, I hoped I would not have to encounter more crowds on the other side of the door. Valentina lived in the center of town, in one of the old pre-revolutionary-era apartments that abutted the city's main pedestrian thoroughfare. Like many city-center dwellers, her stairwell was often crowded with young people, mostly of college age, though sometimes much younger, who hung out in the entrance of her apartment block all day, drinking beer, smoking, leaving litter, and intimidating residents and their guests. She was frustrated daily by the situation. She understood it to be symptomatic of the times: the kids had nowhere to go. Clubs and associations were being shut down and they could not afford to frequent the expensive new bars and cafés that now proliferated in the city. During the winter months, when they clustered in large numbers, she had devised her own ingenious solution to this problem: she went out on her balcony to read drafts of her gender studies lectures to them! It had worked, she told me. The comical intervention took them by surprise and jogged them into a kind of respectful recognition, interrupting the potentially adversarial relation (aggravated homeowner confronts troublemaking youth). Some of the kids had been really interested in what she had presented, she told me – and they promised to keep the noise down.

Fortunately, the stairwell was empty that day. "Success!" I announced triumphantly as she opened the door. Over tea, I updated her on my latest successful mission and shared my trophies: literature and promotional materials from the newly founded regional social welfare organization Vazhnoe Delo (Important Business). By 2006, state-run youth organizations were popping up like mushrooms in the city, as my colleagues put it. Vazhnoe Delo, supported with lavish regional funds, was the most prominent. This project – founded by the new governor of Tver' – engaged young people as volunteers to assist the elderly and orphans. My goals in meeting with the director were to learn more about it and to negotiate internships there for the student members of our research team; we had picked the organization as an ideal site for them to undertake participant observation. Valentina raised her eyebrows at my enthusiastic account of the activities I had learned of, asking sardonically, "But are they interested in the kids that gather in my doorway?"

As her comment suggested, Valentina was highly skeptical of the emergent youth policies and the organizational forms they gave rise to. Rather than tackling real social issues (such as the needs of the youth who congregated in her stairwell, or the elderly they claimed to assist), she considered this organization to be political PR. As an educator, she was also concerned by what these costly new youth projects displaced. As political elites channeled lavish funds to new state-run projects, university budgets shrank.

Each of the eight short research trips I made to Tver' between 2006 and 2011 began with a meeting wherein Valentina, Dmitry, and other colleagues updated me on the latest events. The tone was often sardonic and satirical. Their droll reports and humorous asides always made me smile but underscored our different positioning.

In this chapter, I provide a thick description of our collaborative research process, tracing the goals that prompted it, the moments of dissonance that unexpectedly arose, and the rich insights it generated. In so doing, my goal is to offer a situated response to the challenge of undertaking ethnographic research in Putin-era Russia. As I describe the research process that produced the knowledge this book advances, I also consider the contrast it presented with the project that preceded it: the collaborative work and participatory action research project I undertook with members of Valentina's feminist group Zhenskii Svet in 1997–1998. Conditions had changed in the years since then and the Putin era was a much less hospitable climate than the nineties for international research collaborations. In the course of our project, it became increasingly marked.

Our first collaboration was an experiment in transnational solidarity. Across the fraught terrain of the postsocialist development encounter, Valentina and I sought to forge another, more reciprocal kind of partnership than many of the international feminist exchanges we saw taking place. The participatory action research project we undertook in 1998 had multiple outcomes, one of which was a community-based project: a crisis center for women survivors of sexual and domestic violence set up by members of Zhenskii Svet.[1] An equally profound outcome was the solidarity it generated between the participants of the group and me, based on affective ties and a strong sense of mutual responsibility. Valentina playfully referred to the process of making ties we underwent together as "taming," a metaphor she drew from Saint-Exupéry's beloved children's book, *The Little Prince,* where it was used to refer to the relationship between the Little Prince and his friend, the fox (Hemment 2007a, 19–20). This, our second collaboration, proved to be more complex. Though we began the project from a place of solidarity, we found the ground had shifted under our feet. The reconfigured geopolitical terrain both positioned us differently and elicited different responses in us, stemming from our locations. Moreover, in the latter stages of the project, our feminist solidaristic conception of collaboration came to collide with another, more menacing construction. Between 2006 and 2014, "international collaboration" moved from being a neutral, validating practice (an important part of the symbolic economy of Russian academic life) to becoming marked as "treacherous." New legislation enacted in the spring of 2013 required the Russian recipients of foreign funds (NGOs and scholars) working on "political" issues to register themselves as "foreign agents" (*inostrannye agenty*) – a term strongly associated with Cold War–era espionage – exposing Russian scholars to significant risk.

This chapter explores these themes and tells the story of the relationships upon which this collaboration was based. I portray myself in discussion and debate with my colleagues to offer a window onto this changing field, using our relationship as a diagnostic to communicate the transformations we encountered. I show how, our shared goals and commitment to solidarity notwithstanding, we had different stakes. While not at odds, at times we pursued a divergent politics in this collaboration.

A second goal is to make the case for collaboration within ethnographic research. Despite its challenges, this project was transformative for us all, an example of the richness that collaborative research can provide and the space of connection and possibility it encodes. I show how the complexities of this context led to the adoption of a distinctive ethnographic stance, one that embraced "epistemological humility" (Razsa and Kurnik 2012, 241) and a "politics of possibility" (Gibson-Graham 2006, xxvii). Drawing inspiration from feminist geographers J. K. Gibson-Graham,[2] I conceptualize this as an affective stance that allows for the recognition of commonality in unexpected places. It was prompted both by close, embodied relationships and ties (gratitude toward a mentor and friend, consternation at the plight she and her colleagues found themselves in) and also by the acknowledgment of the geopolitical prism through which they were refracted and in which they were situated. This process yielded rich data that pushed me to new conclusions about the state-run projects we investigated. It was in sum a methodology that shaped the conceptual underpinning of this book.

"A SECOND-GENERATION POSTSOCIALIST (EAST-WEST) FEMINIST COLLABORATION"

I came up with this descriptor ("second-generation postsocialist [East-West] feminist collaboration") as Valentina and I prepared to present on this research at the NYU Gender in Transition Workshop in 2010. I had given a paper at this feminist research forum in previous years; my intent was to signal the differences between this collaboration and the earlier collaborative research we had undertaken.[3]

My relationship with Valentina and her colleagues was forged during the hurly-burly of the Yeltsin years, the now-controversial nineties. We were some of the beneficiaries of this now much derided time; we rode high on the wave of optimism and the increased sense of possibilities the Berlin Wall's collapse gave rise to. Our paths crossed as we traversed the horizontal feminist connections and networks – the first "East-West feminist" scholarly and activist exchanges (Funk and Mueller 1993) – that took shape in the early postsocialist period. I reached out, grabbing a line thrown out in her feminist group Zhenskii Svet's very first online post, a short message posted on the Network of East-West Women's listserv (established by some of the US feminist scholars who now hosted us at NYU),[4] which introduced the group and explained its projects. I first traveled to Tver' in 1995 at Valentina's invitation, returning in 1997–1998 to do my dissertation research, affiliated with Zhenskii Svet. Our collaboration then was a critique of the form of "East-West" collaboration international funding encouraged (as community-based horizontal networks were beginning to be displaced by more formal and professional NGOs).[5] Inspired by both anthropological and feminist discussions (Alcoff 1994; Grewal and Kaplan 1994; Haraway 1991), I sought to explore alternative forms of exchange. Then, our collaboration was a mutual process of investigation, wherein we puzzled and strategized Western aid and sought to forge a different kind of international cross-cultural feminist collaboration.

In contrast, our second collaboration took form out of a shared sense of distress and bewilderment at the sharp turn for the worse that things took in the 2000s, against a backdrop of the escalating East-West tensions I have described. The climate of the university was becoming less friendly as well; at a time of "academic nationalism" (Oushakine 2009), my colleagues found themselves marked as insufficiently "loyal,"[6] problematically Western-oriented, and were disrespected by patriotic colleagues and briskly entrepreneurial administrators alike. Here, Soviet-era patterns of bureaucratic intransigence and hostility toward faculty (who frequently positioned themselves as independent and critical of the party-state) became inflected with a new element: the disdain of neoliberal-style administrators.

This second collaborative research project responded to our shifting personal circumstances as well. When we met in 1995, I was a graduate student and Valentina was a university-based civic activist. Although her feminist group Zhenskii Svet drew on university relationships and resources, it was largely based in the civic sphere. We both had the luxury of time – albeit for different reasons – and were able to devote ourselves to the issues of activism and collaboration that interested us. In 2004, we were both rooted more firmly within the university, carrying a broad and more intense set of university-based professional responsibilities. I was grappling with the challenges of the tenure track at the University of Massachusetts; she was struggling to maintain resources for her Center for Gender Studies. For the center, 2004 was a significant year, as, while it retained university support, it lost the external funding from the Ford Foundation that had sustained it. As US foundations and agencies pulled out of Russia to direct their energies elsewhere (according to the Bush "Freedom Agenda"), Russian NGO activists like my colleagues felt abandoned.

They contended with other problems, too. In Russia, as in the United States and globally, higher education was undergoing a major restructuring. In line with a 2001 Ministry of Education decree, the Russian government has worked to "modernize" higher education. This restructuring is owed in part to European norms and the standardization of education under the Euro zone, in line with the Bologna Process,[7] and in part to market logic. It leaves both teachers and students frustrated. Several teachers lamented that the university was being downgraded to a PTU (technical-vocational school). This comment spoke to their concern about both the devaluation of their own professional expertise and their worsening conditions of employment. The decision to admit fee-paying students placed additional strain on teachers, who received no direct compensation for the increased workload. It also brought in students who had little interest in studying. Valentina put it in terms that resonated with my own concerns about university corporatization: "The educational process is becoming confused with the manufacturing process," she said, adding wryly, "We bring in timber, and produce lumber [trees]" (*Primimaem dubov, vypuskaem lipu*), a play on words suggesting that the university had become a factory that produces materials. Worse, they are false materials, or, rather, false sociologists, as she explained to me – *lipa* means both a linden tree and something false. Her comment also conveyed her dissatisfaction with the raw material in these semiprivatized times – that is, with the students. *Duby* (literally oak) is a colloquial way of referring to someone who is not too bright, in this case students who pay for their degrees but skip class and have no intention of studying.

Against this backdrop, we searched for ways to enact the solidarity and sustain the collaboration and dialogue we had established. The topic that presented itself was our shared interest in and commitment to engaged or community-based pedagogy (or "teaching through engagement and research," as Valentina later recalled it) – here, as a means to reenergize teaching and social science. Valentina had long been committed to a political sociology that was live and engaged with real, pressing (*ostrye*) social issues and problems, and to a gender studies that provided a space for open discourse (Temkina and Zdravomyslova 2003, 52). The relationship between her university work and her civic activism had always been seamless. Zhenskii Svet was university-based but open to the public, and ran consultations and gender studies classes for townspeople via the Evening School in Gender Studies. Until it was forced to shut down in early 2004 – the casualty of shifting political winds in both Tver' and donor nations – the crisis center she cofounded worked together with the Gender Studies Center in an example of university-community partnership.[8] She brought this commitment to her work with undergraduate students as well, going against the tide of dominant pedagogical practice (and "modernizing" neoliberal reforms) to engage her students in hands-on critical sociological projects.

During my stay in March 2005, I had the chance to witness this when I visited a class where her first-year sociology students were presenting their results. Their assignment was stimulated by local politics: the sharp cutbacks in social spending and the retrenchment of the nongovernmental sphere that were taking place in the context of broader federal reforms, "monetizing" social welfare reforms that were causing national protests (Hemment 2012b). Strategically timed to take place before International Women's Day, it sought to elicit women's views on these policies. Students were invited to put one question to women passersby: "What would you like to ask our mayor, if you met him?" Valentina explained that she had devised this assignment after speaking to one of the progressive municipal deputies, who was combating these cuts virtually single-handedly and suffering some abuse in the local media for her pains. Valentina's instructions to the students were to take field notes after each interview and to reflect on the experience, the responses, and what it taught them.

Four of her thirty-five freshman students had elected to undertake the project. As their peers watched, Dima, Volodya, and two young women, Katya and Ira, came to the front of the class. The students spoke of their initial nervousness as they approached people on the street for the first time, and of their learning curve; they also communicated their shock and dismay at the vehemence of some women's responses, some of which were too crude to report. After their presentation Valentina congratulated them and informed the rest of the class that with the students' consent, she planned to organize a public roundtable at the university to present the results of this research, in a gesture of solidarity with the local deputies who were fighting cuts in social spending.

Afterward, as we conferred, she told me how exciting this had been. Her students had amazed her with their enthusiasm. "We colonized Trekhsviatskaya [the main pedestrian thoroughfare]!" she told me, conjuring an amusing image of sociologists taking over the streets. This engaged pedagogical approach was becoming steadily harder to achieve, she told me later; curricular reforms initiated in 2000 meant there was less time for practicums or field-based work.

Valentina's pedagogical strategies and commitments recalled my own and those of many of my US-based colleagues. We were engaged in a parallel project, using the university as a site from which to challenge forms of inequality in our own communities and seeking to intervene in public debates. As I encountered community service learning (CSL) methodologies at the University of Massachusetts and found my feet in my community-based research-friendly department, I felt excited to share them with my Russian colleagues. I saw how anthropologists had used CSL methods as a means of undertaking critical anthropological projects, placing students in productive partnership with community groups, activists, or social movements. This literature provided methodological tools for community-based engagement I thought my Russian colleagues could use. Moreover, at a time when they were struggling, I hoped it would bolster them with a stamp of "international" validation. In March 2005, I led a discussion seminar at Tver' State University, based on a set of English-language readings I assigned (and which my Russian colleagues had translated): four texts that communicated the history and background of CSL in the United States and combined the critical angle and commitment to community-based learning that I felt best encapsulated our shared goals.[9] Our early project thus took shape in a discussion of pedagogy.

Our discussions of CSL led us into a new phase of our collaboration, a new phase of the political "conversation" or feminist participatory process (Gibson-Graham 1994, 220) we began in 1997. We conceptualized this early project as a critical comparative investigation of the restructuring of social welfare provision, citizenship, and neoliberal governance. The comparative element was key, prompted both analytically (the mutuality of processes we saw taking shape) and ethically (by our determination to refuse the binaries of East/West, authoritarian/democracy, that settled on us). Moreover, it was a simultaneous project of scrutiny and involvement. We negotiated placements and internships for Tver' State University students in some local youth-oriented state-run projects using CSL literature and methodologies as a wedge to forge a more critical form of community-based activity.[10]

Indeed, despite the "new Cold War" rhetoric and assertions of radical difference between Russia and the West, I was struck by how much more we had in common than not. In Russia, as in the United States, youth voluntarism and other privatizing initiatives were promoted against a backdrop of economic neoliberalism and concerns about national security (Cruikshank 1999; Eliasoph 2011; Hyatt 2001b).[11] While at first glance these new state-run youth voluntarism-promoting projects looked remarkably Soviet, they were clearly bound up in a very contemporary neoliberal form of welfare state restructuring, where the responsibility for meeting social needs was increasingly met by members of the "community."

A Distinctive Research Collaboration

As Nashi newsletters and flyers from various political parties began to litter the university department and as my colleagues' students began to participate in this state-run youth project, our attention shifted; I sought

1.1. Political recruitment posters, Tver' State University, 2006.

external funding to support a collaborative research project to examine the federal youth projects taking shape. Beginning in 2006, Valentina Uspenskaya and Dmitry Borodin and I led a pilot peer ethnography project with a group of Russian social science majors, wherein they undertook participant observation, completed internships, and conducted interviews with participants of several youth organizations, including Nashi and the organizational committee of Seliger 2009. In 2008 I was awarded a multiyear research award from the National Science Foundation to extend this collaboration.

At the core of the research team were Valentina's students – her advisees who drew close to her and were inspired by her, or those she reached out to and took under her wing. Under the auspices of our project, students undertook their own independent research, following their own interests rather loosely based on the original theme. Several young women – Alisa, Yulia, and Olya – trained by Valentina, were drawn to consider the gender politics of state-run youth projects: pronatalism, neotraditionalism, and sexualization. Others were interested in better understanding their student peers. One student's central preoccupation was Nashi and its Others – notably, he was drawn to focus on the Nats Boly (National Bolsheviks), members of a controversial political party that Nashi activists regarded as their main foe. Others still pursued topic of youth voluntarism, our original point of departure, completing their diplomas on the topic. The ranks of the "team" were fairly permeable. After our pilot project, Valentina issued an invitation to any motivated student to join. In this way, the next generation formed, with older students mentoring younger ones.

While the first generation of student peer ethnographers took themselves seriously as sociologists – objective observers of the processes underway, and bearers of a seasoned skepticism in the face of the promotional materials we gathered – this orientation didn't hold true for all participants. As Russia's Year of Youth gained momentum, there was a magnet effect and different students were drawn to our project. Student co-researchers were insiders and outsiders of state-run youth projects, including those who had participated enthusiastically in state-run campaigns. Kirill, a Nashi komissar, was curious about our project and joined us as an "expert consultant" during the fall of 2006. Andrei, a core team member in 2009, was a former Vazhnoe Delo volunteer who worked as an organizer at the federal youth camp Seliger 2009. Student research team members were at once social scientists, co-investigators, and "paraethnographers," "drawing on their own lived experience and develop[ing a] reflexive understanding of their role in the world" (Razsa and Kurnik 2012, 241, drawing on Holmes and Marcus 2008).[12] They brought with them "a robust critical consciousness and novel registers of politics and experience" (Holmes and Marcus 2008, 83). Some used our project as an opportunity to assess and reconsider their experience, writing about the organizations they had participated in; others maintained their involvement in state-run projects while they took part in our research. The encounters across difference that took place within research team meetings made for an especially rich and reflexive research process.

Research team meetings – held on my schedule, during my short trips – made for some of the most valuable data-gathering opportunities. They took place at the university, where we crammed into the Center for Women's History and Gender Studies' library and in Valentina's apartment as well. Beyond this, we held five focus groups. Student team members recruited their peers and facilitated these meetings. I formed deep sympathy with some of the students I met via focus groups and was able to maintain a connection with them over a couple of years – interviewing them both prior and subsequent to their participation in specific projects.

Despite Valentina's considerable skepticism about top-down state programs, she was sympathetic to her students and their plight. At no point did she condemn them for participating in state-run youth campaigns. She understood well the situation they were confronting and acknowledged the opportunities that participation in these projects promised. Moreover, as she pondered her students' predicament, Valentina engaged in reflexive self-critique about her own prior political involvements. In conversation with me in Amherst in 2010 she told me that it had been a mistake for independent civic activists such as herself to refuse to work with state officials during the 1990s. By holding themselves aloof ("We're clean"), they had abstained from participating in political processes, thus permitting the unsavory nationalist turn of the 2000s to take place. Of course, she told me, she understood that her students had to make a living ("I tell him to close his eyes and think of England!" she told me once, referring to one former student who had accepted a position in the regional administration), but she encouraged them to walk a careful line. As she put it in a meeting with some of my graduate students at the University of Massachusetts in 2013, "[When I was a young person during the Soviet period] I had a principle: not to participate if I couldn't change anything for the better. And [if I don't like something] I can't . . . participate . . . in all these events. And this time, these days when my students again ask what to do, tell me they don't know what to do [when they encounter pro-Kremlin youth projects] . . . I can only tell them my own experience. I tell them, if you don't like it, don't participate . . . don't march in formation [*ne khodite stroem*]!"

ETHNOGRAPHY IN THE PUTIN ERA

The feel of this collaboration was different from the earlier one we undertook – it had distinctive rhythms and pace. Then, I was based in Tver' for an extended period. I lived and worked in the city from 1997 to 1998. Our explorations took place through regular and embodied encounters; our activist projects were situated within the dense fabric of everyday life. This new research was quite different. While I flitted back and forth between Tver' and Amherst, Massachusetts, my presence more peripatetic, my colleagues remained in place.

Moreover, Valentina, Dmitry, and I were differently located within this project; we had different stakes in it and different priorities as well. In many ways, we pursued parallel but different agendas. As principal investigator on the National Science grant that supported our research, I was responsible for the project, and it made for my primary intellectual engagement; my colleagues (formally written in as "research consultants") experienced it differently, as a kind of umbrella that legitimized and dignified their existing engaged pedagogical activities. It validated the hands-on research, the engaged sociological practice Valentina in particular was committed to, and provided a venue, a site, and a topic via which to undertake it. Our project was a hub, or a space to conduct the lively intellectual work my colleagues valued most. It was a venue for mentoring students; under Valentina and Dmitry's careful stewardship, student research team members produced conference papers and their first publications.[13] Our lively meetings – and the tight connections with students they enabled us to forge and sustain – reminded my colleagues of the university they were committed to, the university as it should be – a space of critical thinking, inquiry, and debate. "The university should be a model of an open society," Valentina told me once, "a civil society" – as it was historically in Western Europe. Her primary scholarly and activist objectives meanwhile lay elsewhere.[14]

Ours, then, was a distinctive form of international research collaboration that indirectly provided support for the work that the logic of grants and funding does not acknowledge: the day-to-day work of teaching and mentoring students that is sustained in Russia under increasingly adverse conditions.[15] With each research trip, my sense of its importance was reinforced. Shuttling back and forth, I gained more insight into the indignities and encroachments Valentina and her colleagues faced: wealthy, arrogant students; condescending administrators and new administrative requirements; the for-profit turn that has transformed my colleagues' work conditions and altered academic priorities. Beyond what I witnessed directly, I received action alerts via academic listservs that confirmed my sense of the challenges she and her colleagues were up against. In 2007 a letter of protest and petition from sociology students at the prestigious Moscow State University (MGU), complaining of censorship and escalating nationalism, landed in my in-box. In early spring 2008, I learned of the politically motivated temporary shutdown of St. Petersburg's European University, an event precipitated when scholars at the university received EU funds to undertake elections research.[16] Sociology – particularly the energized, critical kind Valentina espoused and that this project enacted – was, as Russian sociologists Elena Omel'chenko and Anna Zhelnina put it, indisputably "under threat."[17]

In this climate, research had a very different shape and feel. The nineties had been a decade of dizzy possibility for ethnographers. All that had previously been off limits was newly accessible; those of us who began our careers then gained easy access to archives, state officials, and dissidents alike. Until the disenchantments of the 1998 economic crisis, it was also a time of receptivity and mutual curiosity between people. Although the "East-West" feminist dialogue was notoriously fraught, and reproduced many of the tensions of feminist encounters between the global North and South (Funk and Mueller 1993), my feminist colleagues and I achieved an easy solidarity. During the ten months I spent in the city, I got to know Valentina and the participants of Zhenskii Svet well and we reached a place of trust and close connection. Ours was a conversation across difference (nationality, citizenship, economic status) that worked. Moreover, we found an effective way to leverage my foreignness. Valentina sent me to the offices of local powerbrokers (the head of the municipal social services, the president's representative to the oblast, the mayor), deploying, or "exploiting," me, as she playfully put it, in our quest to obtain funds for our crisis center project. "Their doors will open for a Western visitor," she told me, "but never for me." She was right. As I described in my 2007 book, we danced through the offices of state officials and foreign donors alike, forging strategic alliances with relative ease.

Now a different kind of geopolitics intruded. Russia-US relations continued to deteriorate during our project. In this newly configured terrain, my Westernness threatened to be a liability. I found that my Russian colleagues and I responded to this shifting climate quite differently. What is more, we had divergent priorities and responsibilities within the research itself. As PI on a funded research project (one partially funded by the US State Department, moreover), I experienced competing "loyalties" and struggled with a new sense of complicity. Our solidarity and our shared commitments did not prevent moments of discomfort or dissonance. These were not always expressed, but they cohered in my field notes and jottings (moments when I pondered what was safe, what was not, or where I struggled to understand the responses of Valentina and other acquaintances). These were the places I found myself lingering as I shuttled back and forth between Amherst and Tver,' that preoccupied me when I was writing, and that ultimately – out of concern about compromising my colleagues – made me feel compelled to cancel some of my trips.

In the sections that follow, I examine the play of similarity and difference, congruity and divergence, that took place among us, and the rich ethnographic insights this revealed.

Transformative Encounters across Difference in a Polarized Field

This method, this history, and the relationships it rested on gave rise to a specific stance. As in our earlier work, I have been interested in the generative potential of research and the new forms of belonging that can emerge and take shape. Our participatory action research project of the nineties was a process during which we accomplished a kind of consensus and shared research objectives. It gave rise to a "partial but shared, externally related identity" (Gibson-Graham 1994, 218), or a new sense of "we" and the mutual sense of responsibility and ties I have described. Emerging as it did from our long-term relationships and our commitment to each other, this research process also took form as a "space of becoming" (Gibson-Graham 2006, xxii) in ways that were not fully thought out or consciously expressed.

Our research process and the group discussions we held were "spaces of encounter" (Razsa and Kurnik 2012, 249) in which we were all transformed. They prompted my colleagues to reflect on their activist pasts. In their accounts of prior youthful engagements (Valentina's story about patrolling the streets and haranguing smokers as an earnest Young Pioneer; Maria's sardonic tales about her past zeal as a pragmatic paper-pushing, accounts-producing Komsomolka – "I was a superstar!" she joked, using the English term, punning on the multiple meanings of "star"),[18] alternative political subjectivities flitted through the room to join us, the specter of past ways of construing. It led to sometimes earnest (occasionally heated) but often playful debates about the Soviet past, politics, power (*vlast'*), and citizenship.

One of the most memorable moments took place during one of our results-sharing miniconferences in May 2010. We assembled in the library. As usual, it was a space where multiple things happened, the site of a blurry tumbling of events. Alyosha, a research team member who was also employed by the Federal Youth Affairs Agency, brought brochures about the federal youth camp Seliger 2010 to distribute. As he passed them around, many of the students snatched them up enthusiastically, trading commentaries on which session they planned to attend – and simultaneously cracking jokes about them as well.

Switching gears, I made my presentation of findings so far. "Putin's policies ostensibly mark a break from the liberalizing policies of the 1990s," my first slide stated. "However, they actually advance more of the same." Accessing insights from the anthropology of postsocialism I was steeped in, I flagged the complementary processes we were undergoing; as students, as university teachers, as citizens, we were encountering variations of the same neoliberal processes, as relationships between state, citizens, and capital shifted. I showed them a cartoon one of my colleagues had recently shared with me and which I had used in my classes at the University of Massachusetts; entitled "The Evolution of the Professor," it vividly portrayed the transmogrifications of academic life in Europe and the United States (tweedy white men are displaced by lefty radicals, who are in turn displaced by the scholars of my generation: harried hamsters on a wheel).[19] A lively debate ensued about the socioeconomic challenges of the present. Indeed, while I had to leave for an appointment, the students stayed until 7 PM, arguing and talking in spin-off discussions.

The liveliest took place at the end of my presentation, as discussion spilled over into the subject of life more broadly. Vadim was a twenty-year-old left-leaning political science student who had cofounded a political discussion group at the university, to which political actors of various stripes were invited to present (the lineup rather surprisingly included a representative of a banned socialist organization and a Communist Party parliamentarian). At the mention of the Soviet period, he launched into a passionate lament. "Life is so much worse now," Vadim declared. "All my relatives and most of the people in my village [*poselok*] say so." During socialism, he said, "at least there was enough food, the refrigerator was always full." Vadim's longing for socialism – or what he thought it represented – prompted Valentina to intervene. She reminded him about the endemic shortages and the difficulties of finding food. "Well," he said, "they tell me that if there was a shortage, they could always travel to Moscow, whereas today, they can't afford to buy what's in the stores."

"Aha," said Valentina, "exactly, they had to travel all the way to Moscow!"

Vadim persisted, speaking with feeling about how his village had changed for the worse in the course of the last decade. "There used to be crowds of young people, now there's almost no one," he told us. "There's no culture," he went on, "they closed the cinema. Then, people had a belief in the future. I'd like to stay and live in the village, but I won't be able to because there's no work."

Valentina added gently, intent on disrupting this nostalgic narrative about the supposed golden age, "It's just that our expectations have changed. Now we have polarization, there are rich and poor and we can't all afford the same things. This is something we didn't know then. As for the *poselok*," Valentina went on, "well, in Soviet times, they *had* to stay – there was no freedom of movement! As soon as people could move away, they did – to access another kind of life."

Warming to her theme, Valentina told stories about the Soviet past that I had heard before. Once pitched at me, the foreigner, they were now directed at her students. She and her husband had a principle, she told them, a form of principled refusal to play by the logics of the system. If they traveled to Moscow with their children, they would never buy food. Rather, they took their sons to museums, art galleries, and the theater instead. The eighties was a time of chronic shortages, she explained. In these lean and hungry years, most Russian people regarded trips to the capital as an opportunity for provisioning, to stock up on goods not available at home. "It was an anomalous principle," she acknowledged, explaining that her parents and parents-in-law were always upset with them, incredulous that they had returned without sausage! She recalled constraints on political expression in the university as well. Once, during the last years of the Soviet Union, she had been summoned to the *obkom* (oblast committee of the Communist Party), she told us, for having invited anarchists and people from the Democratic Union into class to speak to her students.[20] This was a well-chosen topic, since several other students present were active in the political discussion club Vadim had cofounded, as Valentina well knew.

These kinds of debates between past and present took place in a space of mutually respectful encounter, inflected by my presence as an outsider as well. As Valentina told these tales, she was also telling her students about the possibilities of the present: the university is still open; we can still do this; it has not (yet) come to that!

In 2009, Russia's Year of Youth when federal attention peaked, more and more students were drawn to participate in state-run youth projects. Simultaneously, state officials reached out to us. This led to a series of encounters (and some perplexing moments of misrecognition) that destabilized my notions of who was who, and led to occasions when the distance between our projects seemed less great – for example, when local representatives of the Federal Youth Affairs Agency (Rosmolodezh) attended our miniconference and used it as an opportunity for recruitment. One of the most intriguing moments of blurring was when a participant in one of our focus groups asked if she could keep my Institutional Review Board consent form; while at first I took this to be a surprising engagement with my ethics process, I swiftly realized that she was using it as an artifact of her productivity to give to the oblast youth committee (prior to Seliger 2009, all applicants needed to collect documents and evidence to submit to Rosmolodezh).

There were ambiguous interpersonal interactions as well. In the course of the research, I got to know several Nashi komissars, young people who were conditioned to be hostile toward foreigners; in some of our interactions, we forged moments of deep connection as we recognized common goals and shared frustrations (about the economy, the university, and issues of social rights and social justice). These were micro transactions that – given the discursive field we were operating in – were transformative and prompted me to recognize that the issues that propelled their participation were not dissimilar to the issues that drove the participants in our own research project.

On a few occasions I found myself contributing to these boundary-blurring moments, launching into impassioned legitimacy claims about our collaboration and its intent. The most memorable was with Vitaly, the Federal Youth Affairs Agency representative and Nashi komissar who presented Seliger 2009 materials at our miniconference (described in the introduction). I asked him to tell me about the new international session that was to take place at Seliger 2010. He explained that this session (encouraged by the Foreign Ministry) sought to bring young people of different countries together. There would be two thousand foreigners from different countries of the world, he explained. "[People] from China to the US, from Finland to South Africa – two thousand foreigners! We want to show them that Russia isn't at all as they portray it in their countries."

"So it has this diplomatic meaning," I said. "Like a bridge?"

Yes, he told me. The program would bring foreign teachers as well (he named prestigious institutions including the Sorbonne, Harvard, Cambridge, and Oxford). "We just want to show that in reality, they don't portray the truth in your countries. In reality, [Russia is] a beautiful, normal, peaceful country. The people are friendly, just like in those countries. . . . We will raise the attractiveness of Russia!"

At this, I chimed in: "That's the goal of our research project, actually!"

"Really?" Vitaly replied.

"Yes . . ."

"Explicitly to raise the reputation of this country?"

Jolted by the incongruity of his remark, I launched into a fervent speech about my goals and concerns and the relationships that had prompted our project. "Well, sort of, yes," I stammered. "Our task . . . is to somehow build a bridge. Because we started to do this . . . this was very important to me – because the relationship between America and Russia became so bad. It was just painful to me . . ."

This rather comical exchange, which ended with a pledge to pass on the Seliger 2011 invitation to my own students at the University of Massachusetts, involved recognition of commonality between Nashi, our project, and my personal goals. Vitaly took me to be a fellow traveler!

It was a perplexing moment of entanglement that brought both commonality and divergence to the fore. While my collaborative project's concern with worsened US-Russia relations marked a point of similarity with Nashi's goals as Vitaly here expressed them, his work and mine were animated by quite different cosmologies. My stance derived from my location in the United States and anthropological goals of de-exoticizing Russia as "other," whereas Vitaly's stance was rooted in his training as an unreflexive defender of the Putin-era status quo. At the time, this awkward moment threw me; Vitaly's sudden attentiveness to our project disconcerted me as well. What if he were prompted to reflect on this moment, as I was? Where would this lead and could this bring problems to my colleagues?

On several occasions during the research process I found myself making emotional speeches such as this one about what I was doing. I was tripping over my own anxieties as I did so, prompted by the sense of unease and confusion I felt in this new political climate (What was safe? What was not?). My colleagues were confident, but I was off-kilter and I wrestled with a sense of responsibility that I should figure this out. Yet I was prompted by something else too: a sense of solidarity with and genuine warmth toward individuals like Vitaly and some of the other komissars I came to know through our project.

These encounters took place against a play of assumptions in the Putin era: foreign researchers and Russian scholars and NGO activists who receive foreign funding, especially from the United States, are presumed to be in somebody's pocket (as Putin put it in his 2005 address to NGO representatives, "They can't bite the hand that feeds them"). This suspicion escalated in the latter phases of our project. Indeed, this research and this collaboration felt increasingly fragile as the events of 2011 unfolded – the aggressive, belligerent statist reassertion that took place in the aftermath of the 2011 protests, particularly with Vladimir Putin's return to the presidency. During the spring of 2013, some Russian scholars and research centers came under investigation and scrutiny as the new "foreign agents" legislation was enforced. Although the legislation was intended for NGOs, research institutions and individual researchers who had received foreign funding to work on topics deemed "political" were caught in the crossfire.[21] While my colleagues brushed off these insinuations with humor – indeed, Valentina told me about a poster she had seen at a 2011 protest that read, "State Department – where is my money?" – I experienced twinges of discomfort. The stakes in undertaking critical ethnographic work had radically shifted. I was concerned first and foremost for my colleagues, but I was unsettled by my own location as well. They were partially right: while the State Department did not commission my research and my conclusions may not be to its taste, the department funded portions of this research. It is invested in Russia; it has a specific strategic interest in examining the forms of political activity that take place, as critical anthropologists acknowledge.[22]

These discomforts, then, and the "finding" of my own jumpiness – which was often not shared by my Russian colleagues – had everything to do with the reconfigured geopolitical terrain. At times like these, I realized my critical ethical consciousness had become entangled in the very reenergized Cold War discourses and dualisms our project aimed to disrupt.

Indeed, my colleagues had a different way of coping. We were all anxious on our way to Seliger 2009, but our anxiety had different expression. While I was girding myself for a hostile reception, shaped by the bleak accounts of Nashi I had read in the Western media, my colleagues were ironic and playful. While I dutifully attached myself to our guide and listened to his official account of things, they busied themselves collecting narratives that disrupted it (gleefully reporting to me that, contrary to official claims, a substantial number of young people had come to Seliger 2009 without projects, but in order to have fun and relax). They engaged in forms of mischief as well, alarming me considerably at one point by posing playfully by one of the giant Putin-Medvedev posters we encountered. While I glanced nervously around us, they draped themselves lovingly over the giant images, their embrace a pastiche that called out and mocked the sexualized "cult" of Putin and the eroticized political attachment that has taken shape around him.

There is an important analytic point here, relating to the current configuration of politics and political authority in Russia. At the same time that people like my colleagues are unambiguously critical of the current political regime and do regard it as a form of renewed authoritarianism (the lens I have been leery of reinforcing), they have a very rich and creative satiric repertoire with which to contemplate it (c.f. Cassiday and Johnson 2010).

Moments like this made for repeated sites of collision. Unlike the old days, when I had been in on the joke, I occasionally found myself uneasy with their satire and performative irreverence. My own (stiff) responses and demeanor meanwhile were conditioned by the (US federal) state-mandated ethics conduct I had been socialized into at the University of Massachusetts – the IRB and the consent forms I had produced and earnestly prepared to distribute (or at least orally narrate) to "research subjects."

One of my acquaintances (a liberal-oriented journalist who had been very invested in the NGOs and interventions of the nineties) flinched when she read the consent form I had prepared. I had written, "The greatest potential risk I can anticipate concerns your association with me as a foreign researcher. In the contemporary political environment, it is possible that some people may look upon foreigners and those who associate with them with suspicion." Her response – perturbed, mildly offended – stayed with me. While she was quick to deplore the anti-Western discourses and the political elites who perpetuated them, my allusion to them in this (bureaucratic) form troubled her. I came to see this in terms of "cultural intimacy" (Herzfeld 2005); Russian people's complaints about the state, narratives about it, and strategies for taming it are bonding, they create intimacy. My invoking it in this way marked a crude intrusion.

This came up repeatedly, when my colleagues tried to offset my jumpiness with humor. On one occasion, Valentina told me she had had a call from someone in the university department responsible for security (in effect, a cell of the Federal Security Service, the FSB) in relation to my forthcoming trip. Learning of my visa application, this person was making inquiries about my goals in visiting Russia. As my eyes widened in panic, Valentina insisted it was nothing to worry about; the call had been "from a nice lady" who seemed apologetic for troubling her, she told me. Valentina's account domesticated the state, rendering it benign and slightly humorous, peopled by well-intentioned individuals doing their (absurd) jobs. Moments like these – when our conceptions collided, or where I felt clumsily out of step – were part and parcel of this Putin-era ethnography, alerting me to subtle changes in the political field between 2006 and 2011 and providing rich analytic clues into the ways Russian people apprehended them.

A final example presented itself when in the latter stages of writing this book, I felt compelled to cancel my trip to Russia; in the frenzy of "foreign agents" and furious epithet hurling, I was concerned that our research project could be construed as "political" work and that my arrival might bring my colleagues trouble. As I wrestled with this decision during the spring of 2014 and weighed the advice of my funding agency (not to go), Valentina's response was instructive: she assured me that it was fine, safe for me to come, that it would not result in any harm to her; however, she assured me that she would understand if I decided not to.

She insisted – in what I took as a form of subtle chastisement, or counsel that I should not allow these political matters to encroach on or affect me in this way – that I should decide for myself, and moreover that I should locate the decision within myself, in my heart; it should be a private decision I made in consultation with my family.

Given the discursive terrain I have described, the surprise was how infrequently we encountered hostility toward our project. Any hostility people might have felt was offset by the quality of the ties and Valentina's status and reputation in the city and by the nature of the collaborative process we undertook.

Valentina and I were both invited to deliver lectures at the Seliger 2011 educational forum. Indicative of the different positionalities we occupy, I accepted but she declined (although she agreed to accompany me). My invitation – extended by our old friend Vitaly – was in some ways the price of admission to the camp. He could get me in, he said, in response to my request to attend the Technologies of Kindness session, but how would I like to give a VIP lecture? Thus it was that Valentina and I set off again to the Seliger camp one morning in July 2011. This time, we were chauffeured, accompanied by a young woman who worked in the youth committee of the municipal administration.

At Seliger, we were met warmly by Liuba, a twenty-something Federal Youth Affairs Agency staffer from Moscow. A former Nashi participant (no longer, she explained; she had not joined the ranks of the management [*upravlentsy*]), she was attending her sixth Seliger. After escorting us through the camp and a quiet lunch at the local hotel (wherein Valentina and I joked about her status – my badge signaled my VIP status, while hers was blank. "I'll be your translator," she suggested. "No, my bodyguard," I quipped), she took us to the large tent where I was to deliver my lecture. The tent, "Gagarin" (named after the celebrated Soviet cosmonaut), was empty except for a few kids milling around. I made my way to the small table and chair that were set up, and was greeted by a rather stern woman in her late fifties. As a cameraman with a big mic showed up, I began to get nervous ("Oh yes, all lectures are live-streamed throughout the camp," Vitaly, who met us there, breezily explained).

I encountered a whiff of hostility from two young men who were shopping for a lecture to attend. Upon reading the title of my talk ("Vol-

1.2. My vIP lecture at Seliger 2011. Photograph courtesy of Valentina Uspenskaya.

untarism in the US/Russia: Our Project"), one of the young men curled his lip and muttered something to his friend. Before stalking away, he shared an anecdote, a version of "the lion and the monkey" that disparaged Western arrogance.[23] But aside from this, the audience was warm. I delivered a carefully crafted lecture that emphasized – as always – the mutuality of the research, its origins in long-term relationships, its comparative focus and intent, and its critical stance on both US and Russian state power. It seemed to hit the mark. The young people were eager to hear more about the voluntary sector in the United States. At the end, while some clustered around Valentina, eager to snatch up some of the publications she had brought to distribute (some of her own edited volumes and pedagogical publications on gender studies), several of these young people drew close to me. One, a young woman from Perm, in the Urals, explained that she volunteered with an NGO that worked on HIV/AIDS and wanted to know about contemporary strategies in the United States. We had a lively discussion about the challenge of stereotypes about HIV and I told her about the semilegal strategies of activist groups, such as needle-exchange programs in western Massachusetts (Zibbell

2009). A young teacher from a far-flung provincial university was eager to talk about options for travel and wondered if I could put him in touch with international conferences and circuits.

Meanwhile, just as he had been unconcerned by the research presentations that the student researchers made at our miniconference, Vitaly was utterly oblivious to the content of the talk I had painstakingly prepared and delivered (sensitive to the politicized ways Western efforts could be perceived). Indeed, he took off after dropping me at the tent and did not reappear until the end. When we met outside the tent, his only comment was to inquire about the appropriateness of my audience: "Were they good students [*tolkovyi*]?" he asked me, in a friendly manner.

Despite his training (in earlier interviews he had spoken at length to me about the courses he had taken in "images of the enemy" and on the impermissibility of certain steps by the West), he apprehended commonality, not difference, and he met me as a peer. It became clear that this was a generalized hostility toward "the West" that, given the right circumstances, would fade away in the context of an actual face-to-face encounter.

To my very great relief, at least for the project's duration, it did not attract the kind of savage denunciation that has beset other similarly configured social science collaborations. While I was never aware that our project caused anyone direct problems, I was aware that it contributed to the cloud of grumbles toward Valentina from some colleagues and administrators (some of whom were suspicious of her liberal feminist orientation and international connections) that had followed her for years.

We encountered indifference too – diverse forms of often-bureaucratic indifference toward our efforts from teachers and administrators – that triggered my anxieties about the implications of posing these questions and undertaking this research in this geopolitical domain. There was also the weary skepticism of harried, overworked, and undercompensated faculty members (such as the woman who poked her head into the library during one of our group discussions to say rather sardonically, "Are you still here?"). As Valentina puts it, scientific work has been all but extinguished in the university, where teachers work ever-increasing hours for static pay and are forced to supplement their salaries by engaging in various coaching and admissions-smoothing activities for private clients. There was semihostile indifference as well. Our small, energized, multihour conversations and discussions that spilled out into the corridors and the street did not resemble "international collaboration" as it was usually constituted, or meet the expectations of university administrators, accustomed as they were to budgets, banquets, and formalism. One administrator who had met me warmly the previous year looked quite put out when I showed up at her office the following year, still asking questions. "So you had a grant, did you? Why is it we haven't heard anything from you since? Was there no conference?" she asked me suspiciously, and I could see she assumed we were withholding and hoarding privileges.

At the same time, however, even as international collaboration was marked as suspicious, it was also desired. As one university administrator proclaimed, after collecting Valentina's report of international activities to date, including this project, "Uspenskaya is the brand [*brend*] of our department!"

In *A Postcapitalist Politics* (2006, 1), the authors J. K. Gibson-Graham define stance as "an emotional and affective positioning of the self in relation to thought and thus to apprehending the world." Their discussion of stance emerges from their feminist/queer poststructuralist project of denaturalizing the capitalist economy and the hold it has on our imagination. The central task of their book's project is to jog us out of what the authors call "left melancholia and mourning," in order to free up the imaginary – to make space for alternative visions, or what they call "a politics of possibility." In their formulation, stance is a political decision: here, a decision to be intentionally optimistic. It is also profoundly dialogic, something that's in process, and that evolves and mutates in the push and pull of relationships.[24] It is shaped by history – of relationships, ties, or matters of the heart.

I have shown how the research context, geopolitics, and our history of relationships beckoned forth a similar affective stance: a stance of epistemological humility that permitted ambiguity, opening a space for something new to take shape and form. I maintain that this stance is equally appropriate to this time of geopolitical uncertainty and the calcified dualisms of reenergized "binary socialism" (Yurchak 2006).

Like these authors, I believe that the changing political times call for a change in method – a shift in strategy and epistemological stance – away from a "knowing" to a more tentative stance and positioning vis-à-vis the processes we examine. As Razsa and Kurnik (2012, 241, citing Fischer 2003, 58) insist, "emergent forms demand partnership, conversation, and contestation with 'insiders of all sorts.'" While these discussions derive from the context of collaboration with like minds (these scholars were in political sympathy and solidarity with the movement activists they worked with) and take place in the context of alter-globalization (oppositional) movements, I find them appropriate to my research context as well. I contend that these geopolitical times demand different forms of method/collaboration that I have enacted through stance.

Our research process was a "collaborative encounter of uncertain outcomes" (Holmes and Marcus 2008, 84) that took us in surprising directions and involved some risk as well. It led to a divergence of perspective with my close interlocutors (in comparison with our early collaboration) and unexpected moments of commonality with ostensible foes (Nashi komissars). The productive dissonance between us that I experienced muddied and complicated my conclusions. This "finding" of blurred categories (state/nonstate) and the fuzziness of distinctions emerged from our shared commitments and the affective stance we assumed. As later chapters will explore, young people experienced the state projects offered them quite differently from what was apprehended from outside. Their engagement was not linear, but full of unexpected twists. While some students came to us skeptics and remained that way, others retained their enthusiasm for state-run projects throughout. Some came to us disenchanted by state-run campaigns, only to return and recommit to them, captivated by the latest project renditions.

Our project and the often-playful forms of contestation we engaged in generated excess as well, a kind of energy and sense of agency that was not limited to the terms we might expect – it was neither simply oppositional to the state-run projects or modes of agency offered, nor fully in sync with them. It reenergized us (Valentina, the members of the research team, and I) for the project's duration.

The overspill effects of this project are legion. In what I would like to claim as a welcome instance of reversing the "flow" of knowledge production about postsocialism (Rogers 2010), our discussions about politics and the comparative insights I have gained have energized the work I have done "at home." One of this project's highlights was the 2010

Skype conference Valentina and I facilitated to put our students from the University of Massachusetts and Tver' State University in dialogue around issues that engaged them. This conversation and the project more broadly have added zest to my own teaching and encounters with students at home, prompting ongoing reflection about activism, politics, and political agency.

Recognizing this and traversing these moments of difference have vastly enriched my conclusions. I pick up on these themes in subsequent chapters. I should emphasize that while it is informed by the process of our research and the play of difference that took place within it, the analysis that follows is very much my own.

TWO

NASHI IN IDEOLOGY AND PRACTICE

The Social Life of Sovereign Democracy

ONE FRIGID DECEMBER MORNING IN 2006, I STRUGGLED OUT OF bed at 5 AM to join several hundred local youth at the Tver' railway station. I was joining a campaign organized by the pro-Kremlin youth movement Nashi (Ours). We were traveling to Moscow to meet with World War II veterans, bearing gifts and best wishes for the new year. Our train was one of many traveling from the provinces to Moscow that morning. Kirill, my Nashi activist contact (a "komissar" in the movement who had participated in our research project), explained that the campaign, entitled "A Holiday Returned," was timed to coincide with the sixty-fifth anniversary of the Battle of Moscow – to give back to surviving veterans the New Year's holiday celebration that had been cruelly snatched from them by the Nazis during the winter of 1941. Kirill had explained that the campaign would bring one hundred thousand young people to the capital in specially commissioned trains. Each group of one hundred was to meet with a group of veterans and present them with a New Year's gift.

At the station, I joined a seething mass of young people; while there were fewer than the three thousand Kirill had promised, there still were a lot, and I couldn't see Kirill. A couple of phone calls later, I managed to locate him: he was holding a placard with "Tver 27" written on it – the name of his cohort of one hundred. As I shuffled through the crowds to join him, I marveled at the complexity of the organization. The organizers started to load big plastic sacks of what looked like food onto the train, and then we were told to move onboard. I spilled into a wagon with the others who had amassed under his sign.

As the train pulled out of the station, Kirill and his fellow komissars paced up and down the wagon, barking instructions (there was to be no smoking, no drinking; we shouldn't come to the organizers with any complaints) and handing out supplies. They passed out box lunches, return tickets, and costumes for us to wear as we distributed gifts – Grandfather Frost (*Ded Moroz*) suits for the boys, Snow Maiden (*Snegurochka*) suits for the girls.[1] "These are gifts for you," Kirill called out. "You may keep them, but don't give them to anyone else." I looked around at my fellow travelers. I had ended up in a carriage filled with international students. Jaswinder, Ajit, and Anand were graduate students from India; they had come to Tver' to study dentistry at the Medical Academy. As we rattled along, we chatted in English – newly arrived, their Russian was rudimentary – and I learned something about them. They had not yet had the opportunity to travel much and were excited by the chance to make this trip.

Despite the dark, the cold, and the early hour, there was an atmosphere of excitement and anticipation. For all of us, traveling to Moscow was a big deal; although only 170 kilometers, the trip was costly and beyond the reach of many young people. As we neared Moscow, the Russian kids pulled out their costumes – beard, hats, red suits – and put them on, laughing and mugging for their cameras. A little hesitantly, Jaswinder, Ajit, Anand, and I followed suit.

In Moscow, the excitement mounted. We poured out of the train in the half-light to join crowds of young people – who had arrived on trains from other cities – and lined up in our cohorts. As I took my place next to Jaswinder and her friends, I saw Kirill sneaking a cigarette. From the front of our line (other groups from Tver'), a chant began – "Happy New Year!" (*S novym godom*) – and we were supposed to pick it up. Instead, one of the Indian students, his hat perched rakishly on his head, led a column in a kind of conga and began his own chant in Hindi, which made everyone laugh. "Indian Grandfather Frosts?" cried an astonished and slightly hostile passing youth.

At last, all assembled, we began to shuffle forth. As we rounded the corner and approached the square where the rally was to take place I saw that the streets were eerily empty. The wide boulevards of central Moscow – usually jam-packed with cars – were blocked off to traffic by scores

2.1. Nashi's "A Holiday Returned" campaign, Moscow, December 2006.

of police. We accessed the square through security checkpoints; one of the policemen muttered something incredulous about "foreigners" as we passed through and I tensed slightly, flinching from his aggressive tone (while I knew I could pass as ethnic Russian, clearly my South Asian comrades could not). As we cleared the gate, the space opened up and the crowd let out a cheer: thousands of young people dressed in costumes, snapping pictures of each other with their cell phones, as sound systems pumped out Soviet wartime songs mixed to a techno beat. The words appeared karaoke-like on a large screen as youth sang along.

NASHI: A POLITICAL TECHNOLOGY PROJECT IN MOTION

Nashi, the independent youth democratic antifascist movement, burst onto the Russian political scene in the spring of 2005. Its inaugural mass rally took place in May 2005, as a celebration of Den' Pobedy (Victory Day). An estimated sixty thousand young people from all over the Russian Federation marched in Moscow to commemorate the sixtieth anniversary of the Soviet victory over the Nazis (or "fascists" as they are more commonly recalled). Between 2005 and 2012, when Nashi was finally dismantled, it held a large number of high-profile mass events, mostly in support of the Kremlin and always of a patriotic orientation.

Nashi was the most controversial Putin-era state run youth project. It caused great consternation, both because, with its mass actions and youth in uniforms, it resembled prior Soviet forms (the Komsomol), and because it was taken to signal a new authoritarianism. This "independent youth movement" was state run, founded and funded by top Kremlin aides; Nashi's administrative founder was Putin's chief ideologist, Vladislav Surkov.[2] Its public meetings – always pro-state and often with a pronounced anti-Western or antiliberal orientation – were permitted at a time when oppositional meetings were not. Squares like the one we congregated in were off limits to oppositional protests, yet we had a police guard that day.

But Nashi was more complex than many critical representations allowed. As the above account suggests, there was a play of seemingly incompatible symbols in Nashi campaigns. Nationalist, exclusive discursive elements coexisted with democratic discourses; elements from global youth culture joined emblems of the Russian Orthodox Church. In the Holiday Returned campaign this play of the liberal and the Soviet was striking: discourses of human rights and tolerance mixed with Soviet-era symbols and values. At the same time that it advanced an exclusionary form of solidarity (the name's translation, "Ours," betrays its nationalist core), Nashi promoted cultural tolerance – remember, it is an "antifascist" movement. The designation "antifascist" involved an archetypal melding: in Russia, fascism connotes Naziism; "antifascism" invokes Soviet heroism in saving Europe from the Nazi threat, simultaneously linking this heroic past with contemporary struggles against xenophobia that young people might engage in.

Moreover, it was not static; Nashi was a polyphonic political technology project in motion. Between 2005 and 2012 when it was finally dismantled, Nashi's priorities substantially shifted in response to both shifting state priorities and the interests of its participants, which were usually, but not always, in sync (Atwal 2009; Lassila 2011, 2012).[3] Indeed, some of the forms of cultural production Nashi engaged in had adverse effects, alienating not only many of the young people it sought to attract, but its Kremlin backers as well.[4] Ironically, despite Putin's consistently high ratings between 2000 and 2011, for the duration of its existence Nashi was widely derided and despised (Lassila 2012).

In this chapter, I tell the story of Nashi from a different angle. My first task is to account for the organization by locating it within broader flows and forces. Born of a particular historical juncture, Nashi was a complex political technology project that talked back to international democracy promotion: it simultaneously drew on its resources and critiqued them, undertaking complex "fusions" as it did so. Designed to deal with the "problem" of apolitical youth, it was crafted to occupy their energies and loyalties and enlist them in a specific project of prevention. Borrowing both from the democracy promotion toolkit and from diverse repertoires of rebellion including anarcho-punk DIY culture (Lassila 2012, 142), Nashi offered up distinctive technologies to occupy or take control of the street, in a preemptive project to prevent other unwanted forms of occupation: either radical forms of protest led by domestic oppositional activists (liberals, leftists, the National Bolshevik Party), or democratic revolutions instigated by foreign meddlers.

Nashi makes for an extremely challenging ethnographic object. In many ways the Holiday Returned campaign I attended in December 2006 confirmed its critics' most scathing accounts. The elaborately choreographed and ideologically uncertain event was clearly produced by the central authorities. It was highly mass-mediated as well; TV cameras zoomed down, intruding on the view, capturing signs and snatches of youth enthusiasm, which were beamed back to us on the giant screens before us. Moreover, it was curiously prepackaged. The brochure Kirill handed me on the train read like a precise script for the event that was to unfold ("Ten thousand young people will present veterans with gifts," it proclaimed). The stage where we assembled was adorned with enormous cartoonlike drawings depicting the exchange that was to take place (a beaming, crinkly-eyed elder, surrounded by young people in Grandfather Frost costumes). I later learned that the veterans got short shrift; many participants skipped the meeting to go shopping and there weren't enough gifts in any case. The event was pure spectacle, an "oil-

2.2. Honoring veterans, Nashi-style. "A Holiday Returned," December 2006.

and-gas glamour"–era rendition of Soviet-era work, where veterans were deployed as mere bit players.

The foreign participants were poorly attended to as well. I discovered from my conversations with the Indian students that they had no prior connection with Nashi; indeed, while they had presumably been recruited via a "lesson of friendship" event, the students I spoke with were unclear about the events of the day, or the purpose of the Holiday Returned campaign. While grateful for the invitation to Moscow – they were fearful of traveling alone, they told me, due to the threat of racist attacks – and appreciative of the gesture of friendship extended by Russian youth, they had never heard of Nashi. Nor did they realize the goal of the campaign was to meet with veterans – when I explained this to her, Jaswinder expressed regret that she'd brought no gift.

And yet there was more. As I followed Nashi activists like Kirill home to the provinces, I became aware of other angles to consider:

the meaning Nashi assumed for its participants, the sense they made of the fusions they were offered, and the agency the organization afforded them. Our research showed that between 2005 and 2011 Nashi succeeded in captivating some of its target constituents: provincially located college-bound high schoolers and lower-grade college students looking to invest their civic energies. It articulated an appealing can-do energy, and offered young people a dignified subject position as leaders, active agents (as opposed to "defeatists" and stultified bureaucrats), and worthy heirs to their World War II predecessors. This chapter's second task is to present some of these insights, the fruits of the collaborative project that engaged some of these students as participants. Nashi's critics' formulations ("Putin Iugend" or "nashisty") suggest a docile mass of young people marching in lockstep with Kremlin policies. However, Nashi activists' narratives revealed that although the state provided the framing, its grip was much less tight than its critics presumed. They modified its campaigns as they participated in them, pursuing their own goals. Furthermore, through the narratives I present, we see evidence of similarities with the NGOs Nashi disparaged.

TALKING ABOUT A REVOLUTION: NASHI, CIVIL SOCIETY, AND SOVEREIGN DEMOCRACY

Nashi was born of a time of crisis. The mood in the spring of 2005 was polarized and edgy. The Ukraine's "Orange Revolution" of late 2004 was a largely youth-led pro-democracy movement, prompted by the perception of rigged elections. Like the other "color" revolutions that took place in the former Soviet Union between 2003 and 2005, it was celebrated in the West as a triumph of democracy, an analogue to the pro-democracy "velvet revolutions" of 1989; the youthful bodies on streets that *New York Times* articles portrayed were framed in heroic, civil terms, as a "civilizing force" that swept away authoritarian incumbents. However, this color revolution was highly controversial in Russia. Critical newspaper commentators drew attention to the large amounts of foreign money, especially from the United States, expended in supporting it, and expressed concern about foreign meddling in postsocialist space. Would Russia be next? Journalists debated the potential mobilizations of youth that might ensue. "The 'Orange Revolution' is becoming a brand [*brend*] before our eyes," one article in the liberal-oriented *Moskovskie novosti* newspaper stated, "one that brings together two opposing assumptions – hope for some, a threat for others."[5] As the *Washington Post* reported, "Suddenly in Russia, everybody's talking about a revolution."[6]

The Putin administration, clearly rattled by this unexpected challenge to its authority, was shaken further by a "political tsunami" of protest in January 2005 that accompanied the enactment of a controversial new law on social welfare reform (law 122). Tens of thousands of protesters came out in demonstrations all over the Russian Federation; young people, mostly students, joined retirees bearing Communist banners and placards (the usual suspects). Radical student groups (including antiglobalist leftist ones) began to proliferate on campuses, and some young people formed online communities of protest.[7] I was in Tver' in March 2005, two months after law 122 took effect. People spoke about nothing but the reforms and their antisocial, or antipeople (*antinarodnyi*), character; this term carried great weight, since it had been used to characterize the deeply unpopular "young reformers" of the Yeltsin administration whom Putin positioned himself against. Indeed, Putin's legitimacy was premised on his ostensible difference from his predecessors and the policies they embraced, on his resolute refusal to permit Russia to be dictated to by outside agents. Political protest, which had been unthinkable a couple of years earlier, was now widespread; a new trope of "taking to the streets" was ubiquitous.

As another "color" revolution swept away the regime of Kyrgyz president Askar Akayev, the Russian authorities hit back with an alarmist discourse that invoked the possibility of the dissolution of the Russian Federation (reminding the Russian people of the bloody outcomes of prior revolutions). In an interview that received a lot of coverage in the domestic and international media, Medvedev, then the Kremlin chief of staff, claimed, "If we do not manage to consolidate the elites, Russia may disappear as one state." He went on to say, "The breakup of the Soviet Union will look like child's play compared to a government collapse in modern Russia."[8] To Russians the implications were plain – this was a crisis of statehood analogous to the civil war of the 1920s that followed the Bolshevik Revolution.

In his annual State of the Nation address on April 25, 2005, President Putin stoked these fires with a controversial declaration: the collapse of the Soviet Union, he announced, was "the greatest geopolitical catastrophe" of the twentieth century. For Russians it was a "genuine tragedy," he said, adding, "The epidemic of collapse has spilled over to Russia itself," referring to separatist movements such as those in Chechnya.

As Kremlin political technologists struggled to respond to this crisis, they reached into the toolkit of the disparaged foreign meddlers. Borrowing from the repertoire of democracy promotion, they seized on the civil-society concept as a means to harness this "street" energy and to mobilize youth. They adapted it for their own ends, linking it to a project of modernization and national renewal, drawing selectively on Soviet-era symbols as they did so. Here, "revolution" was rebranded to signal something dire, grotesque, and bloody, rather than the civilizing, democratizing force invoked in Western media reports. These technologists invoked "civil society" in a new way, as something that would deflect and contain these roiling discontents and prevent them from developing further (c.f. Manning 2007).[9]

President Putin had begun talking the talk of civil society during his first administration, and stepped up this rhetoric in his second term (2004–2008). Putin invoked the desirability of a strong civil society in his May 2004 State of the Nation address, declaring, "Without a mature civil society, there can be no effective solution to people's pressing problems." In the same breath, he spoke out forcibly against existing NGOs, denouncing some organizations whose goals, he claimed, were skewed by the fact that they received funds from foreign or domestic foundations. He concluded, memorably, "They cannot bite the hand that feeds them."

The version of civil society he proposed was a corrective project, one that sought to replace the old with the new. As Putin told an assembled group of Nashi activists in May 2006, "Russia needs a society brimming with love for the country, a civil society that would be such not only in name, but in status, that would do its job not just for money, but put its soul into efforts to right the wrongs."[10] While existing NGOs were false, ineffectual, and motivated by self-interested people, oriented toward the interests of foreign states, the new ones would be different. In contradistinction, the civil society he invoked offered a vision of self and nation indivisibly bound; it was a vision of civil society linked to state sovereignty.

To the horror of Russia's NGO community – and the international community – beginning in 2005 the Putin administration placed constraints on existing NGOs, particularly foreign-funded ones, while promoting more politically palatable alternatives.[11] Indeed, echoing the international foundations it denigrated, it launched its own "NGO boom," founding state-run organizations and creating an elaborate infrastructure of grants and funding for officially sanctioned organizations. In the fall of 2005, it founded the Public Chamber (Obshchestvennaia Palata), a new body tasked with facilitating relations between executive authorities and civic groups; in addition to undertaking advisory work, it disbursed federal grants to officially registered NGOs. Douglas Rogers's (2015) ethnography of Russia's oil culture reveals that this borrowing took place at the level of the regions as well. During the same period, Perm regional authorities, together with oil industry executives, held regular grant competitions, stimulating NGOs and individuals to devise social and cultural "projects." These initiatives marked a new technology of governance; in this oil-rich region, cultural and social projects became incorporated into a project of regional state-building, in which Lukoil-Perm was a major player.[12]

This rendition of civil society foresaw a central role for youth. In the mid-2000s, the state began to make serious investment in young people, seeking to channel their energies in productive (state-centered) directions. In a curious echo of early Soviet-era discussions, the key youth policy document (*Strategy*) discussed youth as embodying both the nation's hopes and its fears: "The position of young people in civic-political life, their confidence in tomorrow, and their active engagement [*aktivnost'*] will determine the pace of Russia's movement on the path of democratic development/reformation [*preobrazovannii*]."[13] Recognizing the impossibility of returning to "the model of a single and unitary children and youth organization" that existed in the Soviet period, the state sought to offer young people diverse avenues and projects. A Youth

Public Chamber was founded in 2006, mirroring the Public Chamber, and other organizations as well (Blum 2006, 105).

Western critiques of Putin-era civil society rest on a set of assumptions: they presume that democracy and civil society represent unquestionable social goods whose meanings are transparent and stable. This presumption – like all universalizing statements – is an ideological one that denies the power relations that enable it. In this case, it denies the power relations very visible from the ground.

As we have seen, the civil-society concept brought to Russia in the early 1990s was highly ideological. What had once been a rallying cry of Eastern European oppositionists seeking a "third way" between socialism and capitalism (Ost 1990) became a project of donor states, linked to a neoliberal view of development: the New Policy Agenda. In the 2000s, civil society continued to transform. During the second Clinton administration, US policymakers reframed civil society as a form of soft power with which to achieve regime change (Carothers 2004). US aid flowed to students and oppositional groups in Serbia, Belarus, Georgia, Kyrgystan, and later Ukraine, encouraging the color revolutions I have referred to. Revolution (in the context of democratizing countries, or those considered to be sliding "backward" into authoritarianism) was something that the United States wanted to bring on, to beckon forth (Greenberg 2014). The post-9/11 "militarization" of US democracy aid associated with the Bush administration's Freedom Agenda (Carothers 2006) and the "global war on terror" only consolidated many Russian people's negative impressions of democracy promotion. As they witnessed "democracy building" invoked to legitimize the US-led war in Iraq, many Russian citizens grew disenchanted. By the mid-2000s, democratic discourses had come to signal power relations that many in Russia (and other postsocialist countries) experienced as alienating (Greenberg 2010), and democracy promotion was seen as nothing more than a cynical foreign policy tool. Thus, although many Russian people disparaged Nashi (and other Kremlin projects), they did not have much fondness for the NGOs or international civil-society initiatives it displaced, either.

The Putin-era appropriation of the civil-society concept took place here. This rendition of civil society articulated a specific set of national security concerns: suspicion about Western intervention in Russia and its "near abroad," and the desire to contain the political ambitions of domestic actors – "oligarchs" such as Mikhail Khodorkovsky who began to establish their own civil-society projects and foundations.[14] Based on the principle of sovereignty (*gosudarstvennost*), it advanced a new vision of state/societal relations: civil society in the service of the state (Richter and Hatch 2013, 335).[15] At the same time, this Putin-style repackaging posited its own solution to the "problem" of the crowd and (youthful) bodies on streets, as Nashi perfectly exemplifies.

NASHI IN IDEOLOGY: REBRANDING REVOLUTION, RESIGNIFYING POLITICS

Born of a specific moment of international democracy promotion (the militarization of democracy assistance under the Bush administration's "global war on terror," and the perception of US meddling in postsocialist space), Nashi presented itself as a kind of counterinsurgency movement. Nashi's manifesto – adopted by the organization at its first congress on April 15, 2005, and available on its website – named three goals, one of which was to maintain Russia's sovereignty and values (the others were to achieve the modernization of the country and to form an "active," or functioning [*deistvuiushchego*], civil society). Like its revolutionary predecessor, the Bolshevik-era Komsomol, the organization adopted a military rhetoric, both in its own organizing strategies (active members are komissars) and in its descriptions of opponents (as "mercenaries" who are in foreign pay).

In its early days, Nashi placed great emphasis on undertaking mass events, or "securing the streets," as one komissar put it to me; activists received training in technologies of mass action, as well as education in the arts of "political PR" and "political communication." In so doing, it brought "Orange"-like technologies to political organizing and drew on globally circulating strategies of DIY culture and direct action as well (Atwal 2009; Guillory 2008; Lassila 2011).

One komissar I spoke with explained to me that "political communication" was a new subfield, or area of study, that drew on psychology, public relations, and political science, and which aimed to provide "a combination of skills essential for a young leader." By way of illustration, he told me that the course he attended had focused on images (*obrazy*): the image of the enemy, the image of the hero, the image of the state, and how to construct an image for a political organization.

Reflecting on the early phase of Nashi's work, he explained that the priority was to work with the masses, on the streets (*s massami, na ulitsakh*). Insufficiently attuned to Nashi terminologies, I thought at first that he was referring to the social discontents that brought people (the masses) out onto the street – the dissatisfaction and concern around social benefits reform, for example, roiling forms of political contestation (by 2009, US media commentators were invoking the phrase "the Arab street" – as a place of sometimes disturbing agency – in discussions of democracy and its relative absence). "No," he corrected me, "I meant something different – control of street technology. Campaigns on the streets, a street format [*aktsii na ulitsakh, format ulichnyi*]." This was the time of the color revolutions and the Orange technologies, he reminded me. He had led a bunch of these kinds of actions, he said; one time he brought a train full of young people to Moscow from North Ossetia. Since 2008, priorities had changed, he explained, "but we don't forget about the street. The streets are with us [*ulitsy s namy*]."

I was struck by this formulation. Here, "the street" was a kind of political resource, a site to be managed and an opportunity to demonstrate strength in numbers and the ability to amass crowds.[16] It was curiously disassociated from any social or political issues, and from ideology as well. Kirill, the komissar who invited me to Moscow that day, confirmed this. When I quizzed him about the meaning of the Holiday Returned campaign, he told me that it didn't have any ideological significance and that the veterans were beside the point. If they'd wanted to do nice things for veterans, they could have stayed in Tver'. Growing impatient with my obtuseness he shouted, "The point was that we could pull people together! One hundred thousand people – there's been nothing like it since [the Russian Revolution of] 1905! The point was – the very fact that *we could do it!*"

Beyond these moments, Nashi materials signaled their resistance to and critique of international democracy promotion. The 1990s – the decade of democratization – was a constant referent of Nashi materials and campaigns. Mobilizing what Oushakine (2009, 79) has called the "genre of national tragedy" – the dominant interpretive frame applied to Russia's history in the early postsocialist period – Nashi's published materials "re-fused" disparate historical events to draw a parallel between the nineties and other periods of national trauma – the Time of Troubles,[17] or, more frequently, World War II (Lassila 2012). These materials described the Russian generation that permitted foreign intervention as "defeatists" (*porazhentsy*) rather than as bold democrats and reformers – morally corrupt, degenerate people who sold out the Motherland. The enemy or "other" that Nashi materials portrayed was a complex amalgam of undesirable forces. Nashi extended the epithet "fascist" to a wide variety of political foes, from National Bolshevik Party leader Eduard Limonov to liberal democrats Grigory Yavlinsky and Garry Kasparov,[18] and, grafting a "global war on terror" framing to its critique of nineties-era liberal interventions, proclaimed that its aim was to end the "unnatural union . . . between pseudoliberals and fascists, Westernizers and ultranationalists, international foundations and international terrorists."[19] Nashi presented itself as a solution to the forces of extremism, here a Western-sponsored "liberal-fascist alliance" that sought to hinder Russia's autonomy and strength (Atwal 2009, 746).

Other campaigns specifically repudiated democracy promotion, thumbing their nose at foreign interventions. One example arose after Putin's 2008 jibe against the Organization for Security and Co-operation in Europe's election-monitoring process and their efforts to "teach" Russia, in which he retorted, "Let them teach their wives to make cabbage soup." Nashi activists followed up on the president's remark by presenting a cookbook to the US embassy in Moscow. The gendered character of this retort is significant; it seems to be an implicit reference against Western feminist agitating.

Nashi materials painted an alarming picture of geopolitics wherein Russia was under siege from a rapacious West in a hostile world system. Nashi's army recruitment video (*Nasha armiia*) was a good case in point. The campaign, which sought to encourage young people to enlist by offering them a more agentive approach to military service (You have choices! You can avoid hazing if you sign up in the same platoon with your buddies!), offered an essentialist construction of geopolitics that saw states as inevitably in conflict with one another. "States [*gosudarstvia*] are like living organisms," it intoned – they must consume more, or perish. The United States, the dominant power, "is like a giant fat boy who began to overeat, and now simply can't stop himself. He keeps eating more and more." The message was clear: unless you enlist and Russia's army is strong, the United States will eat you! This message communicated a Marxist-style formulation (as the *Communist Manifesto* [(1848) 1978, 476] put it, "The need of a constantly expanding market for its products chases the bourgeoisie over the whole surface of the globe. It must nestle everywhere, settle everywhere, establish connections everywhere"), but in youth-friendly terms, while delivering a critique of US mass culture (fat people eating burgers). Like some of the texts pitched to young people during the early Soviet period (e.g., revolutionary utopian science fiction), it included a "condensed" version of Marxist anticapitalism and old Slavophile and Russian nationalist fears (Stites 1989, 167).

These images and depictions may appear overblown, however, it is important to recognize that Nashi did not invent them; the critique of the materialism and degeneracy of the West and the dangers it posed to Russia – particularly Russian youth – has deep historical roots in Russia (Alexander Solzhenitsyn's much-cited 1978 Harvard address, his first public statement since arriving as a dissident in the United States, defied expectations by focusing not on Soviet totalitarianism, but on the dysfunctions of Western society and its rampant materialism). This critique was reanimated by the dislocations of the nineties and saturated public discourse by the mid-2000s. Crucially, it was not limited to those who remembered socialism, but was also embraced by young people (Pilkington et al. 2002; Oushakine 2009), who were exposed to it via the media, via the "academic nationalism" that pervades universities in the Putin period (Oushakine 2009), or via the Russian Orthodox Church. While many of the young people I spoke with objected to Nashi, they agreed with elements of the analysis it presented: youth were degenerate and the nation was dying, undermined by a belligerent West (Borenstein 2008; Pilkington et al. 2002; Rivkin-Fish 2006). Here, globalization was a highly intentional Western-emanating plot, with civilizational ambitions (Pilkington et al. 2002). Part of Nashi's success was to tap and acknowledge these constructions, to acknowledge emotion that was denied by "the flattening mechanical functionalism of postcommunist neoliberal ideology" (Oushakine 2009, 85) that prevailed during the Yeltsin period.[20]

It is important to note that while liberal and foreign critics of Nashi (and Putin more broadly) identified their use of "propaganda" and PR as a dirty trick, Nashi actors framed it as an unfortunate necessity for combating nefarious methods of social control that were part and parcel of the liberal governing project. The "political communication" Nashi activists learned was a defensive art, prompted by external meddling and the clever "soft" technologies these foreigners brought to postsocialist Russia (including "new electoral technologies"). Together with "political PR" it was a hybrid technology that drew on these resources, deployed to protect young people and equip them to withstand the political manipulation they inevitably encountered, both from malign foreigners and from domestic "enemies within" (oligarchs who had offshore accounts, servants of capital). As the 2005 *Strategy* policy document put it, apoliticism (*apolitichnost'*) left young people vulnerable to political manipulation. Or as one komissar explained in 2007, "If the state stops funding Nashi, someone else will. America will finance it." He added grimly, "There are only two participants in this election: us and the United States.... Young people ... should be directed in the right direction."

In other words, Nashi materials encoded a power analysis, one that was compelling to many young people in this time of cultural globalization. It built on existing cultural material as it marketed itself to appeal to youth, mobilizing popular anxieties associated with globalization as well as preoccupations with conspiracy – the "deconstructionist" sensibility that was such a fundamental part of the postsocialist political imaginary (Shevchenko 2009). These materials existed in a popular cultural landscape that was suffused with this sensibility. One afternoon in June 2007 at the city library bookstore, I was suddenly struck by the titles I confronted: they included *Social Mass Control* (a textbook) and *Lies in Politics*, "an analysis of political lies and the technology of deceit," by A. N. Tarasov. This preoccupation with power was also manifest in the foreign titles in translation: *Black Rhetoric: The Power and Magic of*

Words, by Karsten Bredemaier, and *The Virus of Liberalism: Permanent War and the Americanization of the World,* by Samir Amin.[21] This was the year Sergei Minaev's novel *MediaSapiens* – which explores the cynical world of Russia's political technologists and the media – became a cultural sensation.

According to Nashi constructions, "(liberal) democracy," like all politics, was apprehended to be a "lie" (this belief was a place of accord between globally circulating alter-globalization critiques and rightist nationalist politics); Nashi was crafted to appeal to apolitical youth, who are sick of "politics" and who would be repelled by anything official or conformist (Lassila 2012). Indeed, I found that komissars frequently insisted that they did not support Edinaia Rossiia (Russia's so-called Party of Power) or any other party. In sync with the Putin team's strategy of pitching him as a man who stepped up to the plate to do the job, as being "above" politics (the "Who else if not Putin?" strategy, as it later became), Nashi supporters spoke of supporting Putin the man himself.

The participation of Kirill (the komissar who invited me to the Holiday Returned campaign) in Nashi was very much inflected with "brand Orange" and the antidemocratization stance this entailed. He had first come to the movement in 2005 when a colleague (*tovarisch*) invited him to participate in a Nashi conference in Moscow. He'd submitted an abstract on the topic of "technologies of the Orange Revolution" (one of the main themes). Then, he explained, he'd taken part in Nashi's election-monitoring project, "Civic Control" (*Grazhdanskii kontrol*), itself a curious appropriation of electoral technologies. "Our task was to stand at polling booths and document any infractions," he explained, "in line with international standards." At the 2006 summer camp at Lake Seliger he had attended lectures by Nashi's leading ideologues, including Nashi founder Vassily Yakemenko's session on mass campaigns – "how to create them, how to disperse them . . . how to properly plan a mass campaign." The ability to do this, he told me neutrally, "is nowadays one of the leading, one might say, stages of human development. Because if a person can bring people onto the street, it means he must be pretty strong. And these are the people who declare [*provozglasiat*] public opinion." Here, channeling the rather condescending tone of political elites toward the young people they wish to mobilize, Kirill adopted a herder's vantage point on "the crowd," those who would occupy the streets.

As he described Nashi's work to me he told me about the organization's tactic of picketing embassies. "No offense," he told me, "but we picketed the American embassy as well." I asked him why. He said it was "in connection with the spread of American democracy. At the pace and the means by which it is trying to do it – with prisons, arms, and money." I pondered the place of the patriotic/national-security dimension in the civil society he invoked. In his account, "defense of national sovereignty" was equivalent to setting up playgrounds (another project Nashi activists engaged in and of which Kirill spoke). Both were examples of "functioning" civil-society organizations mobilizing to meet social needs.

If an important part of the "work" Nashi undertook was to push back and to sternly articulate to foreigners what was no longer permissible, Nashi offered its participants other registers or voices, too. Like other elements of the Putin "cult" (or "brand," as some authors prefer to call it), Nashi was a site of "role play, mischief making and experimentation" (Cassiday and Johnson 2010, 706). Nashi offered its participants a playful repertoire; borrowing on global subcultural repertoires, its campaigns frequently contained an element of the carnivalesque – mass campaigns such as A Holiday Returned, or campaigns against littering and public alcohol consumption where young people dressed up in pig costumes, depicting the swine they sought to educate people out of being. Here, as in alter-globalization movements, we see the privileging of the ludic and the performative.[22] In ways that further suggested the rogue energy of this organization, these campaigns on occasion spilled over into stiob, that is, an overly earnest chastisement directed against the hectoring tone of an imagined always-earnest Western, or liberal democratic, interlocutor (Yurchak 1999, 2006).[23]

Indeed, Nashi activists clearly relished their skirmishes with liberals. Prominent among these provocations were the bawdy and sometimes scatological run-ins with the liberal newspaper *Kommersant*, with which it had a long-running feud. In a protest action in 2008, Nashi activists posing as *Kommersant* employees distributed toilet paper featuring the newspaper's logo, including to parliamentarians; billboards around the city announced the paper's new format. An even more grotesque act was captured on film by the 2012 documentary *Putin's Kiss*: a Nashi activist defecating on oppositionist Ilya Yashin's car.[24]

But beyond articulating a critique of Western-identified interventions, Nashi drew on this complex cultural material to articulate an alternative – a muscular, purportedly national-interest rendition of civil society that provided young people with a dignified and forward-looking subject position (at the same time that it positioned them as heirs to a glorious, if vexed and often blighted, history). This – Nashi materials asserted, claiming consensus – was a version of civil society which existed in the interests of and in the service of the state. Unlike the 1990s rendition of civil society offered by Western foundations and agencies, which posited that people would organize on the basis of "interests" (as women, as ecologists), and distinct from the Bush-era militarized rendition of democracy promotion, this version offered a vision of self and nation indivisibly linked. To quote from the longer version of the Nashi manifesto, the "manifesto with commentaries" posted on the organization's website, "We can say that a regular citizen is a passive person, but civil society is an active people, people who are the subjects of history, people who will build their own fate and the fate of their country."[25] It claimed to advance a particularly agentive mode of citizenship; while liberals just talk, Nashi materials claimed, Nashi activists (as an elite corps of civil society) should take action. As the regular manifesto put it, "Enough talk about the protection of human rights. The verbiage [*slovobludie*] of current liberals is the worst advertisement for democracy. We need to act, moreover to act only together: to protect the rights of every person, including ethnic minorities and the media, to combat hazing in the army and domestic violence, to expose corruption and to subject bribe takers to public ostracism."

One key quality a Nashi komissar was required to exhibit was "historical optimism: faith in the future of Russia." This was an "eclectic patriotic optimism" that drew on diverse symbols and registers (Lassila 2012, 161). Nashi's educational projects articulated this blend, combining patriotism and national pride with some of the skills-building activities internationally sponsored educational projects undertook before them.

Like many of the civic projects funded by international foundations, the Nashi project provided opportunities for professional training and advancement. The most active Nashi members were granted internships (for example, in the media, or in the presidential or regional administration) and the opportunity to travel to attend training sessions in other Russian cities. Some lucky komissars were offered studentships at Nashi's own Moscow-based higher educational institution.[26] Nashi materials addressed activists as leaders, as elite members of a promising new generation who could rejuvenate Russia. The manifesto urged, "Our generation must take the wheel [*smenit' u rulia*] from the defeatist generation who rule this country. Those people who believe neither in Russia's future, nor in themselves." They encouraged young people to draw inspiration from and model themselves upon their grandparents' generation, the heroic generation that saved Europe from fascism. Indeed, Nashi materials exhorted them to see themselves as engaged in an analogous struggle, against a new foreign-identified threat (the "liberal-fascist alliance" Nashi brochures invoke).

Before its restructuring in 2008, Nashi engaged in multiple campaigns. Beyond the high-profile protest actions that attracted international controversy – such as the Bronze Soldier incident in Estonia and the hounding of the British and Estonian ambassadors,[27] which led to Nashi's international vilification and upset even their Kremlin backers – it undertook smaller-scale campaigns that engaged provincial youth at the local level. Our project afforded an ethnographic vantage point on this less controversial aspect of Nashi's work and enabled me to examine the perspective of Nashi activists and their experience of belonging to the organization.

NASHI IN PRACTICE: STATE-RUN ORGANIZATION, INDIVIDUALIZED PATHWAYS

By 2006, Nashi permeated Tver' State University. Nashi booklets and brochures (as well as materials from other political parties, despite the legal prohibition on political advertising in institutions of education) littered the department; members of the research team told me that Nashi activists had come into the university on a number of occasions, inviting them to participate in events such as A Holiday Returned.

Members of the research team shared many of the critical views about Nashi I have summarized. These sociology students were derisive, skeptical of this top-down initiative, and horrified by the crude and "unprofessional" (*bezgramotnye*) materials they encountered, particularly Nashi's use of history. Echoing their teachers and many critical liberal commentators, they refused the "re-fusals" Nashi advanced (c.f. Lassila 2012). That is, they rejected the historical analogies and crude chains of equivalence these materials drew. Several students spoke to me about these materials' (and Nashi komissars') simplistic use of the term "fascism"; as Anna put it to me, it was ignorant, betrayed a lack of familiarity with historical texts, and had no basis in sociology.

My teacher colleagues told me their classrooms were polarized. Nashi activists were not numerous, but they were very vocal; trained in agitation, they took pride in challenging their teachers and bringing their analyses into class.

I witnessed this play out during one of my visits to a classroom in 2006. My colleague Maria had invited me in to talk about my research. I introduced myself to the assembled group of fourteen students, explaining my early interest in civil society and civic activism, and noted that things appeared to have changed: if a few years ago it seemed that young people were allergic to activism, now they were beginning to participate in state-run organizations. The room was silent for a while and then Maria prompted the students, "Have you had any connection with youth organizations? Any dealings at all?" The discussion, intended both as an ethnographic opportunity for me and as a means of recruiting new students for our research, degenerated swiftly into a heated debate.

While the majority kept silent, one spoke up: Kirill, the Nashi komissar, the only student in the room with whom I was (recently) acquainted. Switching into an authoritative mode, Kirill told us that Nashi was the only truly independent youth organization; the others, he said, mentioning the National Bolshevik Party, were "radicals," those who sought to undermine the state. As he itemized Nashi's activities, his peers shifted in their seats impatiently, their posture and eye-rolling indicating their weariness and disdain. Eventually one young man couldn't contain himself and interrupted Kirill to say that in his estimation, all Nashi activists were "bought" – they only did it for the gifts they were promised, such as cell phones and the "uniforms" of T-shirts.

Kirill rose heatedly to this: "OK, we have T-shirts, but it's not so simple! Look at the NBP – they wear swastikas on their arms! We may have T-shirts, but they have fascist symbols!" He went on: "Do you know how hard we have to work before they give us our five-dollar mobile phone account? Yes, there are those who just come for the T-shirts and leave, but never mind them." Objecting to the way I had framed my statement and to the suggestion that Nashi was state-run, Kirill said, "It's not that the authorities [*vlast'*] created Nashi – it created itself. The authorities are only interested in Nashi insofar as it helps them resolve particular issues and problems!"

Speaking impassionedly, Kirill named two local campaigns that exemplified this – an antilittering campaign, and one to prevent cigarette and alcohol consumption in public places, "Live according to the Law." He spoke eloquently about Nashi activists' ambition to challenge antisocial behavior such as public drunkenness and urination in public places. Valentina and Maria nodded, acknowledging that these were real issues, but two young men who had been sitting quietly on my right until now, silently emanating contempt as they toyed with their expensive cell phones, now erupted in complaint. Contesting Kirill's notion of "public space" (*obshchestvennoe mesto*), they insisted that they had the right to smoke and drink on the streets, that the street was not a public place (in their view, the term "public place" suggested a hospital, or a school). Beer wasn't alcohol in any case, they maintained, and where else could young people go? And if there were no toilets, it was not their fault! Kirill jumped in to say earnestly that small businesses should provide toilets; this was their responsibility. Interjecting, Valentina suggested that the question of how we define public space would make for a good research project. "There's no need for any research," one of the young men declared rudely. "There's already a law in place; if you need clarification, you should go and ask a lawyer!"

The encounter revealed not only the extent to which classrooms were polarized, but also what Nashi activists were up against. Except for Kirill, all of the students exhibited "demonstrative emotional disengagement" from politics (Shevchenko 2009). Like their peers in other institutions, the majority of students at the university were politically disengaged and cynical about politics. (Indeed, this was a disposition I knew their teacher shared – Maria was an accomplished satirist and earlier had regaled me with highly ironic tales about her exploits as a Young Pioneer and Komsomolka, and about contemporary politics as well.) But these two students' rendition of it was something more. As if by script, they had leapt to the defense of the materialistic, morally corrupt louts depicted in Nashi commercials, embracing the boorish beer-swilling subject portrayed in them.

The presence of Nashi activists represented a challenge in the classroom; my teacher colleagues were concerned by the analyses they asserted and particularly by the anti-Westernism of their constructions. Yet this exaggerated stance of "nihilism" (as Valentina referred to it) and disdain troubled them as well. These students' rude dismissal of Valentina's remarks suggested a class-based element – the contempt wealthy students had for their economically impoverished teachers (Patico 2008, 2009; Rivkin-Fish 2009). Beyond this, their response was profoundly troubling to my civic-activist teacher colleagues. Their words suggested that they were objecting not merely to Nashi, but to the central premise of its civic campaigns. In their construction, "the street" was a site of consumption and individual expression, a social responsibility–free zone where the powerful held sway; this was a refusal of the social. While they saw no hope of engagement with the nihilist students, my colleagues took steps toward the komissar; Valentina signaled her sympathy with Kirill on several occasions during the discussion by recalling her own youthful activism (as a seven-year-old Young Pioneer, she told us with a smile, she used to patrol the streets wearing a green armband, telling people not to throw their cigarette butts away). Maria told me later that she respected Kirill for holding his ground. After the session, Valentina spoke to him and asked him about his diploma work. "He reminds me of someone I once knew," she told me later, referring to his energy, his determination to make a difference, and his certainty as well.

The classroom interaction I witnessed gave me a sense of the plight of a komissar. Ridiculed by their peers (who frequently regarded them as automatons and dupes and who disparaged Nashi materials as second-rate product), Nashi activists saw themselves as civic warriors, fierce and righteous individuals who, in a corrective to the disparaged politics as usual, engaged in forms of direct action to educate an ill-informed, apathetic public. Kirill later told me of one exchange that recalled what had played out in class. At one campaign, a young man had come up to the Nashi activists and asked, "Why do you need to do this?" This was a meta-question that objected not to the issue (the streets were clearly dirty, urine soaked, and covered in litter), but to Nashi's exaggerated stance of citizen engagement itself.

Portrait of a Komissar I: Kirill

I had the opportunity to talk more with Kirill after that. Indeed, he expressed keen interest in our project. One morning, we met by appointment in the library of the Gender Studies Center at the university. He carefully read the IRB protocol I handed him and agreed to talk, expressing his "willingness for future collaboration."

He was the first komissar I'd had the opportunity to sit down and talk to and I was eager to quiz him about Nashi; Kirill surprised me, however, by starting to talk more broadly about state/societal relations and noncommercial organizations instead: "At the present moment, the creation of noncommercial organizations is one of the main themes of contemporary society; the main driving force in Russia are actually non-profit organizations," he told me. Puzzled, I asked him which kind he meant. "Well, you understand, they are all different, but they spring up when there's a specific social need. Nashi is a youth, democratic [one]."

He explained that he had just completed an internship in the regional administration where he had written a report on NGOs, which he said tackled a very real issue facing noncommercial organizations: the state's lack of a systemized approach to NGO funding. The need was all the greater in the small towns outside Tver', he told me: "There is devastation, the people there have nothing to do. Hence, there's alcoholism, drug addiction, radical groups that are trying to impose a fascist ideology. . . . People need something to occupy them! Nonprofit organizations can focus youth human resources. And it interests them. Because when they work in a nonprofit organization, they *svetiatsia* [get noticed, literally shine, glow], as we say in Russian. They get noticed by some people, by some politicians, [parliamentary] deputies, and bureaucrats and make all kinds of connections."

His internship had been brokered by Nashi and only grudgingly accommodated by his hosts. As he explained it, the officials he'd worked with had given him this task just to keep him out of their hair. "They dumped this project on me to keep me busy," he complained. "They didn't expect such a result of course, but I completed the project. I wrote it up, of course, I wrote it by myself, without the support of any team." However, to his chagrin, the local officials had expressed no interest. They had obstructed his progress, extended no support, and ignored his report when it was done. "I'm just floundering now," he told me, resentfully. "Although I finished my internship on August 17 and it's now September 23, there are no results!"

I was torn between two responses to this declaration. On the one hand, I felt empathetic – both his fervor and his pique recalled the narratives of my civic activist friends during the 1990s. On the other hand, I was incredulous at his impatience. He was nineteen years old and had no prior involvement in the civic organizations he spoke so knowledgeably about.

I asked Kirill to tell me more about Nashi. "The point of the youth movement Nashi is to educate patriots, specialists, and leaders," he explained. "If I am in the movement for more than a year and I'm one of the best activists in the movement, or at least in the region . . . then, by means of the internships, practicums, and other kinds of activities I'll have access to, I'll join the inner circle [*odnim iz svoikh liudei*] in the state structures." Anticipating a possible objection he added, "But this isn't evidence of bureaucracy and corruption; on the contrary, I'll be combating it from within. From within, concretely at the site of this bureaucratic system and with those, to be crude, defeatists who now sit in those places. Because, as a rule, it's the Soviet elite, and its outlook is Soviet accordingly, and it's a little Communist inclined." Ironically, his words recalled Soviet-era campaigns against lazy incumbents (Yurchak 2006).

Kirill joined our team as an "expert" consultant, participating in two roundtables and team discussions. Through these encounters I got to know him better. Of all the komissars I spoke with, Kirill was most firmly in sync with Nashi's manifesto. In line with its constructions (the "unnatural union ... between pseudoliberals and fascists, Westernizers and ultranationalists"), he presented "American democracy" as a threat analogous to anti-Semitic violence (which the other protest he mentioned sought to combat). Yet at the same time, he did not seem like a "joiner." Indeed, he saw himself as distinct even from other Nashi activists (like many of the komissars I spoke with, he didn't have a kind word to say about his peers; rather, his attention and admiration were directed upward). He foresaw a secure role for himself in the "functioning civil society" he described and was impatient when recognition for his efforts was not forthcoming. He had a curiously "critical"-seeming voice and vantage point on Nashi as well, constructing himself as a savvy and discerning consumer of youth projects.[28] In his narrative he subordinated Nashi, spoke of it as a project that was tossed his way and which he was riding for a while as he considered his options.

His work to date had focused on antifascism. He was the leader (*rukovoditel'*) of the antifascist direction and led "lessons of friendship" in schools and colleges – a fact that explained the composition of his cohort during the Holiday Returned campaign. He'd recently traveled to the Russian republic of Karelia on a kind of fact-finding mission regarding a well-publicized incident of ethnic violence. A fight had broken out in a bar in a small town, he told me, and it had resulted in sustained conflict between Chechens and ethnic Russians.[29] Nashi bused in young people to see the consequences firsthand.

Kirill had returned to the university on fire with the "truth" he'd discovered. All was not what it seemed, he told me. The TV reports (which had referred to the violence that followed as a "pogrom" against ethnic Chechens) had shown footage of sunny weather; however, it was raining when they arrived. "It was all a lie!" he told me. He had concluded that the resulting ethnic conflict had been stage-managed; it was a plot, the work of malign outsiders. "Someone's gaining from it," he said knowingly. While he didn't know who was responsible, there was a European magnate, he told me, whose interests would be served by the expulsion of the Chechen community.

His accounts helped me better understand the place of Nashi in this "functioning civil society." Nashi activists are furious cells, tracing leads, following threads, and trusting nobody. Beyond the opportunity to travel for advancement and study, the movement offered a distinctive kind of mobility: travel for a kind of investigative purpose. In a pro-state appropriation of flash mob technologies, Nashi bused its activists around the country to take direct action – in this case to serve as citizen-investigators. This strategy served and catered to the "deconstruction-ist" sensibility (Trust only what you see with your own eyes! Suspect everything! Be alert!). Of course, what one sees with one's own eyes is only ever a partial view – and, as my colleague Dmitry said wearily, re-calling the way these discussions played out in class, "You can't contest a firsthand account."

Kirill only stayed in Nashi one year. Always critical, he grew steadily more disenchanted during the year of our acquaintance. His participa-tion in Nashi didn't bring him closer to the state; on the contrary, it fueled his skepticism about it – he was still bitter about the bureaucratic intransigence and lack of appreciation he'd encountered during his in-ternship. Echoing neoliberal discourse, he told me that interning had only confirmed his sense of the incompetence and inefficiency of lo-cal bureaucrats. During our last interview in June 2007 he told me that Nashi had outlived its purpose. Nashi was over, he said, "because it has outlived its usefulness from within. Not because it is successful or not successful. It is successful as long as everything is done well. And when it has played itself out, even if it is successful in principle, behold, it falls like a skeleton." He was confident that there would be a successor project. "They'll change the name and there'll be a new movement like the old one," he told me neutrally. "It's PR, it's marketing, it's all technologies. It's all just smart technologies." This insight didn't repel him, however. De-spite his critique, he was poised to join another Kremlin project, "League of Equality" (*Liga Spravedlivosti*).

Confirming Kirill's skeptical narrative, one komissar told us cheer-fully in 2006 that anyone could find a home in Nashi: "A person who's interested in something, a person with some kind of problems in his life, if he's interested in things going better in the city or the country, or if he's interested in political activity, or if he's not a very good guy and couldn't give a damn about anything, but wants to make a career and do the minimum amount of work – each one of these people could find their way to the movement." Indeed, interviews conducted between 2006 and 2009 revealed a wide range of identification among Nashi participants. While some – the occasional attendees – were ironic about the organization and saw it just as a means to travel or party *na khaliavu* (at someone else's expense), others were more earnest. Some, like Kirill, had been drawn to the organization by its "anti-Orange" elements, moved by the assault on Russia's sovereignty it invoked, but most of the young people I spoke with seemed moved less by what the organization organized against (Nashi's "others") than by its claims to do good. Our interviews revealed that many young people were drawn to Nashi by its message of cultural tolerance. Several participants expressed their distress at recent hate crimes against racially marked foreigners (mostly African or South Asian students) and people of other nationalities (domestic "others," such as Muslims or people from the Caucasus).

Some were drawn by the opportunity to undertake socially oriented work. Like the Komsomol before it, Nashi had a pronounced service dimension. Most regional branches of Nashi had a social direction (*sots napravlenie*), where young people worked on various socially oriented projects, such as ecological/cleanup campaigns, or worked directly with vulnerable and honored populations such as veterans or orphans. Indeed, within these socially oriented projects, Nashi architects made active use of the Soviet past and drew liberally on Komsomol repertoires. The "Live according to the Law" campaign Kirill spoke of bore a striking resemblance to Soviet-era campaigns against alcoholism (regarded as antisocial, and hence a violation of "Communist morality"), while work with World War II veterans was a staple of Soviet-era youth activity.

Portrait of a Komissar II: Masha

One young person involved in Nashi's socially oriented projects was Masha, a nineteen-year-old Nashi activist I met in May 2009. Masha joined Nashi when she was sixteen years old and became a main player in the Tver' branch's social section. Her main interest was in working with disadvantaged children, and she had led projects that focused mostly on children's homes, or orphanages. Masha spoke earnestly about the work she had engaged in and about the redemptive project Nashi conducted: a project to cleanse and correct both society itself and the individuals who participated in it. In words that strikingly recalled Putin's, she spoke of the need to replace corrupt officials with new people, "those who want to do good for real, people whose moral code won't allow them to live only for their own benefit." In her view, the most pressing problem facing youth was "indifference, to others and to oneself." For Masha, Nashi represented a site where she could contest this kind of citizen passivity and anomie, qualities she, like Putin, associated with the nineties. Participation in the organization allowed her to assume a dignified subject position and to be able to pursue meaningful activities and goals.

For Masha, Nashi was a site of meaningful activities where young people could express their concerns about the nation and their desire to contribute to its improvement, and simultaneously improve themselves. Her narrative about her work with children was shot through with an account of what the movement had given her: training sessions which had helped her to develop professional skills and enabled her to initiate new projects focused on supporting children in orphanages and encouraging a foster system.

During my next visit to the city in 2010 I had the chance to talk with Masha one on one. She reminisced about her path to the movement and her early participation in it. One year later, she was in a different place and looked back half fondly, half ironically at her younger self; yet she also recalled the intensity and excitement that came with being a part of something big. "Honestly, it's funny and a little embarrassing to say," she told me, but she had first come across Nashi quite by chance. A group had come to her high school to hold "lessons of friendship," the Nashi program on multiculturalism and ethnic tolerance, and she'd sat in on it with the sole aim of skipping her physics coaching session. But "the guys turned out to be really friendly, good fun, they were a different kind of acquaintances . . . and because I was feeling that I'd outgrown my peers a bit, I wanted to hang out with older people – well, for me it was a real positive."

Before she knew it, she was entrusted to lead her own lesson of friendship. Her first one took place at an institute (she was still in high school), and it was very intimidating. "I stammered, stuttered, barely made it to the end," she told me. "Of course, I was terribly embarrassed, but I had a mentor. . . . He just sat quietly in the back row, listened, and said that everything was fine," she laughed. "He didn't scold me, or say anything bad." Then one day, she was rushing to a Nashi meeting, feeling guilty about being late yet again, when she met with a surprise. "I opened the door," Masha told me, "and . . . instead of shouting at me, they all began to clap!" It turned out she had given a Stakhanovite performance, chalking up a record number of lessons with a record number of participants. "I really liked it," she told me, "just the fact that I did it. Such a great feeling!" Catching herself, she added, "Maybe it's just egotism of course. Any kind deed is egotistical," she said, a little sardonically. "You want to be congratulated, after all. That's just how it is."

Masha recalled the different campaigns she'd been involved in, some of which were inflected with the Orange brand. In addition to the "social block" (as she referred to the social section), she explained, there was human rights defense (*pravozashchitnik*), where law students provided legal assistance to people who weren't able to get it.[30] There was another block, tolerance, which included the lessons of friendship. One of the largest campaigns was "mass actions," which taught kids how to organize patriotic and socially oriented events. This attracted a lot of young people because "it was fun to be in a social movement. . . . Each campaign was such a boost, a shot of adrenaline for the young people who found themselves in such a campaign – and if [the campaign] was extreme, well, you were left with such intense emotions! It was . . . so positive, it left you feeling so warm because you'd gone through it, not alone, but with your comrades. It was great," she told me. "There was nothing like it. Well," she added, drawing a Bolshevik-era parallel, "probably revolutionaries experience something similar when they unite and do something like this together. Even if it's absolute nonsense [*chepukha*], just a regular flash mob, where people just stand in lines and clap their hands . . . but they like it . . . [because there are so many of them]."

They had collaborated with local veterans' associations in some campaigns. "Day after Day" brought young people together with World War II veterans in the city park. "There was a dance floor," she told me, "boat rides, food. And every young person was paired with a veteran; he had to spend the whole evening with him, to talk with him. . . . They even got a little drunk," she laughed. "Well, our veterans are . . . soulful," she added with a smile. I was struck by this account, as it was strikingly similar to the Komsomol narratives captured by Yurchak (2006, 94). It also provided evidence of the extent to which Nashi tailored itself to the activities of existing civic organizations; the director of the Pensioners' Union had given a similar account of events her organization had initiated.

Like Kirill and many others I spoke with, Masha assumed a metastance on the Nashi project and was able to talk about it with a sense of distance. When I asked her if she still considered herself part of Nashi, she hesitated: "Well, probably not.... They exclude you if you don't show up. And I didn't show up." She had opted out for a number of reasons. What she called the "rituals" (the pomp and the various ceremonies) had overtaken the work (*delo*); in her view this was "silly": "What matters most," she said, "is that a person does the work." What's more, the quality of the education offered and that of the campaigns had declined. Whereas Nashi used to offer top-quality educational programs, she told me, it no longer did. "I no longer consider myself part of Nashi," she went on, "because . . . well, it was certainly my past, and it's given me a great deal, but today I try to be more independent. I think that I, thank goodness, left in time, because I didn't completely lose my mind to it [*sovsem ne do fanatizma u menia eto doshlo*]; I understood perfectly what I was capable of, and thank goodness, I took what I needed. I took what I needed to act correctly. And I didn't become someone who would just blindly follow orders. I mean – I think for myself [*dumaiu golovoi*]." When I suggested that she sounded skeptical about the movement, she demurred: "No, not really skeptical – I'm grateful for it. I'm glad that I was part of it. It's just that everyone grows out of it eventually."

Portrait of a Komissar III: Igor

Igor, twenty-five, was a komissar who, like Kirill and Masha, was involved in Nashi at the very beginning. He participated in Nashi's first mass action, "Our Victory" (2005). When I interviewed him in 2009 Igor told me that the movement had been a major "stimulus" in his life. Disenchanted with his formal education, he had left the university and devoted himself to Nashi. His passion was information technology and he was particularly interested in the scope and potential of social-networking technologies; Nashi had offered a venue for him to pursue these interests. Indeed, he told me the movement had helped him to think about social issues and problems, and to find a way to draw connections between them. "You need a system, or logistics. The movement taught me how to think about this systematically and to be able to analyze situations," he said.

It was clear to me throughout the interview that Nashi had presented Igor with an opportunity for a particular kind of advancement – not the cynical pursuit of his own self-interest or the furtherance of his career, but the construction of self and an engagement in meaningful activities. In fact, although we had ostensibly gotten together to talk about Nashi, Igor barely made mention of the movement. Rather, his emphasis was on the confidence and sense of agency it had fostered in him and the process of self-actualization that it had permitted. When I noted this and asked him about the role of Nashi and his relationship to it, he said, "You understand, the movement is a tool [*instrument*] that helps me; it's like a car that takes me somewhere." Like Kirill, he subordinated Nashi to his own needs. While Masha discussed the collective nature of her participation in Nashi and the experience of solidarity through belonging, Igor's was a more individualized pursuit.

True to the hybridity I have noted, his interview was peppered with references to diverse sources: the Nashi manifesto (which, he explained, expressed his values and orientation); *Rich Dad, Poor Dad,* a financial advice book in the self-help genre written by American authors (which he told me offered an "analogue" to his own experience);[31] *Socialnomics,* by digital marketing guru Erik Qualman; and *Crisi$: How Is It Organized,* a conspiracy theory–ridden detective novel by the Russian author Nikolai Starikov, a copy of which he pressed into my hands as he left.[32] I was intrigued that he embraced such seemingly contradictory texts and that he could refer to them so comfortably in the course of one conversation. While the self-help manual advanced a kind of neoliberal logic and subjectivity, the other two proposed an alternative understanding of capitalism and globalization that viewed them as a hostile political program launched by a rapacious West (Pilkington et al. 2002). Yet Igor drew on all of these texts to offer an internally coherent narrative about himself and his place in the world.

By way of illustrating what he meant, he referred to Facebook. "You know the story of how Facebook was founded, don't you?" he asked. When my face registered inquiry, he explained that it was invented by a student in his dorm, who wanted to make connections with his friends nearby. What struck me was that this Nashi komissar included no national identifiers in this account; Mark Zuckerberg's nationality (American) and institutional affiliation (Harvard) were irrelevant to him as he was recalling the actions of a peer. In effect, he denationalized Zuckerberg. He recalled Facebook because it was exemplary of a form of agency he identified with; it signaled a mode of operation, a way of thinking and operating in the world that he found attractive and which characterized his own life.[33]

I have located Nashi as part of a broader Putin-era civil-society project. Rather than viewing the Putinist appropriation of the civil-society concept as the debasement of democratic ideals, as most accounts maintain, I argue that it makes better sense to see it as the last in a long line of borrowings and local modifications (c.f. Verdery 1996), one that has given rise to diverse social forms at both the federal and regional levels (Rogers 2015). The Putin-era rendition of civil society, linked to the concept of "sovereign democracy," drew on circulating elements, providing further evidence of the instability and promiscuity of these forms and the unintended results of their implementation (Coles 2007; Greenberg 2010; Matza 2009).

Though undoubtedly a top-down project, Nashi was successful in captivating the energy and loyalties of some of its target audience. Designed out of the complex cultural material of the postsocialist period – including forms of disillusion and disappointment as well as the "deconstructionist orientation" mapped by Shevchenko – Nashi both resonated with young people's anxieties and fears and simultaneously empowered them to imagine themselves as agents of change. As these three portraits reveal, youth responses to Nashi were highly individualized. It became clear to me that the "state-ness" of these state-run organizations did not determine their participants' experiences; young people were able to personalize and domesticate them, pursuing their own diverse projects and goals. In a way that signaled continuity with the socialist era, young people were able to entertain multiple models and rationalities within this state-run organization and did not necessarily experience them as contradictory. They did not take its pronouncements at face value and had critical distance from them, distinguishing between what was meaningful and what was pro forma (c.f. Yurchak 2006), and maintaining a sharp sense of their own priorities as they served the state.

I suggest that rather than viewing Nashi as a form of "virtual politics" (Wilson 2005), a way of "faking democracy" (a reconstituted Bolshevik project, as Wilson would have it), it makes better sense to see it as evidence of something new and distinctive – a "post-modern mixture of old school methods and new political technologies" (Robertson 2009; quoted in Cassiday and Johnson 2010, 706), where we can see evidence of considerable agency and polyphony.

Nashi was a political-technology project in motion. Self-aware, it was constantly rebranding and recalibrating its message (Lassila 2012). As we have seen, its activities were less ideological campaigns than "projects," short-lived themed activities that were marketed to youth (in this, it strongly resembled the NGOs it disparaged). In the years of its existence, Nashi underwent substantial mutation. As my frequent visits to the Nashi website made clear, campaigns burgeoned and proliferated, some assuming directions that displeased their Kremlin-based supporters. Indeed, during 2006–2007 the organization undertook a series of controversial campaigns that got it into serious trouble, leading to its reorganization. The year 2008 was a watershed for the organization, due to both this and the Putin-Medvedev-related change in the political climate. In early 2008 it seemed Nashi was finished, but it reemerged a few months later, reenergized and transformed as a number of "directions," including Steel (*Stal'*) and "Our Victory." Until 2012, when it finally disappeared, Nashi engaged in a constant rebranding and respinning, updating and rebooting itself in response to the changing times, and to keep its young constituents interested and lure them from other youth organizations that competed for their attention.[34]

The next chapter turns to examine the new youth projects that emerged (and partially displaced Nashi) during the Putin-Medvedev era. In so doing, it highlights another angle of the realignments that Russia's state-run youth projects contribute to, emphasizing the shifts in subjectivity they beckon forth.

THREE

SELIGER 2009

"Commodify Your Talent"

AS I PREPARED TO RETURN TO TVER' DURING THE SPRING OF
2009, I realized something was afoot. In the aftermath of the 2008 presidential election, state-run youth projects were in flux. While liberal
newspapers jubilantly reported Nashi's demise (it had ostensibly been
disbanded), the media announced the launch of some new high-profile
federal youth events. Indeed, 2009 had been declared Russia's Year of
Youth (*God molodezhi,* or *Godmol,* as it was abbreviated). Its flagship
event, scheduled to take place at a lakeside resort in Tver' region (about
190 kilometers outside the city of Tver') was the summer educational
camp, Seliger 2009.

Official accounts and promotional materials emphasized this event's
distinctiveness from the projects that had preceded it, energetically de-
nying its association with Nashi. This, newspapers claimed, was no longer a narrow Nashi forum (as past Seliger camps had been); Seliger 2009
was organized by the newly founded Federal Youth Affairs Agency in
partnership with the Ministry of Sports, Tourism, and Youth Policy. It
was a competitive forum that invited all "talented" youth to apply from
across the federation.

I arrived in Tver' in May 2009 to find the university students in a
frenzy. In the run-up to the camp at Seliger, multiple recruitment and
training events had taken place and some students had participated in
them. Many if not all of the students I spoke to were at least entertaining
the possibility of participating in Seliger 2009. In another instance of
odd congruence between our research and the state-run youth project,
Seliger 2009 may actually have stimulated recruitment for our research;

at the same time, our research ironically became a magnet for pre-Seliger recruitment events. It was this wave of events that brought Vitaly, the Tver' representative of the Federal Youth Affairs Agency we met in the introduction, to our miniconference at the university. In addition to screening the dark and foreboding "forbidden" commercial, he showed more upbeat "official" ones as well that day, such as "Seliger 2009."

The commercial "Seliger 2009" opened with an image of planet Earth, remote in the dark depths of outer space. A male narrator intoned meaningfully, "What is talent? It's competitive advantage [*konkurentnoe preimushchestvo*] that will allow you to do something new, cheaper, or better than anyone else in the world market." He continued: "Talent needs servicing [*obsluzhivanie*]. You need to find it and develop it – that's time and risk. You need to sell it – that's technology. [On-screen a space-ship was orbiting Earth.] Talent needs environment, community, con-nections, confidence about success, inspiration. You can try to figure it out alone. Or you can go to Seliger . . ."

The pace picked up as the camera panned across a lake, zooming in over small islets. The narrator said, "The all-Russian educational innova-tion forum 'Seliger' is a systemic platform, created by the government to convert talent into products [*dlia prevrashcheniia talanta v tovar*]. [The phrase "Made in Russia" appeared on the screen in English.] The narra-tor then named the ten themed sessions as their logos flashed by: "techni-cal creativity and innovation [picture of a fetus]; youth entrepreneurship [a businesslike handshake]; tolerance [a raised hand]; information flow [a person speaking into a cupped hand]; national tourism [a mountain]; culture and history [a church]; professional orientation [an arrow point-ing upward]; voluntarism [a heart]; leadership [a red star]; creativity [a brain inside a head]." The narrator continued, speaking quickly in urgent tones: "From July 1 to August 15 fifty thousand talented people from eighty-four regions of Russia will be in one place!" he said, as the commercial depicted red Nashi T-shirt–clad youth at past Seliger camps. "In no other place like Seliger can you find such powerful and fast social mobility [*sotsialnyi lift*]."

The video then switched to show some of the powerful politicians who had attended past Seligers and with whom the participants of Seliger 2009 would have the opportunity to meet – grown-ups in their shirt-

sleeves, listening attentively to young people, as the narrator named a
string of ministers and governors: "President Medvedev, First Vice President Surkov . . ." He then promised, "The fine quality of the education
you receive will be comparable to one year of traditional education," as
a computer-generated image of the camp at Seliger was juxtaposed with
black-and-white footage of students staring dully at a professor in a sev-
enties-era lecture hall. At this, I exchanged glances with Valentina. The
video then shifted to portray vigorous-looking men and women bearing
microphones, speaking in large white tents: "There will be lectures by
the best teachers, business games, master classes led by the teachers
from Russia's best teaching institutions. In this autonomous town in
the woods . . . there will be free internet, live streaming of all events;
Seliger will have its own media, its own TV channel – city in the forest,
or an anthill? People will be busy working, glowing, on fire, inspired
from 8 AM until 1 AM! [Here the commercial depicted an entertainment
program – music, a fashion show, etc.] You can present your program,
project, or idea to all interested structures. You will have direct access
to investors, grants, to state corporations, state programs." The narrator
went on to explain that the best projects would receive awards and be
enacted. The goal? "To return Russia to the position of a global leader of
the twenty-first century!"

SELIGER'S PROMISE: TALENT, EMPOWERMENT,
AND THE COMMODIFICATION OF SELF

Talent, global competitiveness, projects, and sellable product – the message was striking. Seliger 2009 really did appear to be distinct. Less the
nationalist-patriotic education program of prior Nashi events, this camp
resembled a giant innovation forum. In line with the "modernization"
theme of the Putin-Medvedev tandem, it sought to encourage innovation
and entrepreneurship. Youth participants would have the chance to learn
skills and develop their ideas to present to powerful corporate sponsors
such as the Russian Nanotechnology Corporation (RUSNANO) and billionaire Mikhail Prokhorov's Onexim Group, both of which pledged
to invest in winning projects.[1] Indeed, as I subsequently realized, the
camp's slogan was "Commodify your talent!"

In contradistinction to the fusty formal institutions of higher education such as the university we sat in, Seliger cast itself as an alternative venue for a twenty-first-century education. Here, young people would be offered dynamic teachers, the opportunity to consult with top experts and learn cutting-edge new technologies, and the chance to compete for funds to enact their projects. Unlike the university (drably depicted in the video), Seliger 2009 was a site of dynamism and fluidity – no calcified hierarchies, or authoritarian styles of interaction here! It promised a fantasyland of opportunity, where structure didn't matter and where talent could emerge and be nurtured. It had reality TV elements too; there you could brush shoulders with minor celebrities, the agents of state power, successful entrepreneurs, and oligarchs, and even catch a glimpse of the president!

Promotional materials promised a firm, capable, proactive, and curiously pliant state, a civil, ethical state that was ready to heed you and your sense of priorities. It promised *glamur* – a flashy and VIP-filled display of wealth, talent, and connections. And it signaled to young people that it (all this!) was at their disposal. In sum, it offered up a specific empowerment script, beckoning forth a particular kind of agency and dynamic conduct in youth as it promised a new relationship with the state.

As I saw when I visited the camp with my colleagues in August 2009, these injunctions and pledges were materially asserted in the posters and placards strung up between trees. "Either study, or goodbye!" read one, quoting Medvedev. "We will do it!" announced another, depicting Putin shaking hands with a young woman apparently clinching a business deal as other young people looked on admiringly. These posters depicted the state offering itself up as a resource, or a tool (*instrument*), as various materials put it. Indeed, at Seliger 2011 (the second Seliger camp I attended), participants did calisthenics against a giant stage bedecked with images of Medvedev and Putin, with a confusingly worded slogan that rather comically seemed to suggest they personally were offering themselves up to the young people: "All tools for the development of talent" (*Vse instrumenty dlia razvitiia talanta*).

In this chapter, I take a closer look at the mode of empowerment Seliger 2009 promised and consider what kind of work or activity it prepared youth for. Which youth did Seliger seek to engage, which were

3.1. "We will do it!" poster depicting a young woman shaking hands with then–Prime Minister Putin, at Seliger 2009.

excluded, and what kinds of subjects did it seek to forge? What kind of talent did this state-run project want to foster and commodify, and which technologies did it deploy in its efforts to do so?

In this Putin-Medvedev-era youth project, we see a shift. While Nashi addressed the "problem" of apolitical youth and anxieties about youth mobilization by foreign powers, Seliger 2009 addressed the problem of youth precarity – of highly educated young people facing uncertain futures, and the instability this threatened. As such, its framing was distinct. Seliger 2009 emphasized youth's role in the global economy, bringing a business-management dimension to youth campaigns. At the same time, however, there were moments of carry-over from Nashi and a great deal of continuity. Like Nashi, this state-run project offered a distinctive blend of logics where patriotic-type programs and goals coexisted with globally circulating ones.

This chapter offers specific insights into the neoliberal renegotiation of the contract between state, civil society, and individual citizens as it plays out in Russia, examining the shifts in subjectivity it entails. Seliger 2009 beckoned forth new forms of commodification of self and coaxed youth into a new relationship with the state. Insofar as it sought to activate and maximize youth and encourage them to self-govern, it resembled other global projects to empower that scholars have critically interrogated (Cruikshank 1999; Eliasoph 2011). Yet the empowerment script it offered departed in crucial ways. While it drew on global repertoires of corporate capitalism and management consultancy, it offered distinctive elements as well. Seliger 2009 offered a repatriated, "socially responsible" form of entrepreneurship to young people and sought to foster a specific kind of "talent" that would serve the nation. At the same time that it offered individualist solutions and strategies, it emphasized the importance of personal networks in a way that seemed quintessentially (post)socialist (Ledeneva 1998, 2006) – connections, acquaintance, and being in the right place at the right time. This, though, with its pledge of celebrity and powerbroker presence, was a distinctively glamorous rendition.

Drawing on interviews with Seliger participants, I explore the imaginative possibilities and the concrete rewards – as well as the disappointments – youth participants encountered at Seliger 2009, tracing the responses of two distinct groups of young people: organizer-activists who were the purveyors of the empowerment script and these technologies and who were at least partially advantaged by it, and some rank-and-file participants.

Situating Seliger

In order to understand this shift in emphasis, we need to consider the shifting field of Russian politics. As the Nashi komissars I spoke to in the spring of 2010 put it, the issue of Russia's sovereignty (thrown into renewed question by the 2004 Orange Revolution in Ukraine) had been resolved by the 2008 elections and the successful transfer of power from Putin to his anointed successor. In the Putin-Medvedev era, the state had new priorities, partly stimulated by the 2008 global economic crisis.[2] "Modernization" (of the economy) was the new buzzword and the most pressing task was innovation and economic development. In a highly publicized September 10, 2009, newspaper article entitled "Forward Russia!" President Medvedev laid out his goal of a sweeping modernization of the Russian economy, politics, and society. The distinctive path to this future he envisaged involved an energized civil society: "A transition to the next, higher stage of civilization will be accomplished . . . not through suppression, but rather the development of the creative potential of every individual." The fate of Russia, Medvedev emphasized, must be shaped "not by raw materials, but by our intellect, our strength, dignity, and enterprise." He proposed a number of steps, including innovation awards, encouraging Russian businesses to contribute.[3] During 2009 the media was full of reports about the flagship of this modernization mission: a new high-tech innovation park to be built on the outskirts of Moscow at Skolkovo, dubbed "Russia's Silicon Valley." The bold state-emanating proclamations and new passion for IT and nanotech inspired Russia's satirists; one friend recounted a joke she'd seen on TV referring to the extremely unpopular, now rehabilitated neoliberal ex–finance minister Anatoly Chubais, director general of RUSNANO, as a "nanonist," a play on "onanist."[4] This joke simultaneously parodies Chubais and the "modernization" policies he (and implicitly Medvedev) espoused, casting those policies as the effete practices of a pubescent boy, a wannabe man (unlike Putin).

This new strategic emphasis on innovation and technology had implications for education;[5] mirroring broader European trends, the Putin-Medvedev administration named education a key target of its ten-year growth strategy (named Russia 2020). The language of modernization, already manifest in earlier educational policy statements, rose to the surface to articulate a "new youth policy." The "modernization" of the Russian educational system deployed psychology as a tool; it involved a move away from learning by rote to a new emphasis on alternative pedagogies with psychologists' input, and focused on "the development of . . . personalities, of cognitive and creative abilities" (Russian Federation 2004, 8; quoted in Matza 2009, 516). (As we'll see in the next chapter, psychologists played a prominent role at Seliger 2009.) Between the lines of Seliger promotional videos, we glimpse the contours of the new entrepreneurial subject this pedagogy sought to deliver – a person who is "moral" and "enterprising," who can "make decisions independently in a situation of choice, can cooperate, who [is] distinguish[ed] by mobility, dynamism, constructive thinking, who [is] open for cross-cultural interaction, feel[s] responsible for the destiny of the country" (Ministerstvo Obrazovaniia, Rossiiskoi Federatsii 2002, sec. 1.2; cited in Matza 2009, 516).

These "new youth policies" were to be enacted by a new institution: Rosmolodezh, the Federal Youth Affairs Agency, founded in 2008. The agency's mission statement echoed these neoliberalism-inflected "modernizing" goals: "The agency considers youth to be the main resource of the country in the 21st century. Rosmolodezh is the operator of this important strategic resource, this most valuable part of the country's human capital."[6] Beneath the new, however, we see substantial carry-over. The agency's first director and enactor of these "modernizing" projects was Vasily Yakemenko, the controversial founder and leader of Nashi and Walking Together.[7]

As I studied the Federal Youth Affairs Agency materials I realized there was some tension within its strategies. In line with the Conception on Youth policies passed by the federal government in 2008 (on the long-term social-economic development of Russia through 2020), one goal was to combat youth social marginalization and disenfranchisement that could lead to political alienation.[8] The conception contained a Komsomol-like pledge of social mobility and advancement; one goal was "the creation and development of 'social lift' systems (support and maintenance for prizewinners and talented young people from small towns and rural areas and the targeted support of government agencies, NGOs, and teachers to prepare them)." At the same time, as we've seen, the agency aimed to serve the brightest and best. It becomes clear that "modernization" as applied to youth was a two-tier plan serving two constituencies: it was undertaken both to encourage innovation among those who might lead (competitions and rewards for the "talented"), and to serve those who were not yet modern (support for the precarious and potentially volatile provincial youth who were the main target of these projects). The hidden referent here is the socioeconomic obstacles faced by these young people; although state documents did acknowledge the global economic crisis, they elided the entrenched hierarchies and

3.2. Seliger 2009 logo, as depicted on the promotional brochure.

inequities provincial youth contended with and the impenetrability of Russia's social strata (Trubina 2012, 215).

As I flipped through the brochures Vitaly had passed out, I learned more about Seliger 2009. Like the promotional video, the glossy brochure was arresting and commanding. The logo on the front page consisted of four squares with hand symbols: a handshake, a thumbs-up, a peace sign, and the final one, a hand with a finger pointing at the reader. While the first three looked like imports from the United States, the fourth recalled Soviet (and US) army recruitment posters. Like the video, the brochure started out by defining the key word "talent" as "competitive advantage";

indeed, I realized that the video and brochure deployed identical phrases and blocks of text.

In addition to the high-profile lectures by VIPs (referred to in the brochure as "vertical connections") and a menu of "master classes" and "training programs" run by experts, Seliger promised "horizontal" opportunities as well, a transformative encounter with the brightest, best, most talented and inspired ("50,000 talented young people from 84 regions of Russia in one place!"). This can-do empowerment rhetoric is accompanied by a stern admonition: "Seliger is not for wimps [*slabakov*]!" the brochure announces. "There's no space for whiners or deserters – there will be mandatory exercise drills and an educational plan."

I realized there was another dimension of the empowerment script. Like Nashi materials, it offered a vocabulary and a knowing vantage point on Russian state power: the "vertical" is something for you to use – here, we'll give you tips – while the "horizontal" is something that's yours to develop and exploit!

Boris was one of several new students I met for the first time during the spring of 2009. He had participated in several regional youth initiatives, but emerged from them disenchanted. Despite his ambivalence about his past experience, he was very excited about Seliger 2009. Indeed, he had recently been hired to recruit young people to attend. The educational forum at Seliger was distinct, unlike anything that had preceded it, he told me breathlessly. "The state will offer an incredible packet of services [*servisy*]," he said. "I don't think there's been anything like it!" His rendition emphasized the megawattage of star power, the elite of Russia's might: "There will be more VIPs than you've dreamed of. ... Putin will be there, Abramovich, Deripaska," he went on, disconcertingly naming oligarchs, people associated with dirty wealth and political manipulation.

When I asked him about continuities with prior Nashi camps at Seliger, he insisted that this event was different, unparalleled and quite distinct. "This is not a Nashi [*Nashistskii*] forum," he assured me. "I emphasize, it's not a Nashi forum. It's a forum of a totally different level!" There will be fifty thousand people," he told me, echoing the video and brochure. The participants would be "the most talented and best, bringing top [*topovye*] projects!" There was a rigorous screening process, he explained: "Each project submitted online will be evaluated and receive a ranking; those who score highest will get to go." At Seliger there would be an intensive training program that would "offer individualized programs of study. . . . They will fully support you . . . and of course there will be a project fair at the end. The best projects will receive financial support, and the best ones will go on to the federal level and they will be enacted at the all-Russian level." While I first took Boris's assertions that Seliger was not Nashi-related to be a form of ideological refusal rooted in disdain for the pro-Kremlin organization, I came to view it differently. In classic marketing speak, he was insisting on the newness of the product; one year later, I learned that Boris had joined Nashi as a komissar.

That day in May 2009 we met in Valentina's office to talk further. In terms that echoed the recruitment speech I described in the introduction, Boris explained, "The main problem young people face is . . . well, let me tell you about myself. Let's say I have a project, but I don't have any connections. I don't have any money, I just have an idea. But if you collect, let's say, a bunch of young people, ten people, we can pool our resources. One person has contacts, someone has sponsorship possibilities, someone else has time, and another person is able to administrate things. And as a result, these projects will be realized."

I encountered various versions of this empowerment script in the course of my research. Individual youth organizers offered different inflections and cadences, but the gist was the same. It promised mobility, education, recognition, and a particular relationship with the state – which would be there to help participants design their projects. It was a democratic kind of vision that promised something attainable to all via the pooling of resources (even those without money or connections had something to give). In its call for young people to look positively at their resources, it resembled the logic of asset-based community development.[9] As with this neoliberal model, there's a slight menace, an element of coercion here. As another promotional video, one that focused on the Russia 2020 youth project, put it, a young person's fate will depend on his or her talent, personal qualities, and activeness (*aktivnost'*); the video showed a young man lying in a gutter as it told viewers that if they didn't succeed, it would be because they didn't try hard enough. The options were stark: "Will you be a leader, or be led [*budesh liderom, ili ve-domym*]? Will you build your life yourself? Or just serve out your time?"

I witnessed a flash of this coercive quality when Boris delivered a recruitment call to some of Valentina's first-year students. When the students did not respond immediately with questions, he quickly moved to chastise them: "It's really awful that there are no questions! It means you're not interested." His response communicated a kind of vanguard-ist impatience with the masses. It also had a national-patriotic inflec-tion – "not interested" implies disloyalty, or indifference to the fate of the nation, as we've seen. At this, Valentina interjected: "Wait a minute, they are still young. They're only eighteen years old." Prompted by this gentle rebuke, Boris recovered himself: "It's just that any stupid question is a super-question – remember that, it's most important. . . . If you don't have a project, we'll sit down with you and will help you fashion one. Or, let's say you have some kind of idea. Even a banal one. A project can be born from nothing!"

Projects from Nothing?

"Project" was the vehicle around which this education was structured and through which this empowerment would take place, and was of-fered as both a means and an end. Echoing the logic of the international agencies that channeled funding to NGOs during the 1990s, projects were central both to the application process and to activities at Seliger. Participants needed to have one to register on the Federal Youth Affairs Agency site, and they were supposed to develop it while there. The key technology – the vehicle through which these things could be accom-plished – was "project design" (*upravleniia proektami*). As one organizer explained to me, "project design" had a "special place in the program"; it was the core of the educational program offered to participants in each eight-day thematic session. It was usually taught during the morning of each day. After that, participants could select among different "master classes" and lectures. They then had the option to compete; events cul-minated in a project fair, where they presented their projects to potential sponsors.

"Project Design: Create Your Tomorrow," the booklet distributed to all participants at Seliger who were coming without their own projects, offered practical steps and skills. It walked the reader through four main stages, from project development to formal presentation – four stages derived from the US management consultancy models it drew on. But "project" represented more; the "project approach" (*proektnyi podkhod*) Seliger promotional materials promised was an encitingly new approach to life and work. It emphasized new qualities and skills for which it offered new terms – a strategic way of thinking (*proektnoe myshlenie*) – and a life stance of appealing agility and flexibility.[10] "The person who develops his ability to effectively manage projects will lay a solid foundation for success in life!" promised Evgenii Sokolov in the lecture on project design he delivered at Seliger 2009. Or, as the Russia 2020 video put it, "Your approach to life will completely change. . . . You'll forget the concept of work, work as a boring necessity that begins in school and ends in the grave, along with the fear of losing work or not being able to find it. The grandiose and precise word 'PROJECT' will now define the rhythm of your life. Your social mobility will increase. You'll easily be able to move from project to project, from town to town, from country to country." At this point, the video switched to an image of a young man with his laptop on the beach. "Your connections will cause envy. Your diplomas and workbook [*trudovaia kniga*] will recede into the past . . . and you'll ask yourself – *do I really like what I am doing?*" Neither wage slave nor *sovok* (the disparaging slang term for passive, dependent Homo Sovieticus), the new subject invoked here was self-directing and dynamic, and experienced work as an aesthetic experience, as creative play. Indeed, in the image of the beach bum with his laptop, work and play blended in an intoxicating fusion.

While this message of choice and mobility may not seem so radical to an American reader (though surely it may seem hyperbolic), it is quite beyond the expectations of most Russian youth. In the twenty-first century, Russian citizens are no longer constrained by socialist-era residency permits, or prevented from traveling outside the country. The global mobility that began in the nineties with oligarchs (who bought up real estate and football clubs in Europe) is now extended to the urban middle class. Professional-class people such as my provincial teacher colleagues are newly on the move; they vacation in Spain and Cyprus and shop in Germany or Finland. However, professional mobility is relatively rare and off limits for most young people – certainly for the kinds of young people who attended Seliger, for whom a trip even to Moscow was costly.

In Russia, there are few domestic opportunities for professional mobility. Twenty-four years after the Soviet Union's dissolution, Russia remains an exceptionally divided nation. Wealth, opportunity, and technology are concentrated in a few urban centers, mostly Moscow and Saint Petersburg. Russia's petrodollar-fueled boom contributed to the further consolidation of wealth and the wide perception of the entrenchment of privilege and the impossibility of social mobility. With its wireless internet, ATMs, and live-streaming plasma TV screens, Seliger, this "autonomous town in the woods," was a high-tech oasis that bore no resemblance to everyday life, as youth participants arriving from all over the Russian Federation would have been aware.

My field notes from August 2009 describe my impressions of the two-and-a-half-hour drive to Lake Seliger from Tver' city. I saw no evidence of trade, industry, or commerce in the neglected hamlets and towns we passed through; indeed, we barely saw any trucks. The infrastructure too was poor and the roads were bumpy. My Russian colleagues – who rarely traveled outside the city, unless it was to go to Moscow, Saint Petersburg, or abroad, and for whom this trip was as "exotic" as it was for me – also noted this. Rather than spending money on these Potemkin projects like Seliger, they told me, Putin should fix the roads. Maria explained that Prime Minister Putin had recently announced that the budget for fixing the roads had been canceled. "But then, he doesn't need roads," Grigory quipped. "He travels by helicopter." (The media had depicted Putin arriving at Seliger by helicopter.) At this Valentina sighed, "And the rest of us are all supposed to just sit at home, as in the old days."

"Made Not in Russia": The Repatriation of Talent

With its talent and project talk and message of individual autonomy and mobility, Seliger 2009 resembled so many global projects that encourage youth into civic activity–inducing, human capital–developing pursuits (Eliasoph 2011). We can locate Seliger 2009 within the global "celebration of talent" Lisa Hoffman (2010) describes in her case study of China; it is one more instance of "human capital development" – the new neoliberal-oriented common sense. It provides evidence of the neoliberal drift into forms of civic activism; indeed, it is frequently hard to tell the for-profit apart from the nonprofit (Eliasoph 2011). With its attachment to "gamification" and its blending of work, play, and civic engagement, Seliger (like other global "youth empowerment projects") is a complex amalgam of the social and the straight-up entrepreneurial, as later chapters will explore.[11]

But there was something distinctive here – a patriotic spin, one that took on a distinctively post-Soviet inflection (c.f. Hoffman 2010). The Russia 2020 commercial went on to define patriotism in similar terms as the Seliger 2009 commercial, as "the ability to compete," adding rather menacingly that talent is "the possibility to do something new, better, quicker, and cheaper . . . than anyone else on the planet."

This extra inflection (which undercuts the promise of global mobility we've earlier seen) peeked through in another Seliger promotional video, "Year of Youth Robot." The narrator is a benevolent robot, "Robot Godmol," the metal embodiment of the Federal Youth Affairs Agency. The robot stands in a futuristic pristine high-tech space, a lab for the changes he seeks to effect. In a tinny voice, he runs through the standard Year of Youth pledges and promises ("The contemporary world needs talented people. . . . There's no task more interesting than to help a young person find his talent, develop it, and sell it"). "Talent needs care" he says then, adding an organic metaphor to the discussion as he benevolently waters the tree that has popped up from the seed he just planted. Echoing the Russia 2020 video quoted earlier, he goes on: "The grandiose and precise word 'PROJECT' will now define the rhythm of your life." But then things switch.

Four minutes into this six-minute commercial, the tone and pace shift from the can-do to alarm. A male narrator takes over, displacing the robot, and in urgent tones lays out the frightening context: Russia is hostage to a hostile world economy. He explains, "All the cool computers, cars, clothes, things we admire were coined not by us, made not by us, not in our country, not using our technology," as a sign appears on-screen that reads "Made Not in Russia." Like the "forbidden commercial" Vitaly also screened, and which we examined in the introduction, it goes on to allude to Russian greatness – Soviet cosmonaut Yuri Gagarin and Russian inventors, now respun in neoliberal fashion as entrepreneurs and innovators. "You need to sell your talent," the narrator insists, "in order that [it] doesn't serve other people."

Other pamphlets and materials pick up this theme. Here, it becomes clear that the Seliger project is not only about encouraging contemporary forms of talent, but about historical restitution as well. Talent here is presented as a form of cultural patrimony that has been cruelly snatched (and which has historically served "other people"). Materials depict lost heroes such as Vladimir Zvorykin (a Russian émigré who left Russia during the civil war in 1918 and who invented the TV) and Google co-founder Sergey Brin, who left the USSR at age six when his family emigrated to the United States. It becomes clear that what is at stake is the repatriation of talent that historically went astray.

Zvorykinsky Project, the session on innovation (one of the most popular sessions at Seliger 2009), was a patriotic incubator of talent, named after this repatriated hero. Youthful innovators were encouraged to follow in his footsteps. Similar inflections were apparent even in the Seliger program on tolerance, "Russia for All." The brochure for that program starts out with a liberal-sounding call to combat extremism and ethnic intolerance; it then switches to a Soviet register to call upon participants to enact "lessons of friendship" (*uroki druzhby*) that will unite people of different ethnicities and teach about culture and cuisine. However, it becomes clear that there is a twist: this is tolerance in the interest of preventing brain drain. As the brochure explains, "A successful country (one that becomes great) is one where people stay, learn, innovate, and pay taxes, and which attracts foreigners, too." It notes the example of the United States: "Thousands of Russian students go there to study, improve English, improve their life chances. But have you ever met an American student doing the same here (working a cheap job, in a café, just to learn the language and culture)? . . . The USA has successfully communicated a myth that everyone there lives well." Resonating with the Nashi projects discussed in the previous chapter, this is a rendition of tolerance that advances a critique of the liberal-democratic notion and calls out its specificity.

In this rendition, brain drain is attributed partially to a rapacious West. While there is some acknowledgment that some people were driven to leave by the anti-Semitism they experienced, we see echoes of what Oushakine (2009, 89) has described: elements of the nationalist revisioning and reformatting of the past that emphasizes the innocence of the Russian people and reframes the Soviet past as something imposed by the Bolsheviks on the Russian nation.[12] In sum, it has a national-security element.

In his address to the participants at Seliger 2009, Prime Minister Putin made explicit these links between entrepreneurship, or "competitiveness" (konkurentnost'), and national security: "In today's modern world," he stated, "the 'defensibility of a country' is no longer exclusively defined by the size of its army manpower, the number of planes, tanks, submarines or rocket carriers, just as a country's 'economic might' is also similarly no longer being determined by the number of its factories." He went on to say, "Quite the contrary, the power of a country and its competitiveness in today's world are defined, first and foremost, by its citizens' readiness to accept all forms of innovations, everything that is new, advanced, and progressive."[13]

Here, the uniqueness of this kind of "patriotic professionalism" (Hoffman 2010) was manifest. Even in this project to "commodify" talent, the critique of neoliberalism and the foreign-identified interventions of the 1990s peeked through, providing evidence of the extent to which a "backlash" against liberal interventions and the discontents they mobilized continued to structure the discursive field in Russia. While Seliger resembled global youth empowerment projects everywhere, it had a uniquely postsocialist spin – it was animated by the nationalist-nativist critique of neoliberalism and the discontents it generated, and by the complex forms of resentment and disappointment that the loss of the Imaginary West entailed.

"NEW" YOUTH POLICIES AND THEIR PURVEYORS

As we have seen, despite the claims of the "new" there was considerable continuity between the Nashi and Seliger 2009 projects. The can-do, entrepreneurial energy of the commercials we've considered in this chapter coexisted with the dark, alarmist tone of the ostensibly contraband film Vitaly screened for us. I came to realize that the two messages, which seemed so distinct, were closely related. Clearly "patriotic education" and "modernization" were dual strategies that operated in tandem. The extent of this coexistence became clear to me only later, when I managed to acquire some of the promotional materials Vitaly had shared with us.

I called Vitaly during the spring of 2010 when I was again in the city and asked if he would have time to meet with me. One year after his presentation at our miniconference, I wanted to follow up with him about the materials he'd screened; at my desk in Amherst, I had been pondering their curious juxtaposition. Unlike the state officials I'd interviewed in the past, he was immediately accessible by cell phone. After some prompting, he remembered me and kindly agreed to meet. In fact, since he was out and about with his driver, he suggested he send his car to pick me up. We chatted pleasantly in the car on the way to his office. When I explained I was teaching at the University of Massachusetts, he confused it with MIT and an amusing little spurt of institutional name-dropping ensued. This Nashi komissar told me he was a graduate student in the Political Science Department at Moscow State University, and was writing a dissertation on the theme of international conflict. At MGU he'd taken courses on subjects such as "images of the enemy," he told me neutrally; he had also taken a distance-learning course at Stanford.

Vitaly had been promoted. He now headed the regional youth committee; however, he didn't feel like a *chinovnik* (bureaucrat); embodying something of the mobile disposition Seliger materials propagandized, he remained relaxed and informal in his demeanor. He chatted pleasantly with his driver, consulting him at one point about a journey to spare him inconvenience; he not only offered me tea, but he made it himself (this took me by surprise both because he was a man and because he was a bureaucrat!); and during my visit he fielded the many phone calls he received from subordinates in the regions with good humor.

I took the opportunity to ask him about the "forbidden video" he had screened. Vitaly explained it was the production of an art studio run by "some young guys of a patriotic orientation." It was "forbidden" because it was not approved by the Federal Youth Affairs Agency, he said; the message was deemed too harsh. When I explained my interest in analyzing the forbidden commercial, he obligingly copied it, together with some other promotional materials, onto my flash drive.

From his account, I understood that the informal-seeming forbidden video had a connection with Nashi and the Federal Youth Affairs Agency, but it was only when I got home and examined the materials he had given me that I understood the degree of their proximity. During his screening in May 2009, Vitaly explained that because the video was "forbidden" we would not find it on the agency's website; he directed us instead to YouTube, where, he claimed, it had gone viral. Yet the file he gave me now, with the Year of Youth logo, contained two videos – the "permitted commercial" (*razreshennaia reklama*) and the "forbidden commercial" (*zapreschennaia reklama*). Both were part of an official Year of Youth package!

My encounter with this purveyor of "new youth policy" technologies was revelatory on a number of counts. I was struck by the diffuse and decentralized way in which Seliger 2009's promotional material had been produced (by "young guys" in a studio) and disseminated (via official screenings, but also via YouTube as well as the diverse sales and marketing pitches I had encountered). I was struck as well by the marked casualness of Vitaly's demeanor. At no point did he signal any discomfort at the seeming disparity of the messages, or at a "technology" inadvertently revealed. On the contrary, he seemed entirely careless about its provenance and about his relationship to it as its custodian – which I found all the more confusing because of my foreignness.

It was the deployment of multiple levels of knowledge that intrigued me. On one level, the strategy of the "forbidden" video recalls a kind of "flexible advertising," where the rebellious is marketed to appeal to youth (the niche appeal of the forbidden). But it recalls Soviet-era management of knowledge as well. During the Soviet period, some forms of knowledge were only available to party or Komsomol insiders, those who were deemed ideologically pure or trustworthy. In his study of the "last Soviet generation," Alexei Yurchak (2006) discusses a 1985 directive from the Ukrainian Komsomol to leader activists – the "approximate list." The list, which itemized foreign groups and artists and detailed the nature of the ideological impurity they represented – from Donna Summer ("eroticism") and Kiss ("neofascism, punk, violence") to my favorite, Julio Iglesias ("neofascism") – did not contain information that was secret or fully off limits to others. Rather, it was just not deemed necessary to the rank and file. The promotional materials – and Vitaly's pitch – contained multiple encodings, i.e., the awareness that different types of young people would respond to materials in different ways (Lipovetsky 2004).[14] What is more, they suggested that young people had a choice. Vitaly's wink to the assembled students ("I understand this isn't for you") invited them to contemplate themselves as savvy, in the know, as potential leaders rather than members of the herd.

RECEPTION

The students I spoke with in the run-up to Seliger 2009 debated the logics the promotional materials offered. While many of them planned to go to the camp, they didn't take its pledges and the empowerment script at face value. Some of the main seams of contestation included their opinions of the key words: talent, leadership, projects, and the quality of education offered at Seliger.

For One, for All? Talent and Leadership at Seliger

Was Seliger an invitation to especially talented youth, as the tough application procedure suggested? Or was it an invitation extended to all, to enable them to find and draw out their talent? What of the question of leadership? The materials were ambiguous. Students picked up upon these ambiguities and debated these themes.

One of the most interesting debates on this topic occurred in one of our student activist focus groups, between Irina, a Nashi activist who was attending Seliger 2009 as an organizer, and Ivan, a young man who had never participated in state-run youth projects and had no intention of going to Seliger. Ivan announced, "I think it's just brainwashing youth. When they say to everyone, 'You're a leader,' and so on. 'You'll be up there [*naverkhu*] forever.' But not everyone can be a leader in the country, you know." In his opinion, the money devoted to the Year of Youth would have been better spent on improving opportunities for students at the university, or put into sports – he'd been in America, he said, and it was just stunning to see what could be done. "I agree that one, or ten, people can be leaders," he went on. "It's clear that you're a leader," he said to Irina, deferring to her authority. "You do stuff, you have a passion for it and you love it, you do it from your whole heart, as we might say. But not everyone can do it, you know . . ."

At this, Irina interjected, "Everyone can, but not everyone wants to!"

Ivan objected: "But we can't have the whole country sitting in the Duma and deciding problems! And not everyone can be president, you know." He went on to tackle the topic of hierarchy: "Not everyone can be selected [as a leader]. Not everyone."

"Yes," agreed Irina, "but those who are not chosen will become workhorses [*rabochie loshadki*]."[15]

"Most people will not be selected," insisted Ivan.

"Be that as it may," Irina replied, "we'll never have managers without workhorses!"

"OK," said Ivan, "I agree that we will have workhorses. But is it good if someone becomes just a workhorse at someone's beck and call?"

But everyone has a choice, Irina insisted. Everyone is given tools.

"You know," said Ivan, "if there is no one to run errands, if everyone is a leader . . . we're really heading for a revolution. That will be it! If there are only leaders, there will be no one to supervise. And what will happen? We will [rip each other apart], trying to lead each other." Irina still insisted it was a matter of choice.

This exchange points to the contradictions of the empowerment script Seliger 2009 promises. The technology of project design is ostensibly offered to all participants; the invitation to become a *proetkovshik* (project designer) is inclusive. To participate and thrive or not is a matter of choice that each person can make ("Will you be a leader, or be led?" as the Russia 2020 commercial provokes). Yet it is clearly more complex. Ivan's words communicated his skepticism about the social fluidity and mobility the campaigns promised; his comments suggested he saw the "new federal youth policies" as a continuation of Soviet managerialism, which produced another *nomenklatura* (the Soviet-era privileged bureaucratic elite). Irina's confusion here revealed the energy that goes into concealing the stratification and hierarchies these projects generate and intersect with (c.f. Eliasoph 2011). I came across occasional slips, as when komissars used the term "caste" to refer to the different strata of youth, a term which of course points to a set of essential, inborn characteristics and aptitudes (the talented ones, predisposed to leadership, and the rest). Here, as elsewhere, we see the elision of social inequality and class.

In fact, as it played out, there was an explicit hierarchy at Seliger. Participants were ushered into one of two "tracks": MAS (*magistery*), those who came with their own projects, and BAS (*baccalavry*), those who did not. Behind the scenes there was a further hierarchy: Seliger was run by Nashi komissars, this already-empowered elite corps of activist-leaders whose presence was denied. Mobility was limited; indeed, prizewinners were few and far between and the rewards were a lot less stable than the promise.

The Critique of Formal Higher Education and the Quality of Education at Seliger

In sync with policy discussions of higher education, Seliger 2009 promotional materials explicitly referred to the institutions of formal education, and communicated a direct "modernizing" critique ("Your worries about your diploma and workbook will recede into the past," as the Russia 2020 video put it, referring to the Soviet-era employment log citizens were still required to keep.[16] The "forbidden" video proclaimed, "Studying is your profession, and the country doesn't need it").

In our workshops and results-sharing seminars, members of the research team (both students and teachers) debated this. While they were concerned about the status of the university (educational reform, increased costs, and the restructuring of academic life were a constant theme of our discussions, and students and teachers alike shared concerns about the quality of teaching some professors offered),[17] they were not convinced that this state-run project offered anything superior. Indeed, they were skeptical about these claims and offended by the critique of formal education these "unprofessional" (*bezgramotnye*) campaigns made.[18]

My colleague Dmitry said he was a little shocked at the formulation – talent as product (*talant-tovar*). As an educator with a very different construction of "talent," this offended him. Valentina joked that the university administrators would like this formulation; it was surely in keeping with the neoliberal-oriented changes that were afoot in the university and which she objected to.

Many of our discussions revolved around the quality of the education offered at Seliger and the extent to which it delivered on its promises. Indeed, there was some disjuncture between what Seliger 2009's
promotional materials claimed and what actually came to pass there.
There had been a rather intimidating-looking application procedure that
required lengthy accounting. Elena, one of the focus-group participants
who had attended the Technologies of Kindness session at Seliger 2009,
told me that between January, when they first found out about the camp,
and May, when they submitted their application, she and members of her
group had spent all their time preparing for it: collecting documentation
of their activities, and compiling a photographic record to post on the
site. However, confirming my colleagues' skepticism about these state-
run programs' capacity to recognize and reward true talent, many students reported that contrary to Seliger's claims of a competitive selection
procedure, many youth participants came without projects.

We found evidence of some of these reported inconsistencies during our trip to Seliger in August 2009. Of the twenty people in the Tver'
delegation we visited, only two or three had come with projects; the
rest had come for "the ride." Anton, the Nashi activist who led our tour,
emphasized the official version. "There was a selection procedure," he
explained. "About fifteen projects were preselected and only the best
five came here. Only the best projects, the most developed, those that
had substance."

Yulia and Sasha, two members of the group he led, contested this.
"Sorry to interrupt," said Sasha, "but those who did not have the best
projects were able to come here, too."

"Well yes," Anton concurred, "they could come to get educated"
(i.e., as BAS).

Yulia then chimed in: "Actually, those who didn't have any kind of
project at all were able to come, too." Later, when we spoke one on one,
Sasha emphasized this point to me. "No one was turned away, " he said.
"There were just those who wanted to come, and those who did not."
Contrary to the official language of "standards," "competition," and a
"tough selection procedure," one research team member, Ira, who attended Seliger 2009, offered the formulation of the "quota" as an explana-
tion – i.e., regional organizers had to recruit to meet their quotas, hence
the large numbers of chance participants (*liudi so storony*).

Sergei, a third-year sociology student and research team member, turned down the chance to go to Seliger. Earlier he had been recruited to attend a four-day preparatory event held in a sanatorium outside the city one weekend in May. The participants were all students from different colleges. The command was sent down from Moscow, he explained, and each institution called upon active students to form an initiative group (*aktiv*). He had not quite understood what he had signed up for, he said: "They just said, don't you want to go to the countryside? There's a convention of activists [*sbor aktiva*]."

At the event he attended training programs – led by Moscow specialists – and worked in groups with his peers to devise, develop, and defend projects. His account recalled a Silicon Valley boot camp – with a twist. At the end of a long day, the organizers screened promotional films. "They fed us well," he said with a laugh, "but those deadly commercials –" Some, he told me, were "aggressive," like the "forbidden" commercial Vitaly had screened at the miniconference. "We were so tired," he told me, "and to watch them made your head split, really. It was all such an outburst. It was more than a regular person could handle, I reckon."

He was ironic about the big talk and "agitation" about Seliger all over the media, including on television's Channel One, and skeptical of its promise: "'There's going to be Wi-Fi there' – well, so what? You can get Wi-Fi in every café! Who are you going to surprise with that? There, there was all this – everything's going to be so cool [*kruto*], the most popular politicians will be there, political scientists, Pavlovsky [a prominent Kremlin political technologist] will be there, Putin. And so what? You can see Putin on TV. Well, perhaps somebody is a fan; some are football fans, and others are fans of celebrities. But a normal person would understand that . . . well, that it's all too much [*chereschur*]." He laughed, adding, "It's a kind of schizophrenia, a little bit sick."

Dubious of the empowerment script and what it promised, he said, "As soon as [Seliger] is over, everyone will forget it. Yeah, so what? Nobody will remember. So, who are you going to tell, are you going to tell an employer, 'I was at Lake Seliger'? And what would he say? 'Oh, good boy, off you go,'" he laughed.

Thus, Sergei declined his invitation to go to Seliger 2009: "I said, no thanks. Not for any career – well, all the same, a person has principles. And I say that I'd never put myself through that for the sake of my career.

. . . No, I don't need it." Interestingly, though, he did sign up to attend Seliger the following year. When I spoke to him in the summer of 2010, he told me he was participating in Art Parade, the session oriented toward creative people. The opportunity to meet talented young architects, designers, and photographers and develop his video production skills was just too good to miss.

Andrei, another sociology student and team member, was similarly unimpressed: "I get a little annoyed with these projects," he told me in an interview, "because the majority of people are just doing them to promote themselves – they want to get somewhere, to get into the youth committee, to the Duma, here or there. Some people just do projects for the sake of projects. . . . Of course, there are people out there who selflessly help others. Maybe it's just me – this is of course a subjective opinion. But that's how I see it – 'Projects, projects, let's do projects. We have projects, projects, projects. There are projects, projects, projects. Promote your projects!' I'm already sick of projects. . . . I can't stand the word 'projects'!"

Andrei told me he liked some of the directions and activities taking shape, such as the blood donor drive and Zvorykinsky Project. For sure, he told me, it's important for the state to fund technological innovation, like in Japan, for example, but he was skeptical about the project format. "You need to do it via legislation," he insisted. "It's necessary to do it within some kind of framework."

Like Sergei, many of the more senior students I spoke with took exception to Seliger 2009's promotional materials. Alena, a participant in one of our focus groups, was vocal on this theme. She contested the empowerment script and pledges offered and scorned the crass commercials she had seen. In her mind, the federal project compared unfavorably to the (private) Potanin Foundation, which really supported youth and gave them what they needed. In her view, it made no sense to invest so much time in going to Seliger. It was OK for younger kids, she said, but it made no sense for someone about to graduate to waste their time camping! She went on: "I see how this really influences young people, those who still believe and are ready to join in. It's an attempt to . . . well you see, I'm a PR major [*piarshchik*], it's very easy to trace these things. I mean, all this 'You're a vegetable, you're a battery' [quoting the "forbidden commercial" for Seliger] and so on. Those commercials ... I just can't imagine who they work on. ... That is, all the people I speak to, with whom I am acquainted, proactive people who are aiming to get somewhere, to develop – they are all in shock, they just don't understand it."

And yet these materials did persuade many TGU students, as we have seen. I turn now to provide portraits of two young people who were enticed to attend Seliger 2009. Igor and Maria were differently positioned; while Igor was a long-term Nashi insider (a participant in the organization since 2005), Maria was an accidental activist who had no prior involvement with Nashi. Both returned transformed by their experience at Seliger and found it empowering, but each returned to the university very differently.

Portrait of a Participant I: Igor the Organizator-Komissar

Although their presence and agency were denied or downplayed in official announcements and promotional materials, Nashi komissars were key players at Seliger 2009. They were "organizers" (*organizatory*), who played a crucial role in recruiting and setting things up. Igor, the Nashi komissar and focus-group participant introduced in chapter 2, was an interesting informant here. I spoke to him in the spring of 2010 and he told me of his participation in the event.

Igor's rendition of Seliger's promise was rather different from the other versions I encountered. Unlike Boris, he didn't emphasize the glitter and glitz of state power, or mention VIPs, oligarchs, or celebrities by name; rather, he emphasized hard work and the experience and fruits of participation. There was a folksiness in his delivery that stood out to me; it was strikingly different from the managerial register I encountered more frequently among young men who advanced in Nashi. Moreover, in his account, the Seliger challenge and the technology of project design took on a distinctive inflection. He applied these tools not to grandiose acts of social engineering, but to grounded, microempowerment schemes – simple solutions for everyday problems.

I was captivated by his rendition of project design. It was a participatory rendition that acknowledged and addressed some of Russia's serious social problems in a practical way and suggested local, community-based solutions. For the problem of isolated *babushki* who can't get to the shops, for instance, he proposed a project designed to put them in touch with their neighbors, and for the problem of derelict buildings and poor infrastructure for children, a project of building sandboxes or playgrounds in courtyards.

His own project, the one he had taken to Seliger, was "auto tourism in Russia." This was essentially another low-tech mechanism for improving daily life, with additional benefits – as he put it, "*obshchenie* [communication, social relations] and a kind of mobilization of people." He explained, "If you look at Russian roads, you'll see most cars are empty. Maybe it's dull to be alone. Or maybe you want to travel to a place that's inaccessible by train, or cheaper to get to by car." His project proposed using social media to put people in touch with each other in order for them to carpool. I found his project compelling because – unlike so many projects I learned of – it was evidently based on his experience. Igor knew all about distance and the far-flung. He explained he had only lived in the city for a few years. He was born in Kazakhstan, then spent much of his childhood in the "deep country" (*glubinka*); meanwhile, his brother was a long-distance trucker.

For Igor, project design was an IT-enabled tactic. Indeed, all of the examples he named used computer technology to good effect (connecting young people with their elderly neighbors; putting would-be travelers in touch with other drivers).

Igor confirmed there were two "tracks" at Seliger and explained the system. BAs were "people who had projects, but they were either very poorly worked out, or at the stage of just a small idea," while the MAs were "people who were not indifferent, who had an idea, and who wanted to implement it." He explained that the two groups had separate and distinct programs of study: while BAs could knock off and play sports or go to the disco after their educational program ended, MAs had a second session of study and were assigned mentors (*kuratory*) as well, young people who had professional or practical experience.

When I asked Igor to comment on Ira's construction of the quota, and suggested it accounted for the difference in orientation among participants, he brushed it off, reacting quite strongly. It wasn't about a quota, he said; it was about people themselves! Echoing promotional materials, he told me Seliger 2009 was a tool (*instrument*) that one could choose to deploy. One could take it or leave it. Here, talent emerged as a personality trait or potential of the self that was revealed at the crucible of the Seliger camp. "You need to understand that people are given an opportunity," he told me, "to sit for half an hour in front of the campfire and think: what don't I like about my environment? What can I do to change it? That's easy. And it becomes your project on which you can work. It may be, I don't know, the lack of sandboxes. . . . For example, you see children in your neighborhood climbing in construction sites, or poking around in the trash or something. And you are concerned that there's no sandbox in the yard. This is also a project! This is something you can ask for money for." Here, Igor launched into another account of the empowerment script – in which, if only young people are bold enough to approach them, the representatives of the state are enlightened enough to listen, and open to persuasion: "Lots of governors come to Seliger," he told me. "You can go up to them and say, 'You know, look . . .' Then you can go on the internet and see how much a playground for kids would cost, how much it would cost to build . . . and go to that person and say, 'You know, this really bothers me. . . . It's necessary.' That is a project. It is an idea you want to realize."

Igor returned repeatedly to the theme of individual choice. It was about a need inside oneself – something, implicitly, that everyone can access within themselves. The ability to be self-directed, to decide and to prioritize, to do it or not do it; as he put it, "If it's important to you – do it! If it's not important – don't do it! Sit and think – important? Not important?" This endeavor was not effortless, Igor insisted, invoking the consumer as a negative point of comparison: "This idea you want to realize . . . it can't be just like popping into a store because you want something tasty for dessert, or because you've run out of potatoes. No. Here, you need to have a very serious deep sense inside yourself connected with the fact that you have to do it. . . . [You have to feel like] if you don't do it, it's going to hurt you deep down inside. You have to feel inside yourself that it's necessary to do it, it's not just simple."

He went on: "Not everyone can handle this pace. . . . It's a skill and psychological preparation. You're in the woods, you live in tents, you don't have your favorite couch, you're far away from your favorite shower, your MP3 player, your electricity and personal computer. For some it's really hard: 'How can you live like this!?' For some it was simple." He explained, "What I really liked about Seliger was that it presented you with the choice: what do you want, *really* want? Because there were situations when a fabulous disco took place at the same time as when you could talk with your mentor [*kurator*] on a really interesting topic. But both were taking place at the same time. And you had to choose. That is, you had to understand deep down what it was you *really needed*. Why did you come? Did you come to hang out at discos, or to receive knowledge? And every person decided this for himself. Nobody pressured you into it. That is, nobody came up to you and pointed with their finger and told you that you had to do it." There were some mandatory elements – no alcohol, lights off, all had to study in the morning – but the rest was by choice.

As he spoke, Igor invoked a kind of John Doe – a regular guy who's a bit of a lazy fool, who is led by his simple needs and characterized by his lack of ambition (the guy who just wants to pop into the store to pick up something tasty for dessert; the guy who prefers to lie on his own couch and who is uncomfortable at Seliger; the guy who prefers discos to study). He invoked this figure as a foil, to contrast with the mode of agency he embraced and proudly modeled. In the pages of the transcript of my interview with him, I see the outline of fond characters that populate Russian literature and jokes – Ivan Ivanovitch, the personification of a regular Russian Joe; Oblomov, the idle, superfluous nobleman of Goncharov's nineteenth-century novel of the same name; and the more recent Masiania, the animated cartoon character that went viral on the internet in the 2000s, who is slovenly, poor, uninterested in success, and without ambition, and who became "a symbol of the lost impracticality, sincerity and warmth of the pre-market social world" (Yurchak 2008, 260).

Later, reflecting on this interview transcript, I realized that the folksy community-based projects Igor cited were not original. Other komissars referred to the playground project; this and the project that invoked internet-consulting *babushki* were clearly circulating forms. Indeed, in subsequently researching the literature Igor cited, I became aware of the extent to which his version of project design and project thinking resembled the IT-enabled microprojects Erik Qualman's *Social-*

nomics (one of the books he had told me he was inspired by) promotes. Still, Igor's passion was real and it was clear that Seliger had effected a transformation in him. He had an agentive, dynamic sense of self that helped him navigate his path forward.

Woven through Igor's account was a contrast between formal education, which he left in disgust, and the kind of education he had gained from Nashi and at Seliger 2009. He spoke explicitly about the university – contrasting it unfavorably with what he'd learned at Seliger. He narrated his path through the movement as a progressive project against the top-down, wooden, authoritarian style of university teachers, which he presented as an outmoded way of being in the world. He told me, "When you see the teachers who teach at Seliger, their high level, their ability to communicate with their audience, their mastery of knowledge, you come back to your university, look at your teachers, and think, yep, something's definitely missing here! [Laughs.] It's like you understand that the teachers are educated, they have a large volume of knowledge that they'd like to share, but they don't know how to do it." He went on to say, "It's a problem of communication. Teachers don't know how to connect with their audience, they don't understand what the audience really needs, because when you give only theory and very little practice, I think that this knowledge is inapplicable, because the person doesn't know how to apply it."

Igor presented the university with all its flaws as another testing ground. He told me that his experience of adversity there, coupled with the tools he gained from Nashi, caused him to emerge stronger. During his run-ins with bureaucrats and teachers he had learned to advocate for himself, to hold his ground; as he put it, "You need to have experience, you need to have a certain kind of strength, you know, internal strength, to explain this to a teacher. Because he's a teacher, and you're a student. ... I know how to do it," he said emphatically, "[how to] approach someone who's higher than me, let's say, for example, by social rank or something. And [I know how to] talk to this person as an equal, to not pay any attention to [this], because it's just another person." He looked at me meaningfully at this point. "You are also a person," he said, "you came to us from another country, but all the same, I can talk with you normally. So this, you see, it's my life path, the line I am following and I like it."

I was already paying close attention to him as he spoke, but this moment summoned me in a new way. In a manner that suggested his Nashi training in "political communication," Igor was calling me out by addressing me as a peer. As I later studied the transcript of our interview, I was struck by how his words recalled the upwardly mobile upstart energy and confidence of neoliberal subjectivity combined with the slight menace of the Nashi project and its bold retort to foreigners. The directness of his address took me aback, but I was moved to sympathy too, for his critique of the university resonated. I looked around me at the tiny room we sat in – Valentina's office that she used to run her publishing house (the proud label "Feminist Press" adorned the door). Humble though it was, it represented Valentina's own run-ins with the forms of bureaucratic intransigence and wooden authoritarianism Igor described (I knew the energy she had expended to secure it from skeptical administrators). She had recently bequeathed the office to her students. Equipped with a kettle and a soft couch, it made for a cozy autonomous space for their own meetings.

Igor made it plain that his experience at Seliger (and Nashi) had transformed him and his expectations. Echoing the Robot Godmol commercial, he rejected the standard life narrative to embrace the new: "A crust of higher education is needed only for the man who wants to follow in the system: school, university, work. Work there on your career, get a promotion, pension. This is standard, this is how it works. . . . You have to follow certain steps. . . . I don't want to take that path."

Igor's project wasn't funded at Seliger 2009, but he voiced no disappointment about this. Despite the firm expectation of concrete rewards that had propelled him to participate, he told me that the learning he had undertaken, the skills he had gained, were more important to him than the funds he didn't secure or the project he didn't enact. In fact, he presented himself as having made an agentic choice not to compete or submit his project yet, but to wait another year.

Igor told me he was going to Seliger 2010 for twenty-eight days, to attend all of the sessions. He was going as an *organizator,* on behalf of the Federal Youth Affairs Agency. This wasn't a paid or staff position, he explained. "It's called being a freelancer," he said, using the English term. "That is, it's when you sit at home and they connect with you by the phone

or e-mail. . . . You know, I really think that this is the future – freelancer-
dom, because it makes no economic sense to rent an office. A person has
their home, their computer, their internet – go ahead and work! Work
away! What's stopping you? Why go out? Especially if we take Moscow,
or large cities. . . . We're talking traffic jams, queues, money." Ironically
recalling the pampered, spoiled individual, attached to his creature comforts, that he had parodied earlier in his account of those who couldn't
handle the Seliger experience, he told me, "I can sit at home, I wake up,
make myself some tasty coffee, have my breakfast, go on the internet,
write to my employee – 'I'm here, come on, give me what you've got.'"
(There's a fine line between the dude on the beach with his laptop depicted in the video – whose comforts enable and sustain his productivity
and creativity – and the lazy Sovok who just wants to lie on his "favorite
couch.")

Igor's conviction and the meaning he found was centrally related
to his privileged location within the new Federal Youth Affairs Agency
structures and the "new youth policies" they effected. Although not materially advantaged, he had accessed the second level of the empowerment script – a sensibility about power and politics, a vantage point and a
vocabulary about state power, a savvy and knowing disposition. As with
many of the Nashi insiders I spoke with in 2010, there was a meta-analysis
peeking through Igor's account. As he explained his own path, he presented it within the broader trajectory of Nashi and the shifting form of
these state-run youth structures. Strikingly, he repositioned Nashi as a
progenitor of Seliger 2009, making the state subordinate. In his account,
komissars like himself were the chief agents – Seliger, like Nashi before
it, was a project of the *komsoobshchestvo* (komissar's society).[19] For that
moment at least, this stance and conviction offset the precarity of his
position.

Portrait of a Participant II: Alisa, the Accidental Activist

Alisa was a fourth-year sociology student I met in the spring of 2010. She
had joined the research team in the fall of 2009. Indeed, she emerged as
a key player who helped us recruit and run one of the focus groups and
organized interviews with activists when I came. Alisa had attended

Seliger 2009, and like Igor, she was planning to attend Seliger 2010 in an organizer's capacity – to lead the Tver' international session. However, she was very much an accidental activist.

Alisa had no prior involvement in state-run projects; she had never attended any Nashi events, nor had she been involved in any of the preparatory events of the spring. She explained that she had attended Seliger 2009 purely by chance. Her girlfriend called and asked, "What are you doing on such-and-such a date?" and she decided to go on a whim. Despite the strict requirements listed on the site, she had no problem being accepted and went without a project. In the end, Alisa attended two sessions of Seliger: "Tolerance" and "Technologies of Kindness." She had gone to the first with her girlfriend, but decided to stay on when she became romantically involved with one of the instructors at the Tolerance session.

Unlike Igor, Alisa returned to the university from Seliger not disgusted by the contrast it presented, but newly energized to continue with her studies. Alisa told me that Seliger had a huge influence on her life, had really turned it around. She hadn't been a particularly good student before she went, she told me, but now she was getting top marks. It was neither the technologies nor the vertical connections that captivated her and effected this transformation – sure, she appreciated what she had learned about project design, she told me, but this same technology was repeated in the other sessions and she wasn't all that interested in voluntarism in any case. Rather, it was the "horizontal" connections that mattered to her, the peers she had met. Beyond her romantic connection, she had encountered impressively goal-oriented smart people there; they had inspired her and their enthusiasm was contagious. She was applying herself to her studies now, she told me. Indeed, in another moment of curious congruence between our research and the state-run youth project, it was in the glow of this post-Seliger inspiration that she first made contact with Valentina and joined our team.

Alisa observed, "I think that Seliger really gives a lot of people, including those who came by chance [*sluchaino*], a boost of energy. That is, people understand that they have support, that they have like-minded people, that they can do something. But then they go home, see the same walls, and everything goes back to normal. That's why I think that it's important to have some kind of system of support for it. In order that it doesn't die out, but keeps going. I was really lucky to meet my boyfriend, someone who was really active. That is, he kept stimulating this activeness [*aktivnost'*]. I don't know if I could have kept it up without him. If not for him, I might have come home and forgotten about it all."

When I told Alisa that I'd learned she was returning to Seliger 2010 that summer as an instructor, she looked at me and replied with a playfully coy smile, "Even better than that! I'm going to be the leader of the international session [of the oblast delegation]." When my face registered surprise, she explained, with a laugh, "After Seliger, my activeness sharply increased!" As she explained her path to greater activity and involvement, Alisa emphasized not pomp and grandeur, or her own importance, but a sense of curiosity and empathetic engagement with people. Like some of the Nashi activists introduced in the previous chapter, she domesticated or personalized these state-run campaigns. "I began to socialize with the guys, that is, with Vitaly and another boy," she told me. "I understood that they're doing something that interests me. I understood that they're good people, and that I can do something to help them, and that they can help me. Yes, that is, that I can collaborate with them." Since January, she had been working with them on various organizational activities, and in return for this, when the job of coordinator of the international session (which required fluency in the English language) came up, they thought of her.

Indeed, the pageantry and hyperbole repelled her, and she saw that they were escalating this year for the international session in a way that concerned her. "Last year," she explained, "we did everything ourselves. We lived in tents, we had a bonfire, and we cooked our own food. Yet this year at the international session there will be cooks! I really don't like that – there's a word for it – *pokazukha* [window-dressing, or show]. That is, we're showing that we want to seem better than we really are. It's a mistake; it's not necessary, because you won't fool anyone. Because when a foreigner, let's say a European, comes to Moscow where everything's beautiful, then he'll go through the fields, the villages, to Ostashkov and he'll see how things are, what life's like, and he'll understand everything – he's not an idiot. And all those big expensive plasma TVs hanging in the trees at Seliger – it's too much! It won't fool anyone."

I asked what her job would be like and she said it wasn't yet clear; she was on her way to a meeting and would learn more then. As she understood it, she was going to coordinate the activities of the Tver' delegation with the Federal Youth Affairs Agency people. As the host oblast, the Tver' team would need to help out with specific organizational issues. Alisa explained that she was collecting a list of possible participants.

As she spoke about her upcoming assignment, Alisa communicated her ironic sense of curiosity about the work in which she was engaged. She was a little critical of the Federal Youth Affairs Agency, which had only announced things very late. "Despite all the rhetoric this year about how only the best, most talented, and most prepared people will go – this may not be true. Time has passed, and they need numbers." She thought the agency was mistaken to organize things this way, as the time pressure was too great. "This year is oriented toward projects," she said. "Ideally, you must be a leader, with a team and a project, but there aren't enough projects yet; the criteria are relaxed [*smiagchaiutsia*] as time passes. The closer it gets, the looser the criteria."

Our interview had a surprising conclusion. In one of those confusing moments of entanglement I have referred to (and which our second-generation collaboration entailed), Alisa actually sought to get me involved in Seliger, by asking if I had students interested in attending the international session there. She could offer them (that is, the state was offering) a 70 percent discount on air tickets and free visas, which would be handled swiftly in one day! I passed this invitation on to some of my students but was ultimately relieved when none of them decided to go. Judging from online discussions, the international session was a bit of a debacle, with lots of international participants complaining that they weren't refunded or that their visas didn't come through in time.

This chapter has explored the forms of empowerment Seliger 2009 offered and the kinds of youth it engaged. Throughout we see an intriguing play of similarities and differences between it and the global empowerment projects it mimicked and resembled.

Like the proliferating projects Eliasoph (2011) and other critics examine, Seliger 2009 was full of contradictions. It was an innovation incubator that existed as an oasis against a backdrop of aching inequalities; despite its bold claims, it was unequal to the task of resolving the social and economic problems it identified. We have seen how Seliger contained partially hidden hierarchies. Beyond the existence of komissars – the shadowy organizers, whose existence was downplayed – there were distinctions between BAS and MAS, or those who managed and those who were led. Although it could not guarantee social mobility or prizes to many young people (though a lucky few did acquire these), like Eliasoph's (2011) empowerment projects, Seliger performed a form of *prevention*. Geared toward youth who were not wealthy or urban, it did perform the socially therapeutic function of keeping them clean, orderly, and off the streets (for the duration of their participation, at least).

The technologies Seliger offered confirm how, in the neoliberal context, class is reconfigured as a measure of individual value. Mobility ("social lift") was predicated on self-improvement; young people were required to improve, build, and develop themselves, via participation in workshops and master classes. These activities resembled the forms of résumé-building activities American students engage in. However, once again, at Seliger this played out in distinctively Russian ways. Seliger, the "autonomous town in the woods," was a celebrity-filled gala; it offered itself as "a right time and a right place" for young people who did not have the connections upward mobility requires. Its chief and most alluring promise was the possibility of acquaintance with (or at least proximity to) the powerful. It was in short an oil-and-gas-glamour rendition of the personal networks that have always been so central to making one's way in (post)socialist Russia.

The portraits I have provided reveal that participation yielded unanticipated dividends. While Alisa thrived on her horizontal connections, Igor's case offers further insight into the Nashi project that preceded Seliger 2009. It shows how, contrary to the idea of Nashi as an authoritarian institution that trained politically quiescent youth, the organization instilled a can-do sense of agency in its participants, as well as a critical edge. They were encouraged to see themselves as innovators, while the enemy was in part "bureaucracy" or a way of being that was in some sense associated with the Soviet era (inadequate to contemporary conditions). Aligned with the Federal Youth Affairs Agency, they were educated into a new form of conduct, a relationship with the self and the world, and encouraged to think of themselves as agents higher than the state and its flawed functionaries. What of the disappointments they would face? Igor's story reveals that these gains were highly ambiguous. While, when we spoke, he was still persuaded and in the thrall of the beguiling technologies Seliger offered him, his position was precarious and unclear. As we will see in the next chapter, Seliger's "winners" found their rewards to be fragile and uncertain as well.

Seliger 2009 marked the first, but not the last, federal youth education forum. At the time of this writing, state-run youth camps continue to take place annually at Lake Seliger. Between 2010 and 2012, the unpredictable and incoherent state form Seliger continued to spin off and mutate. Seliger 2010 contained highly controversial elements that recalled the "rogue" energy of Nashi–for example, a display of liberal politicians' heads on stakes, organized by Nashi offshoot Stal' (Steel). By 2012, Yakemenko and Surkov were out of favor and dismissed.[20] Under the tutelage of Yakemenko's successors, Seliger 2012 tried to channel some of the anti-Kremlin oppositional energy of the December 2011 protests. Organizers invited oppositional figures to attend (members of the "creative classes" who were prominent in the protests), adopted a new edgy logo by British graffiti artist Banksy (an image of a young man preparing to toss a bunch of flowers in the revolutionary color orange), and dubbed one of the sessions (the political session) "Occupy Seliger."[21]

FOUR

FROM KOMSOMOL'TSY-DOBROVOL'TSY TO ENTREPRENEURIAL VOLUNTEERS

Technologies of Kindness

THIS CHAPTER CONSIDERS A THEME THAT ANIMATED MANY state-run youth projects and which featured prominently at Seliger 2009: the promotion of youth voluntarism. Voluntarism was one of eight thematic sessions launched at Seliger 2009. Understanding our interest in the topic, Vitaly brought promotional materials about this session, which included brochures and a video, to our miniconference when he visited in May 2009. After congratulating us on our work ("There are a lot of voluntary projects taking shape now, but there is very little theoretical understanding"), Vitaly urged the students in the room to participate. "I hope that some of you will attend this important session," he said, explaining that voluntarism [*volonterstvo*] was one of the priority directions of the Russia 2020 project, the youth program laid out by the Federal Youth Affairs Agency (Rosmolodezh). Unlike the play of patriotism and entrepreneurship observed in state-run youth projects so far, this one introduced a new and seemingly transcendent theme to the table: human kindness. However, it was rather jarringly linked to technology. Indeed, here the Russian state screamed its governing intent: the session was called "Technologies of Kindness" [*Tekhnologiia dobra*].

As Vitaly sat down, I reached for my glasses and sat back in my seat to watch the video. After the logo "Technologies of Kindness," the following words appeared as if handwritten on a whiteboard: "There is such a thing as cutesy-kindness [*dobrinka*];[1] it exists in everyone, but alas, some people hide it." The cartoon began with an image of planet Earth, quickly zooming in to the Kremlin, then to a Soviet-looking grocery store (*Produkty*). A simple black-and-white animated line drawing depicted a hungry-looking dog sitting outside, set to a pleasant and oddly familiar melody. A young man (in color) came by. Noticing the dog, he popped into the store and returned with a string of sausages, which he offered the dog. Immediately, the dog was infused with color, and a little heart shape (the logo of the Technologies of Kindness session) appeared and began to beat in his chest. The dog then licked the hand of a little boy, who was also changed. As we followed the action, color spread – from the store, to a playground, to a park, to the surrounding trees and buildings, until the entire landscape was resplendent. Although I couldn't place it, I was sure that I had seen this cartoon before, or at least one very much like it, in the United States. The cartoon depicted the ripple effects of good deeds, acts of kindness transforming the landscape. As the melody ended and the scene faded, the video closed with the exhortation, "It's not so hard to change the world, *start with yourself.*"

Later, as I leafed through one of the glossy brochures Vitaly had passed out, I read more about the Technologies of Kindness session. Its announced goal was simply to enable participants to "be people" (*byt' liud'mi*). But what kind of people did it seek to summon forth and which transformations did it accomplish? Despite the charming folksiness this video depicted and the small deeds it celebrated, the session brought a professionalized, managerial register to the endeavors it encouraged. Technologies of Kindness devoted a lot of time to encouraging youth to change themselves, and to believe that they would be able to change the world – but the results proved a little less straightforward.

The promotion of youth voluntarism has been a central plank of Russia's twenty-first-century modernization project, part of the new and distinctive version of civil society the Putin administration has advanced. Voluntarism here was conceptualized as a mechanism via which young people were to be socialized and educated. Indeed, I came to see it as a key site for the redrawing of citizenship and state power. Like the other federal campaigns I have examined, this rendition of voluntarism was a distinctive amalgam. It drew self-consciously and intentionally on a socialist repertoire, adopting the methods and invoking the symbols of the Soviet-era Youth League (Komsomol). In addition to running mass events like Technologies of Kindness, the state passed volunteer recruitment quotas down to the regions (the target was to enroll 11 percent of Russia's youth in voluntarism by 2014). However, at the same time, this state project was infused with the logics of nineties-era neoliberal-oriented international interventions that the Putin administration explicitly disparaged. Federal directives were accompanied by incentives and prizes, such as the Volunteer of the Year contest, and by the invitation to "commodify" talent.

The promotion of voluntarism in the context of state withdrawal is regarded as a quintessentially neoliberal dynamic. Indeed, the jarring linkage between technology and kindness seemed to mark the infiltration of market-driven principles everywhere, which scholars have remarked upon (Harvey 2005; Ong 2006). However, as with other projects discussed in this book, the form of voluntarism advanced in this state-run project was a complex fusion that combined elements of neoliberal rationality with other cultural forms (socialist, Orthodox, nationalist). Moreover, it had uncertain and unintended outcomes; as it intersected with other forms of student sociality and organization, Technologies of Kindness played out in unexpected ways.

Of all the state-run youth projects I have examined, the state voluntarism-promoting project appeared to elicit the least skepticism among its target group. Indeed, I found that it captivated young people. Many of those I spoke with sought venues to undertake socially oriented activities. They were unsure, however, of the form their voluntarism should take, and of its implications. My questions about voluntarism and why the Russian state was interested in it provoked interesting discussions in which young people juxtaposed Russian ways and values with "Western" ones – revealing the persistence of the Imaginary West (Yurchak 2006).[2] It prompted an intergenerational dialogue too, as my teacher colleagues were prompted to reflect on their own youth and prior engagements during the Soviet and early post-Soviet periods. As we contemplated this topic, I realized it marked another instance of friction between us. Our attention was trained in different places; while I was struck by similarities between the voluntarism project and what I saw taking place in the United States, my colleagues focused on its unique and distinctively Russian elements: the self-interest of the politicians who promoted it and their desire for electoral gain.

In this chapter I trace the arc of the Putin-era youth voluntarism project from its early regional and municipal manifestations to the moment when it went federal during Russia's Year of Youth (2009). I base my discussion on the two projects that loomed largest in my research: the regional youth organization Vazhnoe Delo (Important Business) and the Technologies of Kindness session at Seliger 2009. I first analyze the content of some of the materials associated with these projects that agency staffers distributed. Many of the volunteers I spoke to admitted they disregarded the models and pamphlets they were offered. Although largely inert and dismissed by many as "just PR," they are works of substantial state investment; as such, they afford an opportunity to examine the ways "those who seek to govern focus and imagine their world and seek to fashion it anew" (Rose, O'Malley, and Valverde 2006, 100). In the second half of the chapter I turn to examine this project's reception. In selling itself to young people, Russia's state-run youth voluntarism program tapped both popular resentment toward neoliberal-oriented policies and popular nostalgia for purported traits of late socialism that the market displaced: idealism, sincerity, and commitment to the collective (Yurchak 2008). It offered voluntarism as a means by which youth could simultaneously develop or morally redeem themselves and contribute to the nation, articulating a vision of civil society linked to state sovereignty. Many young people were compelled by this vision; however, when they got there, they realized that it had been reformatted. Under the tutelage of the Federal Youth Affairs Agency and the Ministry of Sports, Tourism, and Youth Policy, it had been recast as a form of individualized entrepreneurial activity that also drew on Soviet-era forms.

FROM IMPORTANT BUSINESS TO
TECHNOLOGIES OF KINDNESS

Philanthropy, volunteerism, and "doing good" are as much a site of subjectivation as a straightforward transaction. That is, they have the potential to effect changes in the ways that subjects (both volunteers and recipients) construe themselves. Voluntarism has profitably been viewed as a technology of the self, with the potential to transform people and produce certain kinds of citizens (Cruikshank 1999; Hyatt 2001a;

Lyon-Callo 2004; Matza 2009; Rose [1996] 2006).[3] However, my data shows that in my research context, this did not play out so neatly as some governmentality scholarship suggests.

The state-run voluntarism project was a busy site for *polittechnologi* (political technologists) – the analysts and political advisors who work behind the scenes of Russian political life, and who generated new technologies, methodologies, and schemas to articulate this redrawing and entice young people to participate in it. State interest in youth voluntarism was accompanied by a plethora of new methodological materials, models, and technologies, informed by social science and public opinion research. They were produced by newly founded centers and think tanks and disseminated to volunteer participants. This was a formulation of voluntarism that posited it as an endeavor that had to be learned and mastered, and that required professionalism (c.f. Salmenniemi 2010, 316). As in the other campaigns this book has examined, the governing intent was explicit. Indeed, in voluntarism-promotion campaigns, the extent to which "the self" became an object of concern and investment in Russia during the postsocialist period became abundantly clear, as did the degree to which education became swept up in the "psychology renaissance" of the 2000s (Matza 2012, 804). Another feature was the campaigns' obviousness; the borrowings these methodologists engaged in resulted in awkward terminologies and neologisms that sounded dissonant and jarring to Russian ears and often offended their target audience. They raised the hackles of some who saw them as clumsy, unprofessional (*bezgramotnyi*), and comical, and alienated others for looking suspiciously "foreign." Indeed, despite their ostensible distinctiveness from the nineties-era projects that preceded them, these projects made liberal use of foreign expertise.

Contextualizing Voluntarism

Voluntarism (encouraging unpaid community-based services and forms of civic service) was a vital ingredient of nineties-era international democracy-promotion interventions, funded and prioritized by agencies such as the International Research and Exchanges Board (IREX) and the Open Society Institute. As with other key concepts like civil society and women's rights, the assumption was that voluntarism had not existed during the Soviet period. Working within the "transitions" paradigm, these projects approached postsocialist societies as blank slates (Hemment 2007a; Sampson 1996; Wedel 1998).

Contrary to this assumption, voluntarism did exist during the Soviet period; indeed, it was institutionalized. Distinct from the private initiatives of bourgeois philanthropy, or church-based charity, voluntarism was reorganized as a form of mandatory activity for the good of the collective. Via youth organizations (the Young Pioneers and Komsomol) and later via workplace-based brigades and *subbotniks*,[4] Soviet citizens provided a wide range of unpaid "voluntary" (*dobrovolnye*) services for the state. As the lyrics of a popular Soviet-era song suggest, *Komsomol'tsy* (Komsomol activists) were *dobrovol'tsy* (volunteers), people who served the state and the broader collective at the same time that they developed themselves ("We are strong from our true friendships / Through the fire we go, if necessary / Opening up new paths, Komsomol'tsy-Dobrovol'tsy / We must believe and love selflessly / See the sun sometimes before dawn / Only then can we find happiness!").[5] Beyond the "political" work they undertook (ideological and agitational work), they performed societal work (*obschestvennaia rabota*) as well, such as cleanup campaigns, crop picking and construction projects, visiting orphanages, chopping wood for the elderly, and organizing parties for veterans (Caldwell 2004; Gorsuch 2000; Pilkington 1994; Riordan 1989; Yurchak 2006).

Although derided by many (especially retrospectively) as state mandated, these activities were a source of deep satisfaction for some people at the time (Yurchak 2006). Indeed, remembered today as sites of tight sociality and comradeship in which people could express their concern for the broader collective, these institutions are now the subject of nostalgic cultural production (I found the lyrics above posted in the patriotic songs section of the commercial website Karaoke.ru).

The voluntarism that was promoted by nineties-era agencies had a different hue. An artifact of the post-welfarist, post-1990 neoliberal-oriented development consensus (what Foucauldian scholars have referred to as the "redefinition of the social"), it was premised on the assumption of social inequality. Here, social issues (orphans, care of the elderly) became the responsibility of the community, and informal (voluntary) associations were encouraged to take over social-welfare responsibilities from the retreating socialist state (Hemment 2007a).[6]

Voluntarism has gained traction globally since the late 1990s when I began undertaking research in Russia; by 2001 it had become part of a new international development consensus. The United Nations proclaimed 2001 as the International Year of Volunteers (or IYV),[7] making a series of dizzy claims about voluntarism's transformative effects: "Volunteerism benefits both society at large and the individual volunteer by strengthening trust, solidarity and reciprocity among citizens, and by purposefully creating opportunities for participation."[8] Austerity has only accelerated voluntarism's global appeal. In her study of Italian welfare reform, Andrea Muehlbach (2011) notes that the state offers voluntarism as a form of ethical labor via which marginalized populations (such as youth or the elderly) can redeem themselves and prove themselves productive and worthy citizens. Indeed, ten years after the International Year of Volunteers, the UN's 2011 *State of the World's Volunteerism Report* referred to volunteerism as a "universal value for global well-being," and suggested it was a vehicle for assisting nations in meeting their Millennium Development Goals. This twenty-first-century rendition posits voluntarism as something that is necessary for the health of nations. Voluntarism is seen as performing transformative good, both within volunteers themselves at the level of subjectivity (it is a "reflexive and individualizing" practice) and within the society writ large. As such, it is something that can and must be monitored, tracked, and measured.

It was this complexity that first attracted me to this topic; I witnessed these contradictions at the University of Massachusetts as well. Here too, young people are urged to engage in forms of community-based voluntarism via the service-learning classes they encounter. While service learning can serve as a vehicle for critical community-based inquiry, all too frequently it is a thinly disguised means of engaging students in charity work, projects that accept the status quo and evade the challenge of thinking critically (Morton 1996). In the context of the cutting back of the Keynesian welfare state, some critics view service learning as a "strategy of governance, a technology for the production of neo-liberal citizens" (Hyatt 2001b). Nina Eliasoph (2011) provides us with a powerful and troubling characterization of how this manifests in the United

States. The voluntarism produced by the "empowerment projects" she discusses is fast, flexible, and apolitical, ideally suited to late capitalism. It promises instant (moral) gratification for the well-intentioned yet time-strapped middle-class people, intent on self-improvement, who volunteer their time and also offers, secondarily, an opportunity for redemption for the disadvantaged populations (also "volunteers") they assist. Empowerment projects have two goals – to stimulate civic engagement and to help the needy. In Eliasoph's account, we see how a troubling flip takes place, where the first goal displaces the latter and the needy (recipients) are subordinated or displaced.

In the account that follows, we'll see how Vazhnoe Delo and Technologies of Kindness resembled these projects, but also how they contributed their own distinctive elements. They too focused on the self/the subject (the volunteer him- or herself),[9] however, these state-run social-engineering projects drew self-consciously and intentionally on elements of the reformatted Soviet past (c.f. Read 2010). But just as in the empowerment projects Eliasoph discusses, the needy were displaced.

VAZHNOE DELO: A PILOT STATE-RUN VOLUNTARISM PROJECT

Vazhnoe Delo was a regional youth organization, set up by the governor of Tver' region in 2005. Between 2005 and 2008 when it scaled back its operations, it delivered forms of voluntary assistance to the "socially unprotected" (*sotsial'no nezashchishchennye*), mostly elderly people living by themselves, orphans, and the poor. Youth volunteers (mostly high school students) provided physical assistance to these people – carrying water, chopping wood, delivering medicine and groceries – and organized events and excursions for them.[10]

Like other liberalizing welfare initiatives, Vazhnoe Delo revealed the implications of transforming welfare regimes for client populations (Haney 2002; Hemment 2012b); the recipients of aid it envisaged (those it considered worthy) were exclusively children and veterans. But as I studied Vazhnoe Delo between 2005 and 2008, I was struck by how little emphasis it placed on social issues, or the needy. Its ambition was in the realm of statecraft and its emphasis was on crafting the volunteer.

Vazhnoe Delo's materials were fairly explicit on this score: while the organization's first goal was to assist the socially defenseless, its other, equivalent goals were to assist the development of a voluntary movement and to stimulate society to undertake useful activities.

Vazhnoe Delo exhibited the dual components of state youth policy this book has examined elsewhere; it was inflected with the state's patriotic education programs and with its modernizing and globalizing directives as well. At first blush, it looked very Soviet. Much of the work Vazhnoe Delo volunteers undertook resembled the work undertaken by the Komsomol'tsy-Dobrovol'tsy celebrated in the Soviet-era song: chopping wood, picking up groceries, visiting orphanages, sitting and talking with lonely elders. In their use of uniforms (T-shirts, baseball caps, and bandannas) and mass actions, Vazhnoe Delo volunteers visually recalled the Komsomol and the Young Pioneers. Further, as in their Soviet predecessor organizations, the patriotic element of the education offered via this organization was very pronounced. Vazhnoe Delo materials gave a prominent position to World War II–related events, depicting young people meeting with veterans and taking part in commemorative activities. The organization had a special relationship with a local civic organization, the Pensioners' Union, and worked with it on a variety of events. However, Vazhnoe Delo also bore traces of the Putin-era modernization project. Drawing on the resources of the new experts (the analysts and methodologists empowered by the Federal Youth Affairs Agency), it was engaged in a more technological project of stimulating society as well. Indeed, it won national awards for its use of innovative technologies.

I visited Vazhnoe Delo's director, Igor Borisov, in December 2006. I had a double agenda: I sought both to learn more about its work and to negotiate internships for members of the research team. The organization was housed in small but nicely renovated office in the center of town. After I had been buzzed in via intercom, a young woman greeted me at the door and led me through a crowded room to Borisov's office. It was a chaotic but dynamic scene: boxes of literature lay stacked on the floor and four or five young women sat behind crowded desks at computers. Borisov greeted me warmly and invited me to sit down. As his secretary bustled to provide me tea and cookies, he told me a little of his background. This forty-something-year-old social project manager was a state insider with a youth connection; before being appointed director of Vazhnoe Delo in the spring of 2005, he had worked for years on the youth committee of the oblast administration. He spoke quickly, naming key facts about the program and its activities and handing me leaflets and brochures as he did so. As he reeled off names, dates, and details about competitions and campaigns, I struggled to take notes and keep up with him. I left an hour later with a packet of promotional materials – bulletins, newsletters, and branded items that included a yellow baseball cap, T-shirt, pencil, and notebook – and an invitation to accompany volunteers on one of their next missions to the countryside, as well as a pledge of collaboration (future internships).

Borisov was especially proud of the innovative social-engineering aspects of his organization's work. He explained that Vazhnoe Delo didn't seek merely to provide material assistance to the needy, but to stimulate new relationships and "activate" people, that is, to mobilize them to become more self-directed and agentive and to contribute to society rather than wait to be helped. In keeping with broader global trends, Vazhnoe Delo was an intergenerational project that sought to engage and activate both young people and the elderly as volunteers (c.f. Muehlebach 2012).

As in Eliasoph's empowerment projects, the bulk of the work undertaken in Vazhnoe Delo focused on the volunteers themselves, who were encouraged to engage in substantial self-work, to make themselves over and to participate in in diverse forms of social entrepreneurship. Borisov explained that in addition to the forms of service they were involved in, volunteers joined leadership training programs and psychological training programs, and learned how to design social projects and to fundraise. The program also encouraged its volunteer participants to compete in a variety of locally designed campaigns and competitions. One of the most interesting campaigns I came across was the Social Advertising project (*Sots Reklama*), in which participants were invited to contribute submissions such as posters or video clips. The goal of the competition, as stated in the brochure, was to popularize the idea of social activity and voluntary assistance to those in need. Vazhnoe Delo had a built-in incentive structure as well. Active volunteers were invited to submit accounts of their activities and map their personal growth, in order to advance up a hierarchy (or "career ladder") that was explicitly laid out for them, comprising the following Soviet-named stages: candidate, volunteer (*dobrovolets*), brigade leader, leader, and ultimately chair of the supreme soviet.

Although these innovative technologies were a point of pride for their director, my research suggested that the "new" was outweighed by the "old" in the perception of many local people. My questions about the organization elicited weary skepticism among many of my acquaintances, who regarded it as business as usual, yet another PR/election campaign by political elites. Vika, a local journalist who was well connected with some of the longstanding civic associations in the city, was particularly scathing about Vazhnoe Delo's claims to empower the elderly. In her view, such claims not only were condescending, but undermined and even appropriated the work of independent pensioners' associations that had been active for decades. Indeed, it appeared that many local residents shared this skepticism.

Our research suggested that Vazhnoe Delo failed to attract many college-age youth. While it claimed to have a huge base of volunteers – three thousand at its peak – research undertaken by my team members revealed that many were one-time participants and had weak connections with the organization itself. An average volunteer could slide by without participating in training programs or really encountering the technologies and methodologies the organization purported to advance. According to our data, the majority of youth volunteers appeared to be schoolchildren and students at vocational schools which offered secondary education to those aged sixteen to eighteen.

Marina, whom I met during one of our focus groups, participated in Vazhnoe Delo as a schoolgirl. She joined Vazhnoe Delo campaigns to assist the elderly, spending time with them in the countryside and chopping wood, but she never attended any training sessions or workshops and didn't consider herself a Vazhnoe Delo volunteer. Like many participants, she had been recruited by one of her teachers. Vazhnoe Delo had representatives in many municipal and regional schools, teachers or administrators who were responsive to this state-run organization's directives and who required their students to engage in these activities

(sometimes even canceling classes in order for them to be able to participate in Vazhnoe Delo campaigns), much in the way the Komsomol did
during the Soviet period. This is not to say that this signaled anything
unwelcome; my sense is that teachers and administrators welcomed
Vazhnoe Delo's input as a source of additional resources. The organization's campaigns afforded them the opportunity to sustain the forms of
culturally familiar activities they had always engaged in, and to undertake the project of *vospitanie* (moral education) for children.

Marina was aware of the technologies and methodologies Vazhnoe
Delo used, but she neither took part in their training programs ("I was
too small then") nor thought very highly of them. She told me that she
didn't see the point of the hierarchy and the career ladder and regarded
the initiatives to document volunteer activity as "red tape" (*bumazhnaia
volokita*).

Andrei, a member of the research team, was much more closely involved in the organization. He volunteered with Vazhnoe Delo for one
and a half years, during which time he moved through all the stages of
the hierarchy. In his estimation, Vazhnoe Delo did not follow through
on its promise to deliver advancement and personal growth: "I was able
to achieve the highest position in a year and a half," he told me, "but
afterward they didn't offer me anything, they didn't offer me the chance
to realize myself – instead they said, 'Do what we tell you.' So I left."

In sum, many of the young people I spoke to regarded Vazhnoe
Delo as a bit crude, a bit in the old mode, and dismissed it as a clumsy
PR device. While the organization appealed to the two main subsets of
volunteers – high schoolers and pensioners, who found in it a vehicle for
continuing their culturally familiar activities – it did not offer much to
college students, who felt it did not deliver on the "new" opportunities
it promised. By 2009, the look of projects promoting youth voluntarism
had changed. Hitched to the Year of Youth bandwagon, these technologies were overhauled, pepped up, and advanced much more forcibly.
Here, the entrepreneurial dimension was pronounced.

In the next section, I turn to analyze two motivational texts associated with the Federal Youth Affairs Agency's Year of Youth project.
Described as "unique social innovations" that would jump-start vol-

untarism in Russia, they were posted online and distributed to young people during 2009 by the Federal Youth Affairs Agency and its affiliates.

KIND ADVICE: ACTIVATING VOLUNTEERS AT SELIGER 2009

"Dobrye sovety" (Kind advice) is a motivational text issued shortly before the Technologies of Kindness session began at Seliger 2009. In a can-do tone, it exhorts young people to participate in voluntary activities. Like the promotional video Vitaly screened, it calls upon them to "be kind," to change themselves, and in so doing, to change the world around them – the brochure's subtitle is "Kind You; Kind City; Kind Country." Implicit here is a critique of the "unkind" social relations that prevailed during the dog-eat-dog neoliberal nineties and the individuated selves this period gave rise to.

Like other Seliger promotional materials, the brochure addresses youth in an informal, direct way, referring to the reader as "you" (c.f. Lassila 2012). It too lays out a bold teleological vision whereby goodness advances, though here this is expressed in planners' terms. Goodness spreads not from branch to tree to blade to lawn, but from the individual (you!) to the city and then the nation (*strana*).

There is another draw here: the booklet suggests that these acts of kindness will be attended to and appreciated by agents of the state – the regional officials and offices it instructs young people to enter into partnership with and address. Indeed, although written in a chatty tone, the booklet is clearly written from the vantage point of the state. It opens with a lengthy quote from a speech by President Medvedev to the federation council, in which he urges young people (or those who are not indifferent – *neravnodushnyi*) to participate in forms of voluntary activity. The section entitled "Voluntarism Today and Tomorrow" describes the urgent need to do this for Russia's future, using the same conception of Russia (as strong and grand, but beleaguered) we have seen in prior materials. It concludes, "Everyone can become a volunteer!"

Like other Seliger 2009 materials, the booklet offers voluntarism as an opportunity space for youth. It addresses them as empowered and agentive individuals whom the state will heed, and invokes a world of patriotic, socially responsible business leaders (capitalists with human faces), who honor young people's efforts and do the right thing.

The young people I interviewed were drawn to this vision and compelled by this call; however, when they got to the Technologies of Kindness session at Seliger, they found it was a little more complex. Illustrating the blend of entrepreneurial and socialist elements observed in the previous chapter, a volunteer here was a kind of entrepreneur – someone who devised projects. Despite the brochure's serial overuse of the root word *dobro* ("good" or "kind"), "doing good" or "being kind" was not enough; participation in this realm required self-improvement.

Further, although "everyone can be a volunteer," there were hierarchies within this field. Like Vazhnoe Delo, Technologies of Kindness offered its participants a career ladder; here, though, new (and rather awkward) terminologies displaced the Soviet terms. The "Kind Advice" text explained the three "stages of growth" through which volunteers could advance. The lowest rung, or rank, was *dobrovolets,* the simple volunteer. The next was *dobrovoller,* an awkward neologism with no obvious Russian equivalent that recalls (to my Russian colleagues' amusement) the word for scooter (*motoroller*), and referred to a team leader. The highest rank was the *dobrotekhnik,* the technologist, or mechanic of kindness. To rise on the career ladder, one had to both master certain skills and "activate" other volunteers. Goodness and doing good, then, were linked rather jarringly to the logic of performance audit. Promotion or advancement within this new terrain was tied to numeric performance evaluation (Kipnis 2008) – a kind of network marketing logic (*setevoi marketing*) in which the more people one sells to, the further one advances.

Youth were invited to advance through this hierarchy by means of performance audit, recorded in a ledger, an "unofficial passport" called the "volunteer's personal booklet" (*lichnaia knizhka volontera*), issued and overseen by the state. This second motivational text offered young people a format in which they could record and monitor their growth as volunteers. The booklet was distributed to participants in the Technologies of Kindness session, and to those who registered on an official website. Each good deed was to be recorded, monitored, and confirmed by an official stamp from an agent of the state. Like a moderated form of the "asset-based mapping" technology that is used widely in neoliberal urban-development projects, this document suggests that the state was less interested in society and social problems than in the agents it sought to activate, the volunteers.

At the Technologies of Kindness session at Seliger, these logics were enacted. Youth participants had the chance to develop their skills and work on their projects via workshops and VIP lectures, led by experts (political technologists, business leaders, and academics). As at all sessions at Seliger 2009, the key technology they encountered was project design, here retailored to become "social project design" (*sotsialnoe proektirovanie*); participants learned how to design, pitch, and market a social project and how to produce a "product" that would appeal to potential sponsors – representatives of business and the state, who offered grants and contracts to the best projects. What struck me was that the focus was not on social issues themselves, but on two other things: the innovative product, and the qualities of the person or the entrepreneurial self. One of the student organizers I spoke to told me he coached the volunteers he supervised ("my volunteers") to give a thirty-second "elevator pitch" (he used the English term) so that they could better compete. The elevator pitch simultaneously delivers a convincing product and a convincing salesman. Indeed, this was confirmed when one participant explained that winning projects were selected by teams of psychologists, who were dispatched by the organizers to observe some of the most promising volunteers in action, and to examine their skills, behavior, and conduct.

This focus on the individual and his or her performance became most clear in the Volunteer of the Year contest, held immediately after the summer camp at Seliger 2009. The competition focused on assessing the person, the candidate, rather than the project each one devised. As the contest announcement explained, contestants would need to demonstrate a set of skills and aptitudes, including personal effectiveness, the ability to strategize and make quick decisions, the ability to be adaptable, the ability to "think outside the box" (*nestandartno myslit'*), psychological stability, and "self-discipline" (*samoreguliatsiia*).

I had the opportunity to discuss some of these materials with one of the architects of this kind of methodological work – Lidiia Alekseevna, the director of the Scientific-Educational Center for Innovative

Technologies for the Development of the Professional Careers of Youth (Nauchno-Obrazovatel'nyi Tsentr Innovatsionnykh Tekhnologii Razvitiia Profkar'ery Molodezhi), a semi-independent center within Tver' State University. Established in 2003 to provide psychological counseling and professional development to students, it has since narrowed its focus to concentrate on "the professional preparation of volunteers."[11] While university departments have remained chronically underfunded, the center receives generous federal and regional funding. In addition to the work it has undertaken with local university students, it has published methodological-technological materials as well.[12]

One afternoon in May 2009 I went to visit Lidiia Alekseevna in her well-appointed and newly renovated office – the center was located on the ground floor of the main university building, prime real estate – and we chatted pleasantly over tea. She was interested to learn about my research project and saw in me someone with common interests. She explained that her center ran training programs for students to help them figure out a professional direction: "Some jobs don't suit all psychological types [*psikhotipy*]," she told me. She also informed me that the center trained students in teamwork and leadership and assisted them in developing their own projects so that they could enter regional (state-run) competitions.

Lidiia Alekseevna shared some of her recent publications with me – methodological works that were published during the federal Year of Youth (2009) and which focused on stimulating, motivating, and engaging young people. As I flipped through the pages, I recognized some of the sources she used – the International Declaration of Voluntarism, and Edward De Bono's "De Bono's Hats" exercise, which I had used in class with my students at the University of Massachusetts.

Lidiia Alekseevna had not been directly involved in Seliger 2009, though she had attended it as a VIP lecturer, delivering a speech on the professional preparation of youth. If anything, she appeared a little leery of the camp, regarding it (like many I spoke with) as a Nashi-affiliated event, the rogue product of the Federal Youth Affairs Agency.

While she had not been involved in developing the personal booklet, she was a key node in its dissemination, authorized by the regional youth committee to distribute copies of it to volunteers. Lidiia Alekseevna was happy to discuss the booklet with me (although she hesitated slightly before giving me one; "I don't think it's a state secret," she said). The one she had on file was a small book, like a passport, with a space for a photo and an official stamp on the first page.

Lidiia Alekseevna described the book as a new innovation, one that was drawn up from other methodologies ("It's not our idea; it was taken from abroad, I think," she told me, acknowledging the dialogue with Western authors). She said it was being distributed all over the country, after having won support at Seliger. "This book has state status," she explained. "It's like the [Soviet-era] labor book [*trudovaia knizhka*]. . . . The idea is that it will enable the government to collect statistics on voluntarism – how many youth volunteers there are in each region." Young people would go to a website and register in order to receive one; in this way, "they regulate themselves," she said, "so it doesn't look like it's something forced." From her account it became clear that the book had another purpose as well. In addition to helping the state compile statistics, it was intended to be a device that would encourage young people to participate in voluntarism. "The book is intended to be a stimulus for participants," Lidiia Alekseevna told me. "For example, if a job candidate has this book in addition to his regular portfolio, people will pay attention. . . . We think it will be interesting for our kids, because it will help them find employment – it has the potential to be a really effective mechanism." She explained that any agency except commercial structures – that is, educational establishments, nongovernmental organizations, and state structures – were authorized to provide a stamp to vouch for a young person's participation. Here, "voluntarism" was defined rather broadly.

As in the previous chapter, we see how this self-monitoring and self-audit resemble neoliberal forms, but also that there are substantial differences between them as well. In Lidiia Alekseevna's account, the booklet was an extra resource for young people that could work alongside a cv. Its ambition reveals an interesting delineation of spheres between the individual, the organization, and the state. While young people participate in their own regulation, they need to collect official stamps from agents of the state as well.

Lidiia Alekseevna sounded rather ambivalent about the personal booklet; certainly she was not evangelical about it ("There need to be different mechanisms"), but she thought perhaps it could make for a useful tool. She told me that many kids were resistant – they didn't want to bother with collecting stamps for the booklet, because to them it signaled formality (*formalnost'*), but she still thought it could work. Alluding to recent public opinion research, she told me (in apparent contradiction to what she had just said), "Recent research shows that today's youth are oriented toward formal stuff. They want official status, they are concerned about their careers; hence this will appeal to them." She mentioned a recent newspaper article she had seen that compared Generation X with Generation Y. "Those in Generation Y," she said, "value stability and are very career-oriented, hence they appreciate official symbols."

When I remarked on the newness of the state project, Lidiia Alekseevna demurred: "I don't see anything new in voluntarism; it was taken for granted. We may not have discussed it as such before, but it was very well established. We didn't even see it; it was so taken for granted. We were all in effect managers of social projects." A former Communist Party insider, she was comfortable with the continuities she recognized.

Via our miniconference and discussion sessions, the members of the research team – the teachers, the students, and I – debated these technologies and the projects we saw unfolding. Many of our conversations circled around these moments of resonance with the Soviet past. Elena Ivanova, a university colleague who had been very active in the Komsomol as a teenager during the eighties, threw up her hands in exaggerated horror when I showed her the "Kind Advice" materials. "Oh God, it's the next utopia!" she gasped, confirming that they strongly resembled the work she had done as a young Komsomol secretary (*komsorg*). Valentina, who had been only minimally engaged in the Komsomol during her youth, shuddered at the text and its schemas. In particular, she recoiled from the hierarchies and the formalism. In her view, both state projects – the Putin-era project and its Soviet predecessor – exploited youth and inhibited their capacity for individual agency. "They [the former Komsomol activists turned architects of youth policies] only know how to manage [*upravliat'*]," she said. Many of the student team members agreed with Valentina and viewed this state project as a crude state attempt to appropriate student labor. They saw the use of the term "volunteer" as duplicitous, another attempt by the state to pull one over on them.

These discussions proved to be bonding for the members of the research team. In an ironic inversion of the "Kind Advice" booklet's promise ("Everyone can be a volunteer!") my university teacher friends joked, "We are all [already] volunteers!" Here, they were picking up a joke I remembered from the late nineties. They meant that while their students were exploited by these campaigns, they themselves were exploited as well – referring to their miserly public-sector salaries. In their ironic debates I found little evidence of the critique of voluntarism made by skeptics in the United States, who regard it as a cunning neoliberal ploy, a means of justifying the appropriation of social services from the needy, or a means by which "neoliberal citizens" are produced. But here it had different resonance, and people voiced a different kind of skepticism, seeing it as a distinctively (post-)Soviet cynical ploy, an attempt on the part of political elites to gain moral capital and transform it into electoral gain.

RECEPTION

Ethnographic research revealed insights into the contingencies of state-run youth projects. I came to realize that there was considerable disjuncture between the resources expended on these materials and their apparent effects. True to what Valentina referred to as the "virtuality" of these projects, they were hatched, launched, and funded, and yet rarely seemed to graze the surface of daily life. Most youth participants appeared oblivious to these technologies; they either did not know about them or merely ignored them. Many of the students I spoke to had copies of the personal booklet, but they did not use them. As we shall see, this didn't necessarily mean they rejected the activities themselves, but – in another continuity with forms of Soviet-era political identification scholars have noted – they tuned out aspects that they considered pro forma and not meaningful (Yurchak 2006).

Meanwhile, I found that some of the adults who might be presumed to be supportive of these state-run youth projects expressed impatience with both these materials and (some of) the offices they emanated from. They viewed it as PR or *pafos* and were quick to call it out.[13] Irina, a junior municipal official I met in July 2011, was tasked with disseminating and collecting the booklets. When I asked her about them, she rolled her eyes and groaned dramatically. It was she who explained about the new directive to enroll 11 percent of young people in time for the Sochi Olympics in spring 2014. She thought this was crazy, an unrealistic target. Moreover, the booklet was no way to keep track of participants' progress. "It's not clear how many good deeds one has to do to get a stamp," she told me. "It's totally subjective!" Describing it as "absurd," she said that she and her colleagues preferred to adopt a more qualitative approach. They didn't just hand the booklets out or award stamps willy-nilly, but tried to really understand what the person was doing – was this person really doing voluntarism?

Portrait of a Dobrotekhnik I: Andrei

Andrei, the research team member mentioned earlier, was an interesting interlocutor as I pondered these models. After leaving Vazhnoe Delo, he had participated in other state-run youth projects. Now employed by the regional youth committee as an organizer of the Tver' delegation to the Technologies of Kindness session at Seliger 2009, he was also writing his MA thesis on the topic of voluntarism and was eager to talk with me.

Andrei was pondering voluntarism from different angles – his past engagement in Vazhnoe Delo, his current work as an organizer for Seliger, and his MA thesis. In our interactions he switched frequently between registers. As a recruiter, he gave upbeat accounts of the projects and campaigns; as a social scientist, he voiced frustration with some of the promotional materials and the formulations they advanced; and as a participant, he spoke of his own investedness, ambition, and desire to realize himself. A technologist in training, he was simultaneously excited at the prospect of Seliger 2009 and frustrated by what he perceived to be the inconsistencies in the state project so far. Like many people I spoke to (young and old), he dismissed Vazhnoe Delo as a rather clumsy PR campaign for the governor. While he allowed that it did some good work and offered some decent training programs, he felt that, like its Soviet predecessors, it implemented a flawed form of voluntarism (what he called "pseudo-voluntarism"), wherein youth were coerced and bribed and "good" was instrumentalized.

More than most of the young people I spoke with, Andrei was attentive to the materials and technologies distributed by the state; indeed, he was quite knowledgeable about them and was able to refer me to some of their authors (he informed me that the "Kind Advice" text was written by high-ranking twenty-something Nashi activist Yulia Zimova). He spoke a lot about the moments of dissonance and contradictions within the models offered. His discussion focused on making sense of the Western models and the Russian or Soviet conceptions they competed with and displaced. Andrei contrasted *dobrovolchestvo* with *volonterstvo* – where the former was Russian and signaled the direct provision of aid to the needy, the latter signaled a Western conception of voluntarism as professionalism, and Andrei was infuriated that state youth projects sometimes used the terms interchangeably ("It's a scandal!"). While he felt some change needed to be made – a Western-style opportunity structure had to be introduced to motivate volunteers, and it was important that there should be professionals – he didn't believe that the two conceptions should be confused, or that voluntarism should be remunerated. As he explained to me, "Russia must aim to achieve true [*istinnoe*] voluntarism, where people really want to do something for the social good, and not just because they've been made to do it, or because they have to do it at work." He believed it necessary to come up with a new word to express this, since the two terms *volonterstvo* and *dobrovolchestvo* were overburdened by their Western and Soviet associations. Even as he was critical of Western models, he was settling accounts and taking issue with the discredited socialist state (c.f. Read 2010).[14]

Although he grumbled about some of the tasks he was given and the quality of the work that took place, Andrei positioned himself as a trainee architect of these programs. Indeed, he embraced the managerial role and spoke consistently from the vantage point of one who was trying to stimulate, promote, and manage voluntarism, rather than someone on the front line of social issues. One of the first and most urgent topics of our conversation was the issue of volunteer motivation. "We have a problem of people's consciousness," he told me. "In Russia, people are not yet mature enough for voluntarism. Only that, that . . . *caste* of people who can be inspired on the basis of their personal motivations [understand it]." In addition to working as an organizer at Seliger, Andrei intended to present four of his own projects there. One project was a kind of school, or cultural center ("A kind of *dom kultura*," he explained, "but like you have in Western Europe") to educate and inculcate youth with values. He presented it as a kind of incubator for "true" (*istinnoe*) voluntarism (rather than the "pseudo" or "quasi" voluntarism that existed in Soviet times and which was being produced by state policies such as Vazhnoe Delo). He explained that his ultimate goal was to establish a school of voluntarism that would train and encourage people to participate in voluntary activities.

Andrei was a valuable guide during the buildup to Seliger 2009. His work on the regional committee meant that he had access to many volunteers and was ideally positioned for helping us recruit interviewees. Thanks to his efforts, we were able to organize two focus groups of student volunteers in May 2009. The two groups brought different models of voluntarism and leadership into juxtaposition. While one comprised volunteer activists involved in state-run youth projects (including Nashi), the other was a "grassroots" volunteer project, as my colleagues referred to it, comprising students who had thus far not had anything to do with the state-run programs.

Through these focus groups, I met Marina and Masha, two young women Andrei was eager to acquaint me with, "super-volunteers" with "top projects" (*topovye proekty*) who were planning to attend Seliger. At first blush the young women exemplified different modes of voluntarism – one the old, the other the new. However, as I came to see, they were not so distinct.

Portrait of a Dobrotekhnik II: Masha

Nineteen-year-old Masha, whom we met in chapter 2, was a student at the local Medical Academy. Long active in the Tver' branch of Nashi, she now worked as coordinator of one of the Tver' delegations to the Technologies of Kindness session at Seliger.

Masha was a poster child for the kinds of social projects the state encouraged. Indeed, one of Seliger 2009's promotional brochures included a photograph of her engaged in one of these campaigns, with members of her team on the front cover. Like Andrei, she had first come to voluntarism via state-run youth organizations, though her voluntarism – as described in her profile in chapter 2 – had been nurtured and fostered by Nashi. She told me that the welfare section (*sots napravlenie*), which she had led for two and a half years, was one of the largest Nashi projects; at one point it comprised forty people. Masha explained that her team (*rabochaia komanda*) undertook a wide range of activities in the areas that interested them, e.g., they organized blood drives, helped at animal shelters, and worked with orphans and disadvantaged children in children's homes – Masha's special interest. On the basis of the work she had done (her volunteer portfolio, as it were), she was invited to assume an organizational role at the Technologies of Kindness session at Seliger 2009.

Like Andrei, Masha also described Technologies of Kindness as offering a distinctive version of voluntarism – new, modern, more evolved, not a backward-looking Soviet program that just trained people to deliver forms of assistance. In the course of explaining her work, Masha described a switch she had made via her engagement in state-run youth programs: "Earlier, of course, we went around collecting monetary and material donations. But we've outgrown that stage [*moment*] and now we're mostly doing fundraising, and writing grant applications." She now organized events that were "more oriented toward raising awareness of problems than trying to resolve them." Her project, "Tver', a City without Orphanages," which she had developed under the auspices of Nashi and now planned to present at Seliger, manifested this enlightened orientation. She and her team held educational sessions about adoption during parent-teacher meetings in schools, in which they explained the benefits of adoption and fostering, and informed the parents about the forms of state support available for adopting families.

Masha's project, I realized, was very much in sync with federal policies. In the 2000s, the Russian state began to try to stimulate domestic adoption, both to reduce dependence on state orphanages and to curb the controversial international adoption process.[15] She spoke authoritatively about how adoption was "better for society at large" than orphanages.

During the focus group, Masha came across as an intense and earnest activist-leader, an insider of the state projects we were investigating. She spoke with gravity and authority about the education she had received and the work she had done so far, and she remarked on several occasions that her efforts had prevented her from getting involved in some of the more relaxed and fun aspects of Nashi's work and the summer camps at Seliger. She was very invested in the work she was doing for the Year of Youth and committed to the project of professionalizing voluntarism. Her job, she explained, using the Soviet term, was *agitatsionnaia rabota* (agitation); she was charged with recruiting promising young people to take part in the Technologies of Kindness session at Seliger and to help them design successful social projects. Indeed, she took advantage of the focus group to invite the other students to participate in it.

Masha interested me because she was something of an anomaly. This is a gendered terrain, where those who constitute themselves as "technologists" are mostly young men, while young women engage directly with needy populations and enact forms of care or "kindness." Masha participated in both forms of activity and was able to comfortably switch between registers – the managerial and the caregiving. It was this quality, I suspect, that won her the respect of her peers and made her a successful recruiter. She presented as austere and disciplined – every inch the manager-leader – and yet she was passionate about social issues and very concrete in her discussion of them. Although there was substantial disagreement among the focus-group participants regarding the intent and purpose of state-run youth programs, about which many spoke very critically, all of them deferred to Masha. She radiated a sense of integrity, authenticity, and commitment that clearly impressed them.

It became clear that Masha's work with children in orphanages had been transformative. In addition to the educational campaign she intended to present at Seliger, she had a second project, smaller in scale and evidently more personal. It was less a project than "an idea [she] had long cherished," prompted by her relationship with one child, a six-year-old boy she had met and befriended at the orphanage. He was wild, unloved, and written off by the orphanage staff (they called him "Mowgli"), but she had gotten through to him. Her project sought to "rehabilitate" children like him so that they might have a chance of being fostered.

Portrait of a Dobrovoller: Marina

Our second focus group brought me into contact with Marina, Andrei's other "super-volunteer." Marina also worked with children in orphanages; however, while Masha's voluntarism emerged and was nurtured by state-run youth projects, Marina's voluntarism had a very different hue and a different provenance.

Marina was a second-year student in the Department of Foreign Languages at TGU. She was well known and widely respected at the university as the initiator of "Children First," a voluntary campaign to assist children in orphanages in the region. Children First was not an organization or a project in the Seliger sense. It was an informal initiative that had begun a few months previously among students of the university. I subsequently learned that Marina had organized and fundraised with the support of the university administration (the dean's office – *dekanat*); she had held a series of quite successful funding drives there, collecting toys, candy, and money from students and delivering them to local orphanages.

Nine members of Children First participated in our focus group – eight young women and one young man. They were enthusiastic to participate and eager to talk about their work with the children. Indeed, our session became the occasion for a very soulful and moving coming-together. Marina and her friends spoke with feeling about their work and screened a slide show they had made especially for us, depicting their activities. These sophomores, all foreign language majors and classmates, modeled a form of tight sociality that is characteristic of the Russian educational system. Although they spoke in unison – adding, chiming in, and fleshing out each other's points – they all deferred to Marina.

Marina did not see herself as a "leader"; indeed, she eschewed such a designation and resisted it. In all of our interactions, she presented herself as carried along by a series of serendipitous events, buoyed by people (peers and authority figures) who saw promise in her ideas and intentions and who were persuaded by the importance of the work she wished to undertake. Although clearly identified by others as the initiator of the project, Marina avoided any proprietary statements about it and ducked any suggestion that she had played a particularly important role. As she put it, "I got involved in this only because I saw that there was support, and I understood that I'm not alone and that there are very many people who are ready to help. . . . It wasn't that I called people to the project, rather that people called me and I agreed to participate."

This was a distinctive form of leadership, one encouraged by the Russian and Soviet educational system, in which children work together in "collectives" from an early age. To be a leader in this sense required the confidence of one's peers. One had to be able to talk to them, and, it seemed to me, also able to take guidance and direction from them (Yurchak 2006). It also required a certain charisma, which Marina had in abundance. Indeed, although this was not the form of leadership propagated at Seliger, Marina was respected not only by her peers, but by the student leaders involved in organizing the Tver' delegation to the Technologies of Kindness session. Indeed, she was one of Masha's favorite recruits.

Children First modeled a distinctive mode of voluntarism, too – one that was quite different from the model promoted at Seliger. Throughout her narrative and description of her own activity, Marina asserted an implicit contrast between Children First and what she saw taking form elsewhere in state-run projects. Children First was not a "project," she explained, because that implied something more thought out. Rather, it was an initiative that came from the students themselves. In her words, the campaign began as a "kind step" that snowballed, propelled by the participants' inner need or desire to do good. "It surprised me that people have this need inside themselves," Marina said, "and that it's possible to help selflessly." The initiative was deliberately informal; rather than engaging in formal fundraising, the group began with student participants pooling their own meager funds to buy balloons and candy and mobilized their own resources and networks. In words that ironically recalled the empowerment script repeated by some of the youth activists involved in propagandizing Seliger 2009, she explained that someone had a car, someone else had a well-placed acquaintance. This was not "sponsorship," she carefully made clear, but "support straight from the heart." They secured pledges from local stakeholders as well, mobilizing local channels that were well known to me from my prior research – a prosperous local bakery, whose director was a political player and prominent philanthropist in the city, had donated baked goods.

In contradistinction to the approach Seliger modeled (where project design was an innovative art form requiring skill), Marina and the other young women asserted the self-evident nature of the issue they mobilized around. Rather than needing to be made up, crafted, branded, and skillfully pitched, Children First spoke for itself. "We don't need to agitate," Marina said. "It's enough to show a person the photos. If a person is interested, their eyes light up and they join our team." Another chimed in: "People come themselves." Indeed, there was no whiff of the "new" in Marina's construction of voluntarism. Devoid of social-engineering goals, their projects didn't seek to activate the needy, nor did they have any publicistic component, but there was plenty of soul.

Marina and her friends spoke eloquently of the deep spiritual and physical satisfaction they got out of the work they did. As one of the girls put it, "When the kids come up to you, they take you by the hand, and then hold onto it, they don't let go. And when you see their eyes, you understand that you have something to live for, that your life is not in vain." Personalized, face-to-face connection was important too, and Marina insisted that this was what made their work successful and appealing to the children they helped (compared with the more bureaucratized forms of support offered by Vazhnoe Delo).

It was clear that Children First offered Marina both a venue for personal fulfillment and a site where she could express her commitment to society; the key words of her narrative included collective, team (*komanda*), and team feeling (*komandnoe chuvstvo*). She derived satisfaction from having close, personalized connections with others, both the children she assisted and the classmates who joined her in this work.

In May 2009, Marina and her team were on the brink of something new. Their goal was to secure more substantial sponsorship to enable them to continue this work. They had already approached the oblast youth committee to request funds, but to no avail. Infected by the buzz of excitement and possibility among their classmates, they were now turning to Seliger. Although a little put off by its formalism (Marina told me she found the strict selection procedure quite intimidating), and not altogether convinced it would be different from prior interactions with the authorities ("I'm afraid [the project] will just remain on paper"), they registered at the Seliger website and began the series of bureaucratic steps participation required. Marina explained that the application procedure required them to quantify and submit records of all the activities they had undertaken. In ways that confused her, they were required to provide measurable evidence of their kindness. As I contemplated the girls' willingness to participate in our focus group, I realized that the research team and I were caught up in this as well. Through the focus group, the girls were undertaking their own form of "agitation"; they associated us in some way with the people they were trying to reach and impress. The slide show they made for us – especially for us, as Marina explained – was an artifact of the kind of accounting they were encouraged into. (Unlike most of the young people I interviewed, Marina and her team expressed great interest in my consent forms. I later realized this was so they could present them to the oblast committee; they planned to claim participation in our group as evidence of their own voluntarism-oriented activity.)

During subsequent interviews with Marina I was able to learn more about her background and what had attracted her to voluntarism. She explained that she had moved to Tver' from Tajikistan in 1997 when she was eight years old. As she narrated her trajectory, she emphasized the role and kindness of a few individuals. Although her family arrived in the city at the beginning of the school year, she was fortunate enough to be admitted to a prestigious school. The principal was very sympathetic, and indeed made a real effort to ensure that Marina fit in to the *kollektiv.* It was at this school that she first became involved in voluntary activities. There, she encountered a remarkable teacher who played a pivotal role: "He was like a volunteer [*dobrovolets*]," she told me, because he really loved kids and took them on field trips [*turisticheskie pokhody*] – to lakes, to the sea. Marina spoke with feeling about the sense of belonging that these activities afforded: "I think perhaps that this was the moment when that feeling of being in a team arose [*chuvstvo komandnoe takoe*]. Because when you live outside in nature, these feelings, they just come together. You understand immediately what you need to do, that you have to do things a little differently, you start to live independently." After that, she became involved in the teacher's toy drive initiative for a children's home. She described this more recognizable experience of voluntarism as "the first step."

It was through this teacher that Marina came to participate in some of Vazhnoe Delo's campaigns. Then, when she entered the university, her voluntarism got another boost when she received an award from the Potanin Foundation. Through her account, I came to realize that Potanin fellows (*stipendiatory*) form another tight collective within the university; further, this foundation acts as an incubator of social projects like Seliger. Marina explained that fellows are encouraged to devise these projects in teams, the most successful of which are awarded funding so that they can implement their projects.[16] It was here that she first proposed the idea of supporting children's homes.

When her Potanin peers did not select her proposal, she took it to her classmates. It was here that things took off. What began as a simple toy drive became something much more. Since this took place just before the New Year holiday, someone suggested they put on a play, or dress up as Santa Claus and give the gifts to the children in person. According to Marina, the plan snowballed: "The information quickly spread through the whole university, and the whole university began collecting toys. By the end of December, there were twenty of us wanting to go." She had thought it would be a one-off event, but "those people supported me and said, 'Let's not stop this, because it's really great, it's necessary.'" Between January and May 2009 they traveled to the children's home a number of times, laden with sweets, balloons, and small gifts. They traveled when they could manage it, mostly on national holidays such as the Day of Cosmonauts and New Year.

Marina told me that she wasn't drawn to Seliger because of the opportunities it presented for self-development; rather, she was going because she hoped to secure support for the project. Strikingly, she didn't speak of competitions or grants, but of contacts: "We're participating in the Year of Youth because, well, we're not so much drawn by its promise to develop our opportunities, but because it offers a small chance to connect with people who could offer us real support. You see, at Seliger, we'll present our project before special guests – directors of different factories, members of the administration."

In contrast to the forms of activity emerging in state-run programs, Children First did appear more "grassroots"; it struck Valentina and me as very similar to the energy of the "societal movement" (*obshchestvennoe dvizhenie*) of the early 1990s, before the arrival of foreign agencies, grants, and funding (Hemment 2007a). Meanwhile, Marina was exceptional, but recognizable – an exemplary practitioner of a long-practiced and culturally sanctioned activity. Her voluntarism owed something both to specific forms of sociality afforded students in Russian higher-education institutions and to the new opportunity structures offered them during the 2000s, such as the Potanin Foundation and the new trend within the state higher-education system that encourages young people to develop their professional credentials.

Empowerment Rendered?

The following year, I had a chance to talk with Andrei, Masha, and Marina about their experiences. The three super-volunteers had all attended Technologies of Kindness (Marina with fourteen of her peers), but their projects had fared quite differently. While Andrei and Masha's projects were recognized and awarded sponsorship at Seliger, Marina's project was not.[17]

In May 2010 I spoke with Marina about her experience of Seliger 2009. While she had not won the substantial support she had hoped for, she insisted she was not disappointed. "It's just that things were a bit different from what we'd expected," she said. Although they had not won a grant, she told me the group had secured a number of "agreements" with sponsors at Seliger – more, in fact, than she could recall or name. She had also made useful contacts there, most notably with the local representative of a national charitable agency, Who If Not Me?, which now provided them with transportation to the orphanage and donated baked goods.

She gave a glowing report of the event and insisted she had gained a lot there. First, she had to learn how to be assertive, to win the attention of the invited experts; second, she had to learn how to make effective and fast presentations, practicing a skill that she and the other Children First team members had been taught. There were additional optional activities such as advanced classes on different themes – one foundation ran a class on art for children, another on how to adapt fairy tales for them. "I liked it a lot, we were tired, but it was fun," she told me, and there were interesting VIPs there as well, she said.

Through her account I got a more textured sense of what Seliger offered – a kind of gala, wherein participants could for a few moments enter the orbit of minor celebrities and political figures. Marina explained that participants set up stands to display their projects along "Seliger Road," the main path that ran through the camp. This was the route that newcomers – including VIPs – arrived on. In this way, one of the girls had managed to chat with a famous actor. Indeed, to my amazement, Marina told me she'd even met Putin himself: "It was a chance in a billion. . . . They told us we weren't allowed to call out to him, as he had such a complicated schedule. Really, everything was planned down to the last minute." The girls were dressed as angels, she said; they invited passersby to make donations in return for a yellow star. Marina, our exemplary volunteer and charismatic angel, caught Putin's eye. Without thinking, she called out to him, asking, "May I give you a star?" To her surprise, he broke ranks, violating the tight protocol to walk over and speak with her. "It was utterly unexpected!" she told me breathlessly, as she rummaged for the photo she wanted to show me. "I don't know how I dared!"

No social science major, Marina was not directly critical of the models offered (or the politicians she had encountered). However it was clear from all she had to say about her project that she found these models disconcerting. Marina was kind, but not technological; the "innovation" and quantifiable objectives and results Seliger sought were at odds with her thinking. "Kindness is something abstract that you can't classify," she told me. "I still feel the same way. If you really want to do something and if you do it from the heart, you can do it without funding. I know from my own experience this is true."

In sum, although she was appreciative of the opportunities Seliger presented, Marina rejected these technologies and refused to develop her project along the lines that were recommended to her, articulating a different form of personhood and subjectivity as she did so (Dunn 2004). When I asked her if she planned to return to Seliger in 2010, she told me, "No, unfortunately, I'm not going this year, because I don't want to go alone.... It's not [about] me, it's a team thing, because if the others weren't there, I wouldn't [get on well]. And I can't picture myself there by myself." Her work with children was meaningful to her when undertaken in the company of her friends.

She didn't give up on her project, however. On the contrary, Marina and her team emerged from Seliger more tightly bonded and – it seemed to me – more committed to their way of doing things. In ways that were partially, though unexpectedly, attributable to Seliger, the past year had proven to be more successful than the first. This had less to do with the new acquaintances she had made at Seliger than with the goodwill she encountered locally. With a glow, she named the events they had participated in: one was a fundraiser, a concert. The university had allowed them to use one of its auditoriums, and a local print shop had agreed to print flyers for them for free. The event was a big success – a lot of people came, bringing donations. The concert not only served as a means of fundraising, but infused new energy into their campaigns as a great many more students signed up to participate. The way she spoke communicated that these were more meaningful forms of support than those offered at Seliger. Unlike the agreements (*dogovory*) she'd received at Seliger, which she had struggled to remember and itemize for me, she reeled off details about these forms of assistance ("support from the heart") effortlessly.

Meanwhile, Masha's skillful work of social-project design had won her the ultimate prize: her pro-adoption project was named one of the top three social projects at Seliger. It won a grant and was presented to Prime Minister Putin. When we spoke in May 2010 I found that despite her success, she was a little disappointed at the way things had played out. Her favorite projects, the ones she had recruited for, worked on, and considered most worthy, like Marina's, were not honored at Seliger.

Masha mused regretfully on Marina's failure to prosper at Seliger. Beyond the usual investment of an organizer, motivated to see her recruits win awards, she admired and was fond of Marina. She described her in glowing terms as "an amazing girl, a really kindhearted person, a total sweetheart." However, she explained, "unfortunately, at Seliger they didn't really take her very seriously, because, well, her project isn't, well, her project is a bit run-of-the-mill, a lot of people do that." Moreover, unlike Masha's own project, Children First worked within the discredited state orphanage structures and was thus out of sync with official state policy. Masha insisted that Marina could have tweaked her project: "I told her a few times that she could just correct the project a little in order to get funding, but she . . . that didn't come together [*chto- to ne sroslos'*]. I don't know. But it's a real shame, because her project is really excellent."

However uninnovative the project, Marina and her team were remarkable, Masha insisted: "Nobody does it so warmheartedly, nobody does it so frequently and so – well, for themselves. They don't beg for money to help them go to the orphanages, they don't ask anyone for transport, they just collect themselves, throw in money for gas, take a car, and go to orphanages to organize a play. They don't need any sponsorship. They collect occasionally – they hold charitable concerts but it's all very minimal. I agree that one can do any project for pennies. The thing is, though, to do it that way for a hundred rubles, you have to work twenty-four seven."

She told me there was no room for her own small, intimate project at Seliger, either: "I didn't get to present it unfortunately . . . because, well, because it was the same case as Children First, I suppose." Smiling ruefully (one year on, her ideas had changed a bit), she told me that what had mattered was "innovation" – it wasn't enough to do good, to just organize events, or do nice things for orphans; one had to introduce some new technological dimension. Indeed, she told me that most of the winning, or "top," projects at Seliger were products, socially oriented goods that could find sponsorship and be branded, marketed, and sold – she named a dog waste disposal system, sponsored by a dog food company; a nicotine-free cigarette, and a biodegradable bag. (Andrei confirmed this; as he put it, "In general, they look at things as products, which can be sold, which you can sell, which the government needs.") Moreover, these prizewinners were technologies that had little to do with kindness.

Masha spoke with eloquence about the frustrations of projects and funding, the shortcomings of the PR and promotional work she'd been rewarded for accomplishing, and the complexities of the issue she'd taken on. The price of success was steep. While she had been elevated, the project that mattered to her had not. She'd had to move away from the work with orphaned children that was meaningful to her. The work she'd been funded to perform was, she felt, empty – the grant money went exclusively into advertising and P R work, not direct work with children. Moreover, adoption was a complicated issue and it was hard to stimulate it. She spoke concretely and with knowledge and insight about the complexities, the structural impediments, and the deep psychological problems many children in orphanages faced (most of those in the oblast orphanage are unhealthy; they have deep psychological issues that make it unlikely that parents will choose to adopt them). Further, she had run up against some serious real-world obstacles when she tried to enact her project, in the form of hostile bureaucrats who felt her project encroached on their territory. She said she would like to work with children again, but is "afraid to, afraid to invest [her] energies now, in case something similar repeats." Instead, she had stepped off the youth-voluntarism career ladder to focus on her studies.

One year later, then, Masha – the girl I had taken to be the ultimate Nashi insider – had come around to share Marina's point of view ("I agree that one can do any project for pennies"). She too had decided not to attend Seliger 2010, since she understood it was pointless (*bespolezno*).

Andrei's projects, meanwhile, were met with acclaim at Seliger. When I talked with him in May 2010 he spoke with pride about their reception ("All three were well regarded; the last one was honored [*ot-mechen*] by Putin"). Although he had not won sponsorship or material support, he had won a number of "agreements" with sponsors who had pledged resources (*resursnaia podderzhka*). One agreement was with the representatives of *Star Factory,* a reality T V show where young people compete; one of its stars had pledged to participate in an advertising video for his project, in collaboration with a mobile phone company.

Rather than moving away from state-run youth projects, he was more tightly integrated than ever. However, he had moved away from voluntarism. Andrei told me that during the summer of 2009 he had moved "to the level of Western voluntarism." He explained, "I started to do voluntarism [*volonterstvo*] in a professional sphere, that is, to teach myself to be a professional in the realm of innovation." By May 2010, he had let go of voluntarism entirely to move into more specifically entrepreneurial activities. He informed me that he was working full-time (unpaid) as an official representative of the Federal Youth Affairs Agency's Zvorykinsky Project (on innovation) – "It's a life hobby," he said. Furthermore, he told me solemnly that he had joined the elite komissars' society (Komissarskoe Soobshestvo), by becoming a Nashi komissar.

In talking with other young people I came to recognize this dynamic. Voluntarism is sold as a space of opportunity, a space where they can undertake meaningful work addressing urgent social problems, while simultaneously developing themselves. Distinctive from the 1990s-era NGO or civic projects sponsored by international foundations and agencies – perceived by many in Russia to be suspiciously internationalist in orientation – this work claims to serve the common good, the broader collectivity, and is done for the sake of the nation. However, the social reality of these projects is somewhat different. The latter project (self-work, skills building, and career development) eclipses the former (addressing social problems); the career ladder that young people are offered actually encourages them to move away from social issues and concentrate on their own careers.

This research showed that like their global counterparts, Russian youth were motivated to engage in state-run voluntarism projects by the desire to do good, to contribute to society, and to develop themselves. The federal rendition of voluntarism they encountered at Seliger 2009 was rather different from what they expected. Russia's state-run voluntarism projects strongly resembled the form of voluntarism put forth by the empowerment projects Eliasoph (2011) discusses and which theorists of neoliberal governmentality have critiqued. These too were focused less on the needy or on social issues than on making over the volunteers themselves. The Technologies of Kindness session at Seliger 2009 invited each volunteer to become an "entrepreneur of himself or herself" (Gordon 1991, 44), one who was constantly invested in reworking his or her human capital. At the same time, providing evidence of the "resonance" between neoliberal and socialist logics that scholars have noted, these competitions and this self-work also recalled Soviet rationalities and social engineering (Hoffman 2010; Matza 2009). Throughout the Soviet period, citizens were encouraged to compete via contests between work collectives, and via the Stakhanovite movement.[18] There were other points of resonance as well. In their emphasis on health and clean living (antismoking and antialcohol campaigns), competitions like Vazhnoe Delo's Social Advertising project closely resembled Soviet-era agitational work, such as the campaigns to encourage the population's culturedness (*kulturnost'*) (Rivkin-Fish 2009; Kelly and Volkov 1998). The managerial work the Russian state encouraged young people to undertake strongly resembled Komsomol work during late socialism. Party or Komsomol work was a form of voluntarism, or activism that was already entrepreneurial (or managerial-entrepreneurial) in nature (Yurchak 2002, 279).

While voluntarism-promoting projects such as Technologies of Kindness bore traces and tidemarks of both Soviet and 1990s-era neoliberal projects, they yielded something distinct (Eliasoph 2011). These were incoherent technologies produced by multiple (often low-ranking) state actors; their results were far more uneven and unexpected than those seeking evidence of neoliberalism's penetration might suppose. Beyond the manager-leaders we have considered, Technologies of Kindness constructed different kinds of subjects as well. It also spawned irony, critique, and (as Marina's case reveals) a kind of intense idealism and affective excess. The logics these young people were exposed to were not immutable, but morphed as they moved forward; my own entanglement and incorporation into the campaigns provided further evidence of their uncertain and unexpected subject effects.

The narratives I have shared reveal that, far from marching in lockstep with Putin, the youth participants at Seliger were leery of the technologies offered them. When they talked about the state, they often did so with irony, to call it out as engaging in PR or electioneering. The next chapter develops these themes as it examines a project with an even more intimate reach: the much-touted eroticized "cult" of Putin and the technologies associated with it.

FIVE

"AROUSING" PATRIOTISM

Satire, Sincerity, and Geopolitical Play

ON THE ROAD TO THE SELIGER YOUTH CAMP THAT DAY IN August 2009, my Russian colleagues were in high spirits. As we pulled out of the city, the jokes began. "I wonder what food they serve at Seliger," Maria pondered, suggesting that it would have to be patriotic; perhaps they would serve food in the colors of the flag, she hypothesized, "something red, something blue, with a dollop of [white] Smetana [sour cream]!" As we sped through the Tver' countryside in Maria's husband Alexei's comfortable Ford Focus, we listened to various songs, debating which should be our "anthem" for the day. Somewhere between Torzhok and Ostashkov, Maria slipped a CD into the player to entertain us – the soundtrack to the satirical film *Election Day* by the popular band Neschastnyi Sluchai. One song in particular had my friends in stitches; as I struggled to follow the lyrics, Valentina explained to me that it was about village girls who were unable to achieve orgasm until Putin arrived in their village.[1] A version of the film, based on a play and familiar to them all, had been shown on television prior to the 2008 elections.[2]

It was only in retrospect that I realized how fitting that song was and what an apt theme song it made for our day. Gender and sexualization were very much on our minds as we wended our way to Seliger. On the one hand, this fact spoke to my colleagues' preoccupations – they were gender studies scholars, after all. On the other, it spoke to what they knew about these state-run youth campaigns and the notoriety of the camps at Seliger.

In line with state policies more broadly, the youth projects I examine here are pronatalist; they seek to talk young people into neotraditionalist values associated with the Russian Orthodox Church and usher them into a markedly gendered redrawing of citizenship (Rivkin-Fish 2010; Sperling 2003, 2012). At the same time – and seemingly contra-dictorily – state-run youth campaigns are frequently sexualized, illus-trating the commodified and sexualized rebranding of politics and the eroticization of political authority that has taken place under Putin (Bo-renstein 2008; Goscilo 2013b). Indeed, they have generated some of the most controversial "patriotic" performances. In sum, they have borne the hallmarks of the contradictory gender politics of the Putin era: the simultaneous embrace of Russian Orthodox cultural values (gender tra-ditionalism, pronatalism) and the sensational sexualization of politics and commodification of sexual discourse.

GIVE BIRTH AND STRIP! THE CONTRADICTORY
INCITEMENTS OF RUSSIA'S GENDER REGIME

Nashi swiftly emerged as an enthusiastic participant in these perfor-mances (Sperling 2012).[3] In 2007 the media buzzed with reports about the Nashi-sponsored youth camp at Lake Seliger where young "leaders" were to demonstrate their patriotism while engaging in heteroprocre-ative sex. There were mass weddings, the "Love Oasis" (as titillating me-dia accounts referred to it), a cluster of tents intended for young couples to embark on their procreative lives,[4] and a number of pronatalist cam-paigns including "I Want Three," in which young people were persuaded to pledge to have three children.

In 2008, Nashi komissar Antonina Shapovalova launched her own "patriotic" fashion line.[5] This commercial Nashi spinoff project – which debuted at Seliger and was subsequently presented at the state-sponsored Moscow Fashion Week – prominently featured T-shirts with a variety of slogans that reflected this contradictory mix: pronatalist ones such as I Want Three were accompanied by other more racy and sexually sugges-tive ones, such as "Vova [a diminutive of Vladimir, i.e., Putin], I'm With You!" emblazoned on bikini bottoms (Lassila 2012, 162). These eroticized patriotic performances continued in the Putin-Medvedev era, intensi-fying as Putin prepared to stand for a third presidential term. In 2010, Nashi was implicated in another ostensibly youth-led campaign – the re-

lease of an erotic calendar on the occasion of Putin's fifty-eighth birthday
by women students in the Journalism Department of Moscow State University.[6] The calendar ("Vladimir Vladimirovich," it read, using Putin's
first name and patronymic, "We Love You; Happy Birthday Mr. Putin")
depicted scantily clad young women on each page, with phrases that
expressed both their political and sexual devotion: "How about a third
time?" as Miss February put it, or Miss August's "Who else if not you?"[7]

Perhaps the most bizarre was the "Putin's Army" campaign, which
invited girls to strip, or rip their clothes off for Putin, in support of his
2012 presidential candidacy.[8] While it was unclear who orchestrated
the online campaign, it bore the hallmark of Nashi and was posted on
the blog of parliamentarian Kirill Shchitov, from Putin's ruling United
Russia party.[9] A promotional video released by the campaign, which
went viral online, depicts a young woman striding purposefully through
the Moscow streets, wearing a black jacket and stacked heels. Toting
a slim black shopping bag, she is part businesswoman, part shopper.
The camera lingers on the cross that dangles in her cleavage. "Hi, my
name is Diana," she says. "I am a student. I am crazy about a man who
changed our country." She takes out her iPhone, which has a logo that
reads "Putin, We Trust," and as she does so, we gain a glimpse of a box
with an Apple logo in the shopping bag. "He is a worthy politician and
a handsome [*shikarnyi*] man," she continues. "He is Vladimir Putin. He
is adored by millions of people who believe in him, but there is a small
group of people who throw mud at him. Perhaps it's because they are
afraid of him; maybe it's because of their own weaknesses, because they
will never be in his place."

The camera moves ahead of her to zoom in on two girls in sundresses,
lying on chaises longues by the Moscow River. As they sip cocktails
through straws, chat, and play with their MacBooks, they look simultaneously sexy, expensive, and businesslike. They wave smilingly as Diana
approaches them. "Young, smart, and beautiful girls have come together
to form an army for Putin, an army that will strip for him," Diana says.
"We announce a competition – the rules are very simple. You shoot a
video in which you tear something or someone apart for Putin, then
you upload your video to the group VKontakte." The girls look at the
website on their computers; it depicts girls with laptops doing just that,

going to the VKontakte site. Diana takes out a red lipstick and writes the phrase "Strip for Putin" (*Porvu za Putina*) on a white vest, then kisses it and says, "The author of the most original video will become the owner of an iPad 2."

At this, one of the girls reaches into Diana's bag, to take out an iPad 2. Diana stands to face the camera directly, now clad in the tight-fitting vest T-shirt she emblazoned with "Strip for Putin," and asks, her head tipping in a kind of hip-hop jerk, "So what are *you* ready to do for your president?" As she says this, her hands reach for her shirt, and prepare to rip it open.

Valentina alerted me to this campaign (with great disdain) when I was in Tver' in 2012. As I watched the video on YouTube in my home in Amherst, I was struck by the curious fusion it represented: political campaign meets product placement ad, army recruitment tool meets soft porn. It was no wonder she found it alarming!

SATIRE, SINCERITY, AND GEOPOLITICAL PLAY:
INTERPRETING THE GENDER POLITICS OF
RUSSIA'S STATE-RUN YOUTH PROJECTS

This chapter investigates the place of gender and sexuality within state-run youth campaigns and examines the bewildering fusions that take place within them. Building on my analysis in prior chapters, I first move to account for them. As with other manifestations of the Putin era, I argue that to comprehend them, we must locate them within broader trends, including neoliberal-oriented social and economic policies, the backlash against Western models and liberalism, and the growing influence of the Orthodox Church in Russia. Quintessential oil-and-gas-glamour manifestations, they can be viewed as "geopolitical performances" that articulate both a critique of a popularly defined "liberalism" and ambivalence about Russian national identity in light of globalization (Heller 2007), and use sex in a provocative display of Russian power and might.

The "sexualization of Russian politics" (Sperling 2012, 245) in the Putin era has been well noted. Commentators and feminist scholars have documented the sexualized "cult" of Putin the leader (hypermasculine, shirtless) and the ways young women's bodies (and fertility) have been recruited in pro-Kremlin political campaigns and deployed for pro-regime purposes (Goscilo 2013b; Johnson and Saarinen 2013; Riabova and Riabov 2010; Sperling 2012; Wood 2010). It has been highly controversial, both in Russia and internationally (though for rather different reasons). While many Russian commentators dismiss these sexualized elements as marketing strategies and do not see them as radically different from other political PR ploys, US- and Western Europe–based journalistic and media accounts often interpret them as further manifestations of Russia's authoritarianism. As British journalist Edward Lucas put it, writing about Seliger 2007, "The *real* aim of the Nashi youth camp – and the 100,000-strong movement behind it – is not to improve Russia's demographic profile, but to attack democracy."[10] Some of the Western feminist scholars who have documented these excesses appear to concur; Johnson and Saarinen (2013, 561) describe them as manifestations of "neomasculinist semiauthoritarianism."

In this chapter, I consider this proposition and grapple with the challenge for feminist interpretation these provocative forms present. These performances of erotic attachment to Putin are indeed troubling, yet it is important to be reflexively aware of our own location in the analyses we produce. I argue once again that we can only make sense of these patriotic performances if we situate them within a "broader political geography" (Gal and Kligman 2000, 4). What at first glance appears to be a uniquely (and exotically) Russian phenomenon, confirmation of Russia's authoritarian turn, turns out to be something much more global and shared. We need to consider not only the historical forces that propel these performances, but their location within broader trends – here, the fusion of politics/consumption and new media culture that has reshaped politics globally (Goscilo 2013a; Cassiday and Johnson 2010; Salmenniemi and Adamson 2015).

Like the other governing projects I have examined in previous chapters, these sexualized patriotic performances are uneven, multiauthored, and unstable, permitted but not directly endorsed by state officials. Moreover, they have had unexpected and unintended results. As my colleagues' appreciation of Neschastnyi Sluchai's song about orgasm-deprived village girls reveals, the sexualized characteristic of the Putin "cult" has been a rich source of satiric cultural production (Mikhailova 2012). Indeed, despite their ostensibly pro-state character, erotic patriotic performances are a venue for satire that critiques state power in the Putin era and the commodified and corporate forms it has assumed (oil-and-gas *glamur,* or the ideology of glamour). Here, in an interesting transmutation of late socialist forms, satire (stiob) is turned simultaneously against the Russian state and against a presumed ossified and dogmatic liberalism and feminism as well. In dialogue with recent works in Russian cultural and performance studies, I consider the implications of this satirical production for understanding these performances and consider the challenge of putting local responses in dialogue with our own.

In the second half of the chapter I return to ethnography and the insights our collaborative project provided. Drawing on interview data, I explore youth activists' ambivalent responses to these campaigns and how they negotiate the contradictory incitements of pronatalism and sexualization. As in previous chapters, we see how young people do not take the campaigns at face value. I also reflect on the centrality of the topic of gender politics to our collaborative project and sketch the alternative gender-education project state-run campaigns overlapped with – the feminist educational project undertaken by Valentina and her colleagues. Our collaborative project had a geopolitical range and intent as well, insofar as it was conceptualized as an intervention that would call out and contest the xenophobic constructions that worked to prevent international collaboration and signaled "feminism" (and other liberal values) as "other." Once again, our collaborative research afforded special insights and revealed something distinctive. Our discussions, debates, and divergent responses to the campaigns made me aware of another angle of my entanglement in this project: as a foreign liberal feminist I was positioned within these geopolitical performances in a particular way. Where politics is "spectacle" (Goscilo and Strukov 2011b), there is a special obligation to examine all dimensions of the performance, including our own reactions. I include a reflexive account of my response to the campaigns, tracking these moments of entanglement as a means of pointing to the representational dilemmas they presented. My analysis in this chapter is stimulated in part by my uneasy sense of having been drafted as a bit player.

The theme of gender continued during our stay at Seliger. While we did not encounter any of the most controversial things we had read about

Молодежь Селигера!

У Вас есть возможность совершить невероятный и героический поступок! Жениться на Селигере!

Прием заявок на бракосочетания проводит Комаров Дмитрий
Контактные телефоны: 8905-604-28-40 Дмитрий, 8916-201-39-64 Аня

5.1. "Get married at Seliger!" poster, displayed at Seliger 2009.

(love oases, or stripping), we found ample evidence of patriotic pronatalism. One poster we saw taped to a tree announced, "Youth of Seliger! You have the opportunity to undertake an unbelievable [*neveroiatnyi*] and heroic act – Get married at Seliger!" While I attached myself to our guide Anton, my colleagues busied themselves seeking out other gendered themes. Maria proved to be a photographer with a keen eye. In addition to the wedding incitement, she took photos of a poster announcing a Miss Seliger beauty contest, sponsored by the Russian cosmetics company Faberlic, and a handwritten poster advertising "intimate services."

Back at the Tver' encampment to which Anton led us after our tour, we met more Tver' State University students, several of whom rose from their chores to greet us. While young men chopped wood, a couple of young women sat by the fire. "The girls are guarding the hearth!" Valentina quipped, invoking neotraditional discourse, and she insisted on having her picture taken with them. "Who does the dishes?" she asked playfully, to which they all replied that each did their own. Ira, Yulia, and Katya were students at Tver' State University (indeed, Ira was a sociology student who had taken classes with Valentina); they had not come with their own projects, but spoke enthusiastically about the events they had attended and their experience at Seliger.

After showing us around their small but cozy compound – there were three tents (one for boys, one for girls, one dedicated as a pantry), a shower, a large wooden picnic table, and the fireplace – the students invited us to sit down for tea and some food: berries, bread, salads, and cheese – a veritable dacha feast! After chatting with them about their experience and the running of the place, we sat and took advantage of the companionable moment to put some of our questions to them about the gender politics – was it true that weddings took place at Seliger? Oh, yes, Anton assured us earnestly, some couples had gotten married that past week. It was a wonderful opportunity for young couples, he explained; after registering the union at the ZAGS (civil registration office), they could come back to the camp to be congratulated by four thousand people and go out on the lake in a boat to celebrate! The four young women appeared a little less sanguine. Yulia, a woman in her thirties who was attending Seliger both as a participant and as a teacher, signaled her disapproval, adding archly that some of these couples had met and decided to marry on the basis of just a week's acquaintance!

Unexpectedly for us all, our irony dissipated in the course of our visit and we left the camp impressed. The provocative pronatalist elements were very much on the periphery and other impressions overtook us instead. The students met us with warmth and solicitousness, and they spoke with enthusiasm about their activities – the sports, the music, the pleasures of camping, as well as the workshops and lectures they had attended. It was impossible not to be affected. Our mood, however, was soon to shift. Before setting off for home, we decided to pay a visit to the local monastery, a short walk from the camp. The Nilova Pustyn monastery is a celebrated historic Tver' landmark. During the Soviet era the dusty, crumbling, prerevolutionary relic was a popular site of secular tourism. In the post-Soviet period, like all church-owned sites it has acquired new wealth, status, and ideological charge. We were aware of this, of course, but we were unprepared for what we found there. "Woman!" barked the burly, camouflage-clad security guard posted at the gate. "Read that sign!" We realized as we stepped back and looked around us that there was a neotraditional dress code: women (and men wearing shorts) were required to cover up in order to enter the monastery, to don apron-like garments. Disgusted, Valentina and Maria turned away and we walked back to the car.

SHIFTING GENDER REGIMES AND HISTORICAL CONTEXTS

In order to make sense of these sexualized gendered performances – and my colleagues' complex reactions (from their well-honed satirical responses at Seliger to their disgust at the monastery) we need to step back a bit to consider the context. Their ire was not prompted solely by a dress code, or by the disrespectful and aggressive tone of the guard (although this certainly contributed). It was what the interaction signaled that irritated them: the status of the Russian Orthodox Church and its influence on politics in the Putin era. They objected both to the "neotraditionalist paradigm of family and gender politics" (Zhurzhenko 2008; cited in Rivkin-Fish 2010, 711) it has advocated and which has become institutionalized in the Putin era, and to the church's cynical involvement in politics.[11] But what of the history that led to this?

Gender equality – specifically, the elimination of forms of domestic slavery for women and their elevation into the workforce – was a key legitimacy claim of the Soviet Union. Initiated by the Bolsheviks and sustained – unevenly – during the entire Soviet period, women enjoyed substantial rights: full suffrage, political representation, the right to abortion on demand, and access to education and professions (Khasbulatova 1994; Aivazova 1998; Edmondson 1984). However, official proclamations of gender equality were undercut by persistent traditional gender arrangements and naturalized presumptions about women's roles. This was due in part to the backlash they engendered; Bolshevik egalitarian policies undermined church-sanctioned patriarchal family relations and were highly controversial (Goldman 1991). Since the 1930s, when Stalin proclaimed the "woman question" to be resolved, women were constituted as nurturers, mothers, and homemakers. While Soviet power sought to reformulate gender divisions by encouraging women workers to pursue male-dominated professions (recall Soviet posters portraying women tractor drivers and laborers), they did not encourage men to move into traditionally feminine areas of work. Women remained occupationally concentrated in the "caring" professions (health, social, and educational services) and retained most domestic responsibilities as well. Moreover, Soviet state policy was pronatalist.

Michele Rivkin-Fish has examined the complex and contradictory contours of Soviet pronatalism. Stimulated by concerns about a "demographic crisis" in the early Bolshevik period, it coexisted uneasily with socialist gender egalitarianism, waxing and waning in line with the priorities of the state. Concerns about low fertility in the 1960s–1970s reenergized "demographic crisis discourse" and led to a host of interventions: "sex role socialization" classes for high schoolers (Attwood 1990), didactic projects that instilled family values, and maternal leave policies. Significantly, there was no space for discussing sexual pleasure; indeed, the state censored discussion of sex and sexuality throughout the Soviet period (Rivkin-Fish 2003, 292).

In the postsocialist period, debates about reproduction raged as political actors throughout the former Eastern Bloc made legitimacy claims and sought to burnish their nationalist credentials (Gal and Kligman 2000). In Russia, demographic-crisis rhetoric sharply accelerated, stimulated now by the dislocations of market reform (Rivkin-Fish 2003). Ignoring long-term trends, Russian nationalists and Communists, together with Russian Orthodox Church representatives, attributed low fertility to market reforms. They decried the destruction of the nation's "gene pool" and issued ominous warnings about the death of the nation. They were alarmed by the liberalization of sexual discourse as well. These conservative actors (politicians and parliamentarians) launched public-morality debates that invoked the erosion of values and the crisis of the family (Chandler 2013, 75), making incendiary claims against Western organizations for purportedly contributing to these processes. For example, in 1996 a UN-sponsored sex-education program for grade schoolers was canceled, following a conservative-led campaign to cast it as a program that would open Russia's door to "Western cultural evils" – including homosexuality, governmental failures, and depopulation (Rivkin-Fish 1999, 806).

This, then, was the stage Putin stepped onto. As with the other areas examined in this book, the Putin administration cannily took on this complex cultural material, co-opted some of these nationalist/Communist demands, and harnessed them to forge something distinctive: a "New Russian Patriotism" rebranding of these decades-old discourses. Here, too, the decade of the nineties was discursively mobilized – this time to signal a period of gendered humiliation (depicting the fall of the USSR as the fall of Soviet manhood, connected to the much-discussed "crisis of masculinity"; likening international interventions to the rape and pillage of the Motherland; attributing the "crisis of the family" and demographic ills to the market reforms of the 1990s and a malign West).

Beginning in 2006, the Putin administration undertook a series of high-profile social-policy initiatives, including the extension of benefits ("maternity capital") to mothers of two or more children.[12] These were accompanied by splashy PR campaigns and the launching of new "pronatalist technologies." The Kremlin announced that 2008 was to be the Year of the Family, and a new nationalist holiday was instituted – the Day of Family, Love, and Fidelity (Johnson and Saarinen 2013, 549). Reflecting the contradictory blend we have seen elsewhere, these campaigns melded Soviet-era techniques with reality TV elements. For example, in 2007 the governor of Ulianovsk announced the competition "Give Birth to a Patriot on Day of Russia [Den' Rossii]," pledging the prize of a jeep to women who gave birth on this national holiday. In 2009 President Medvedev revived the Soviet tradition of granting medals for motherhood – the "Order of Parental Glory" (awarded to the parents of four or more children).

These federal actions were reflected at the regional level as well. Enthusiastically fulfilling the demands of the "power vertical,"[13] Tver' governor Dmitry Zelenin declared 2008 the Year of the Family for Tver' oblast; in December of the same year he organized a "Father's Forum" that propagandized and moralized the family and the woman's role as its "guardian." Local churchmen chimed in as well. At the regional administration's annual International Women's Day reception, an Orthodox priest publicly suggested that the holiday should be renamed the Day of Women Guardians of the Fatherland.[14]

In sum, pronatalism offered politicians an effective platform – a muscular, forward-looking set of Russia-first policies that diverted attention from the state itself, toward issues beyond its control and toward a malign West. These pronatalist policies – most energetically enacted in the aftermath of the 2005 mass protests against social welfare reform discussed in chapter 2 – offered a means by which Russian state actors could reposition themselves and expunge the stain of association with neoliberal policies (Chandler 2013). In so doing, these actors have drawn closer to the positions of the Russian Orthodox Church. Indeed, the relationship between church and state became extremely tight-knit during the mid-2000s. In 2011 the media reported the Kremlin's chief ideologist (and "author" of the Nashi project) Vladislav Surkov's claim that Putin had been sent by God. Meanwhile, Patriarch Kirill, head of the Russian Orthodox Church, described the twelve years of Putin's rule as "a miracle of God." These cynical moves infuriated liberal observers like my colleagues, which helps to account for their disgust outside the monastery.

Indeed, though I did not realize it at the time, the Seliger camp's location spoke to this symbiosis of church and state. I subsequently learned that Seliger 2009 was jointly hosted by the governor of Tver' oblast and the church; the camp took place on church-owned land, belonging to the Nilova Pustyn monastery. Back in Tver', some of the students told us that young girls from the Seliger camp were required to go and clean the monastery (objecting to this form of gendered subservience, Valentina muttered, "What's the matter, can't the priests [*batiushki,* literally fathers] do their own dishes?").

This revamped and reenergized pronatalism coincided with the creation of a sexualized "cult" of Putin. In contradistinction to the flabby, flaccid Yeltsin, Putin's "brand" was that of a firm and resolute leader, a "real man" (Borenstein 2008, 227), uniquely able to restore Russia to its position as global leader. Russian gender studies scholars Tat'iana Riabova and Oleg Riabov (2010, 55) trace the crafting of Putin's masculine image and how it morphed during the course of his presidential career, from a Western-type manager (sober, rational, practical) in his first term, to a "father tsar" (a man who defends his subjects both from the West's intrigues and from corrupt officials), to a "*muzhik,*" a macho "he-man," in the early-to-mid-2000s. Indeed, in the mid-2000s the Putin administration made good use of the media to broadcast hypermasculine images that portrayed a bare-chested, steely-eyed Putin undertaking physically challenging and risky pursuits – engaging in judo, bearing guns, even hunting tigers (Goscilo 2013b). Putin became the "ultimate celebrity" (6) as well, sharing the stage with Russian and foreign performers at televised gala events. The sexualized Putin cult and the performances I have discussed restore the image of the leader as "father of the nation," adding male sexuality in an additional twist (Mikhailova 2012, 67; see also Goscilo 2013b, 8), and reinforcing the sexual contract that its pronatalist policies advance. Ironically, given conservative anxieties about sexual discourse and materialism, the leadership of the Russian Orthodox Church is on board with this, participating in elements of the Putin administration's glamorous "show" (Menzel 2008).[15]

Clearly there is much that is troubling here. Young girls are encouraged to demonstrate patriotism via procreative heterosexuality and displays of erotic attachment to the leader, in a way that is disturbingly reminiscent of fascist political identification (Gal and Kligman 2000, 22). Indeed, some commentators take these gender performances and the hypermasculinity of the Putin brand as further evidence of Putin's authoritarianism, as I have noted. But there is more going on. To leave the analysis at the point of authoritarianism suggests a more coherent, directed, intentional process of sociopolitical engineering, and a more unambiguous reception on the part of society, than have been happening. Distinctive from Soviet-era pronatalism, this neotraditionalist pronatalist expression and the eroticized expressions of devotion I have presented take place in a commodified field where sexual discourse proliferates; further, they consist of commodified forms that engage multiple actors (c.f. Goscilo 2013a).

THE COMMODIFICATION OF SEXUAL DISCOURSE:
POSTFEMINIST RECALIBRATIONS

As we can see, these sexualized patriotic performances do not emanate solely from the state. There are ambiguities around all of the artifacts and performances I have discussed. The Shapovalova fashion line was a commercial Nashi spin-off project; while it got a lot of press, it was merely tolerated, not endorsed, by the Nashi leadership (Lassila 2012).

No organization claimed responsibility for the MGU calendar. There are multiple authors and multiple interpretations at stake, and this cannot be reduced to authoritarian politics.

Illustrative of the fusion of entertainment and politics and the centrality of spectacle in the Putin era (Goscilo and Strukov 2011b, 2), the energetic commercial media picks up and amplifies these stories, which are consumed eagerly by the (sometimes scandalized) public. Further, these stories exist in a mediascape that is supersaturated with sexualized images. The Russian mediascape – no less than the Italian, North American, and British ones – is suffused with globally circulating popular-culture images, and shares the same distinctive sexualized depictions of postfeminist media culture (Salmenniemi and Adamson 2015). Like Putiniana (elements of the commodified "Putin cult") more broadly, these products are "grotesquely varied" (Cassiday and Johnson 2010, 684), and they include postfeminist images of sexualized female empowerment as well as objectification. As Salmenniemi and Adamson (2015) define it, drawing on Rosalind Gill (2007), postfeminism is a contradictory and highly unstable discourse that includes the following characteristics: "a focus upon choice, individualism and empowerment; the crucial role of a 'makeover' paradigm; the celebration of a 'natural' sexual difference; a sexualisation of culture; and an emphasis on consumerism and the commodification of difference" (Salmenniemi and Adamson 2015, 89). It adapts as it intersects with other cultural logics – in these authors' analysis, with the Soviet-era trope of labor.[16] Indeed, in the era of petroleum wealth and glamour, the media, glossy magazines, and TV are full of images of young women, insatiably consuming and pursuing an exhausting set of sexualized strategies as they labor to improve themselves. Women consume them eagerly, as the robust market for magazines such as *Cosmopolitan* and *Elle*, reality TV shows documenting the lives of the rich and famous (*Rublevski Wives*), and self-help magazines attests (Ratilainen 2012; Salmenniemi 2012b).

In this milieu, it is extremely difficult to identify political intent; the complicated relationship between *vlast'* (the state), political technologists, cultural producers, and consumers makes for a profound ambiguity. Indeed, some of the authors of sexualized Putiniana have been propelled mainly by the profit motive, enlisting "Putin" as brand. Consider the 2002 pop song "A Man like Putin," by the girl band Singing Together

(*"I want a man like Putin, who's full of strength / I want a man like Putin, who doesn't drink / I want a man like Putin, who won't make me sad"*). The song, penned by Alexander Yelin, topped the music charts and became an unofficial theme song at Putin rallies, yet its author's intentions were highly ambiguous.[17] The reactions of my Russian acquaintances and friends prompted me to realize the diversity of responses to these eroticized political campaigns. While these campaigns certainly have plenty of domestic critics, including Valentina and her colleagues,[18] I found that many people were inclined to regard them with a shrug, or even with appreciative humor. The use of sexuality and sexism is not limited to pro-Kremlin groups; as Valerie Sperling (2012, 2014) notes, it is a tactic widely adopted by political actors from the National Bolshevik Party to liberal oppositional groups. At the same time, the sexualized Putin "cult" has had surprising participants. Liberal oppositional politician Irina Khakamada (one of the few women in politics during the nineties, a Yeltsin protégé, and a presidential candidate in 2004) is a good case in point. Although no fan of the Putin administration – she ran against Putin in the 2004 campaign and quit politics in 2008, objecting to the status quo of the Putin era and the impossibility of accomplishing anything in Russian politics – she participated enthusiastically in a 2008 radio talk show discussion of Putin's sex appeal.

I have long collected and pondered these performances, the strangest of which was perhaps the Anna Chapman case. Chapman, a twenty-eight-year-old social media and real estate entrepreneur living in New York, was deported in 2010 on suspicion of working for the Russian Federation's external intelligence agency. As I followed the case of this unlikely spy, I learned that the affair was not denied by the Russian authorities, but rather celebrated – and sexualized. Upon repatriation, Chapman received a great deal of attention from the Kremlin and the Russian media (which dubbed her "Agent 90–60–90" to signal her perfect figure, in centimeters). Chapman received state honors and was appointed to the leadership of the state-run youth organization Molodaia Gvardiia (the youth wing of the party of power, Edinaiia Rossiia). Moreover, she was granted a personal audience with Putin where – according to Putin's own media-circulated claim – she sang nostalgic Soviet songs with him, including "From Where the Motherland Begins," a 1960s-era song beloved by Soviet intelligence officers.[19]

It got stranger still. In November 2010, a scantily clad Chapman appeared on the cover of the glossy Russian men's magazine *Maxim*, wearing lingerie and bearing a handgun. The article claimed that "Anna has done more to arouse patriotism in Russians than our football team and the Bulava missile put together." Entitled "International Woman of Mystery," the six-page article (studded with seminude photographs) is a spectacular artifact of nostalgic Cold War cultural production that recalls James Bond and Austin Powers simultaneously. Both the product of the commercialization of sexual discourse and its parody (c.f. Heller 2007, 206), Chapman's performance delivers satire and nostalgia simultaneously.[20]

In this dizzy commodified realm there is an unstable boundary between satire and sincerity at the moments of these images' production and reception, as the Chapman case most clearly reveals. Indeed, as Tatiana Mikhailova (2012, 67) has pointed out, in their racy poses, girl patriots like Chapman and the erotic calendar–producing Moscow State University students drew on an existing satiric repertoire, established in cultural forms such as the song we listened to en route to Seliger (the act of offering oneself up sexually to Putin had already been satirized).

But there was another angle to this. The more I pondered the case, the more it seemed that Anna Chapman's performance – as represented in these photo shoots – expressed a form of erotic patriotic attachment that was also a retort – a "geopolitical performance" (Heller 2007) that represented an intentional stiob-like nose-thumbing at the United States, from which she had been deported, at the liberal democratic (hypocritical) pieties that the United States and the West more broadly are currently taken to represent, and at the figure of the "feminist" (stern, sexless, and humorless).[21] The more I contemplated it, the more it seemed to me that it sought to incite a (particular, presumed) Western feminist response.[22]

Indeed, the figure of the liberal scold (earnest, humorless, and self-righteous) was a frequent target of Nashi materials between 2005 and 2011. One example that stands out is a Nashi spoof of a 2010 *New York Times* online interactive feature that invited Russian citizens to post videos discussing social problems. While the *Times* site featured videos documenting serious abuses of power or the negligence of officials, the

Nashi site (entitled "Help Us, America") consisted of a series of faux-earnest posts from individuals who parodied liberal subjects, identities, and sexual politics. For example, one male subject complained of discriminatory treatment because he wore a skirt; another demanded rights for transsexuals.[23] Via these crude caricatures, the "Help Us, America" campaign pilloried the "narcissistic, self-indulging" liberal subject who is compelled to engage in these forms of self-expression (Klingseis 2011, 111); in so doing, it also incited the liberal response it wished to parody – the liberal (feminist?) viewer who would spring to that subject's defense and earnestly insist on his or her right to so engage.

Building on this example, it appears to me that Nashi's use of young women's bodies was a provocation that deliberately sought to flout liberal norms and pieties (Heller 2007) as they are currently construed in much Russian popular discourse, in a context where "liberalism" and "liberals" are widely disparaged (I am thinking here of "political correctness" as it is popularly understood in Russia, to signal US hypocrisy and double standards,[24] or the popular television comedian and satirist Mikhail Zadornov and his anti-American/anti-Western shtick).[25]

There is no question that Nashi undertook deliberate provocations. Between 2005 and 2011 the organization at times went aggressively on the attack, leading homophobic campaigns and making inflammatory statements against LGBT rights. Members of the research team reported instances where komissars spoke out about the "threat" posed by LGBT values, and Nashi's mass campaigns displaced LGBT-rights marches. This is to say that once again, Nashi was being purposely offensive in its assertions; here, as we have seen in earlier instances, it was deliberately spurning and ridiculing liberal democratic norms, and it thrived on the liberal outrage it generated.

This backlash against feminism and liberal gender politics became ever more explicit during the course of our project. It came to the fore during the 2011–2012 Pussy Riot affair, when the activists' "punk prayer" actions were lambasted as "demonic jerking" and feminism was cast as an obscene or satanic practice. Members of Pussy Riot were celebrated in the West as feminists and LGBT rights crusaders, but they met with a highly ambivalent reaction in Russia, even among liberals and feminists.[26] Objecting to draft legislation prohibiting gender discrimination under discussion in the federal Duma during the spring of 2012, Russian Orthodox Church activists sprang into energetic online agitation. One site referred to the term "gender" as an "antifamily technology" which would lead to acts of "terror" against the traditional family. Here, in yet another morphing of "global war on terror" discourse, feminism is configured as a threat to Russia's national security (c.f. Riabova and Riabov 2013).[27] Another Orthodox site referred to gender as a "loophole for sodomites." There have also been sustained attacks on LGBT rights, climaxing in a series of anti-gay legislative measures during 2013 that banned the "propaganda of nontraditional sexual relations to minors." These measures represent a retort to "Europe," or "the West," and to the liberal gender regime they have come to represent. Indeed, as Brian Baer (2009, 6) puts it, in Russia, Western-style homosexuality, or the "global gay," has become a convenient symbol of Western cultural imperialism, involving the encroachment of Western values (over sexuality, nonreproductive sex and consumerism) and Western political concepts (tolerance, diversity and civil rights)" (see also Rivkin-Fish and Hartblay 2014). This sense of civilizational clash has escalated in recent years, as exemplified by a new term which has emerged in popular discourse: "*Geiropa*" (Gayropa). The term, which associates Europe with gay rights, is intended to signal European degeneracy and is often combined with allegations branding Europe as "sexually deviant" (Riabov and Riabova 2014a, 2; see also Riabova and Riabov 2013, 32).

I contend that Putin-era sexualized patriotic performances talk back not only to the decade of the 1990s and the humiliations and unwelcome international interventions it entailed, but to the disciplining reach of global liberal norms and global governance that continued in the 2000s as well.[28] Gender mainstreaming and gender equality are an integral part of EU membership requirements; between 2004 and 2013 their reach expanded, as many Eastern European countries joined the EU and signed on to these norms as part of their accession campaigns (Gradskova 2014). In short, feminist principles and values have become associated with a broad liberal cultural project at which most Russians – not just state officials, churchmen, and political technologists – chafe. I suggest that we can see Putin-era sexualized patriotic performances as propelled in part by the desire to confound the Western gaze, or "judging western eye" (Greenberg 2010, 44). These campaigns direct themselves not only to foreign liberals, but to despised domestic constituencies as well – the liberal-oriented urban professionals, or "creative classes," who in recent years have expressed opposition to the Putin administration (Gapova 2011).[29] Indeed, the 2011–2014 period saw an escalation of these logics. Riabov and Riabova (2014, 7) note that during the spring of 2014 some critical commentators recast the wave of pro-EU integration demonstrations known as "Euromaidan" into "Geiromaidan," a term suggesting "Gay Europe demonstrating at the Maidan." At this time of heightened tension, nationalist commentators and Putin administration officials found an effective way of signaling the menace of Western encroachment and casting those who beckoned it forth as "traitors."

This then is the performative context within which these campaigns arise. The patriotic-erotic blend that is offered to young people exemplifies the transformations that take place as globally circulating postfeminist discourse hits the ground – here, as it is seized upon by the political technologists who serve the state (Salmenniemi and Adamson 2015). This blend carries a particular inflection – it articulates here with aggressive nationalist patriotism, but also with the energy of stiob and with the mischievous desire to confound the Western gaze. From this perspective, the outraged liberal democratic (feminist) response – such as my own – is part of the performance itself (c.f. Heller 2007). As I viewed these sexualized patriotic performances, I felt as though I were being baited.

FEMINIST TACTICS, FEMINIST
CRITIQUES: VALENTINA'S VIEWS

Valentina has been a source of perceptive commentary for me about these gendered shifts and this complicated terrain. In conversation in June 2007, she told me wryly that "gender is already a dissident term." By this she meant that the term "gender" (in Russian, *gender* as well) – which here signaled a commitment to gender equality and a stance against discrimination on the basis of sex in line with international norms and legislation, and which had been incomprehensible to state officials during the 1990s – had now emerged as the object of very conscious backlash.

During the 1990s she, like other Russian feminist activists, had been engaged in a project to educate state officials (as well as other people) about the liberal feminist concept of gender and its importance to policy, and about international norms as well. It was an uphill struggle, to be sure. One of the most intriguing phenomena of the postsocialist period (for Western feminist observers like myself) has been the deep-seated hostility that both men and women express toward feminist formulations (Funk and Mueller 1993). Part of the distancing from the Soviet Union involved a rejection of its gender regime – in this case, the state-mandated, quota-enforced "egalitarianism" that most women experienced as an unwelcome (and "unnatural") form of social engineering. In the postsocialist era, women and men were eager to explore their "natural" differences as a means of rejecting the "equality" purportedly enforced by the Soviet state – via consumption and the freedom to opt out of the labor market. They welcomed the proliferation of sexual discourse as well. As Katharina Klingseis (2011, 90) puts it, officially endorsed and ethically required "modesty" coexisted and competed with a "yearning for eroticized 'flamboyance'" during the Soviet period; in the postsocialist period this was granted full expression. Thus the startling prominence of sexualized images of women – images of naked women posted in workplaces, or displayed on plastic shopping bags – which alarmed Western feminist visitors (often forgetful of the extent to which these same images pervade public space in the United States and Western Europe as well) failed to shock at home. Instead, they were welcomed as liberating instances of self-expression. Since people widely accepted Soviet-era state declarations that women had been granted "equality" and were protected from discrimination, the gender-equality framing made little sense, and a "feminist" was popularly understood (and discussed in the press) in the most derogatory and stereotypical of terms. Meanwhile, "feminism" as expressed by Western foreigners was popularly taken to be an overcorrection; Russian people had no knowledge of the 1950s social relations that prompted the second-wave women's movement and viewed Western feminist concerns about equal pay, equal treatment, and sexual harassment as somewhat absurd.

    Despite this skeptical climate, Russian feminist scholars and activists made modest inroads in the 1990s, stimulated by the foreign foundations, NGOs, and colleagues with whom they entered into productive dialogue. Scholar-activists like Valentina founded the first gender studies centers within universities (Temkina and Zdravomyslova 2003). These scholars' services were required by the state, to track and monitor gender patterns of employment and other factors as mandated by the international treaties to which Russia was signatory. By the 2000s, it was rather different. In the Putin era, the term "gender," Valentina told me, together with human rights, was no longer considered relevant (*aktualnyi*); Russian feminists' modest gains of the nineties in institution building and political recognition were being systematically dismantled and state officials (following orders from above) were vociferously rejecting this liberal democratic framing. Indeed, alarmingly, Russian politicians and bureaucrats now regarded talk about gender equality (again) as something alien, something "other," something "dissident," as she put it.[30]

One of the most striking pieces of evidence of this pushback against international norms that Valentina shared with me was a 2005 report documenting Tver' region's official response to CEDAW, the UN Convention on the Elimination of All Forms of Discrimination against Women.[31] It had fallen into her hands via an acquaintance working in the regional administration; this woman (who had formerly attended Valentina's feminist-oriented group, Zhenskii Svet) was horrified when it landed on her desk and picked up the phone to call Valentina immediately. The report, authored by an anonymous "expert," used the occasion of a recent meeting with visiting Swedish women to point to substantial cultural differences between Russia and the rest of Europe. The document stated that whereas in Europe (Sweden) the trend is for women to leave the family to have careers, in Tver', as in Russia as a whole, "a new direction dominates: the defense of the family, maternity, and childhood, not gender equality."[32] The document goes on: "Women-leaders of Russia today support the saving of the classical model of the family, where the woman plays the role of guardian [*khranitel*] of the family, and the man is her defender." The document concludes, rather contradictorily, "The [CEDAW] convention is observed [*sobliudaetsia*]. However, it doesn't fit the mentality of the country. Our ideal today is the classic large [*mnogodetnaia*] family, which is supported by the Russian Orthodox Church." Interestingly (and unusually), this document does favorably invoke Bolshevik-era policies ("Women in Russia have had legal equality since the Great October Revolution, and are guaranteed these rights by the RF Constitution") at the same time that it dismisses the liberal democratic framing of gender equality.

Valentina was troubled by the new antiliberal and antifeminist discourses that circulated within the university. She told me of a conversation she had recently had with a couple of her students, wherein they credulously reported media-circulating claims that "feminism" was a foreign import, brought to Russia to undermine the nation. "It all builds on the image of the enemy," she said. During the same research trip, she told me about the controversial jeep-pledging "Give Birth to a Patriot on Day of Russia" competition. "They tell women, 'Give birth, give birth,' but there's absolutely no support!" she said bitterly.

She was eloquent about the plight of contemporary Russian youth. Unlike her own generation, or those who came of age during the late Soviet period, she felt that young people today have extensive freedoms. Via the media, the internet, and consumer culture, they encounter diverse gender scripts and repertoires and have avenues for self-expression. However, these same freedoms signal constraints as well. As she put it to me in a conversation in 2007, "If during Soviet times there was pressure to be a worker-mother, now the pressure is to be a sex object and successful businesswoman. And at the same time, this traditional, Orthodox message is put out. These are children of the postfeminist generation. They have de jure rights, nothing to fight for, but at the same time the old stereotypes are recycled."

There was all the more need for her gender studies classes now, as young people encountered this confusing terrain, Valentina told me. Indeed, there was an increased student demand for them. However, administrators resisted and wanted them cut back instead.

Valentina's words resonated with me. I confess to finding the era of petroleum wealth and *glamur* quite oppressive. In this environment, the popular media proclaims that a girl's best asset is her body and its enhancement her surest investment. My well-meaning old friend Gosha (a relatively affluent man in his forties who lived in Moscow) told me musingly that if a woman of a certain age (i.e., over thirty) did not use Botox, it was presumed it was because she could not afford to. Meanwhile, chick lit, such as the books by popular author Oksana Robski, announces that social mobility is guaranteed through a man. Reality TV shows call upon provincial girls to make themselves over to win the attention – and protection – of an oligarch (Ratilainen 2012). At the same time, disparaging images of provincial girls on the make circulate too, as the young women who undertake these strategies are discussed, scolded, and dissected in the media.[33]

The case of "Sveta from Ivanovo" stands out. Sveta Kuritsina was a nineteen-year-old activist of the pro-Kremlin Nashi offshoot project Stal' (Steel) who achieved national prominence in 2012 when a journalist's video interview of her went viral. Sveta, in the Moscow subway on her way to a campaign run by Stal', spoke poorly, in phrases that recalled the uneducated reverence of the masses for Stalin (since the pro-Putin party United Russia came to power, she gasped worshipfully, "We started dressing more better" [*my stali bolee luchshe odevat'sia*] and "the amount of land increased" [*stalo bol'she zemel'*]. Sveta was initially reviled in the liberal media by intellectuals who took her as confirmation of the dire outcomes of the state's youth policies, but her story had a classic "oil-and-gas glamour" ending: she attained celebrity status when she was subsequently offered her own talk show by federal channel NTV.

The Sveta from Ivanova case speaks to the aching economic disparities young people confront. Like US working-class pop-cultural antiheroes (such as Honey Boo Boo), Sveta's case gave rise to endless rounds of moralizing discussions and debates – a mortifying set of representations my provincial informants must have been aware of. In a way that has made me conscious of another aspect of my entanglement in state-run youth projects, I have found myself feeling every inch the caricatured stern, humorless "feminist" as I have navigated this terrain, baited equally by the sexualized excesses of *glamur* and by its class-based forms of gendered disparagement. My sympathies have shifted and I have pondered how in this environment, it is small wonder that young provincial women are drawn to state-run youth organizations and find events like Seliger – with its comradely campfires, mass calisthenics, and gender-neutral T-shirts – appealing.

Valentina's own work (teaching and scholarship) has long sought to disrupt gender stereotypes – specifically the "women must" (*zhenshchina dolzhna*) trope that she believes is oppressive for both women and men. Through her teaching and civic activism she has consistently sought to call out these stereotypes. This work has had a geopolitical angle too, insofar as it implicitly undermines the neotraditionalist agenda. Since her graduate training during the 1980s, she has been engaged in a research agenda of exploding dichotomies, one that insists that feminism is not an exclusively Western-emanating ideology, but something with a long and contested history in Russia (her scholarship has examined the historic connections between first- and second-wave feminist activists in Europe and the United States, as well as the history of feminism, including the work of Bolshevik feminist Aleksandra Kollontai). Since feminism was viewed as a "bourgeois deviation" during the Soviet period, and as an unwelcome "foreign" ideology in the post-Soviet period, these studies have marked her as a maverick, subject to castigation.

Valentina's own "feminist tactic" is to consistently challenge xenophobic or discriminatory (sexist, anti-Semitic, and also anti-Western or anti-US) statements, by poking, disrupting, or exposing them. She fulfills this mission in her self-presentation as well, undertaking her own PR when she has the opportunity. During any encounter with journalists she takes pains to upset stereotypes of feminists as man-hating women, emphasizing her own harmonious family (she is married with two grown sons). Her tactics have changed in the years I have known her. In 2007 she told me she had a different idea about "glamour" and did not oppose it as she once used to. Now in her early sixties, she takes pleasure in defying local notions of age-appropriate conduct by dressing to the nines in Euro elegant style; via the glamour magazines she collects and distributes, she coaches her young women students about fashion as well, encouraging them to see it as an empowering strategy that is not incompatible with intellectual life and self-realization. (Her Center for Gender Studies colleagues celebrated her fifty-fifth birthday with a playful tribute, a publication entitled "Sui Generis" that celebrated not only her intellectual and activist contributions to the city, but her style and love of fashion as well. It was subtitled "Tver' Glamour, or Style By Valentina," and described her apartment as "the Uspensky Museum: price of admission, a good bottle of French wine!")

Her feminist tactics also include elements of a mischievous repertoire. Invited to give a lecture at Seliger 2010, she jokingly proposed a training session entitled "Gender Equality Is Profitable for Russia" – in keeping with the commodification of talent framing. Though humorous, it had a serious intent. It would offer a different model to the current demographic policies, she said: "If you want to raise the birthrate and strengthen families, there's an alternative approach – to educate young men and women about ideas of gender equality." Here, she meant to signal her commitment to gender egalitarianism in child rearing, where fathers as well as mothers were understood to have an important role.

UNSETTLING STEREOTYPES, PONDERING POWER:
INSIGHTS FROM A SECOND-GENERATION COLLABORATION

One afternoon in June 2008 I made my way to the university to join Valentina, Dmitry, and members of the research team for a results-sharing session. As usual, we were in room 222, the room bequeathed to the center a few years back for its library. The bookshelves were crammed with Russian, English, and German texts – testimony not only to Valentina's own prodigious output, but to twenty years of international feminist collaboration as well (many of the foreign-language books had been purchased with international grants or donated by feminist agencies or visiting scholars, among them several anthropologists). Valentina referred to the room as the center's "oasis." She meant that the room was a safe space for real intellectual activity (endangered in these corporatized times), from which she and her students could not – for now – be kicked out. It was the one place where they could engage in free discussion, a site of "resistance from within," as she put it.

The room bore testimony to her playful pedagogical tactics as well as her intellectual connections and erudition. Posted on the sliding door of one of the bookcases was a startling photograph of a youthful Vladimir Putin holding an infant child (his daughter?). As with other artifacts of the commercialized Putin "cult," it was unclear what motivated the producers to release this piece of Putiniana (Cassiday and Johnson 2010). But the intent of its commentary-free display in this room was clear: it signaled a playful disruption of the militarized and hypermasculinized image his spin doctors have fostered. Indeed, it was clear Putin had been deployed as a bit player in one of Valentina's gender-stereotype-challenging projects, the art exhibition "Men with Children in Their

Arms, Not Weapons." The exhibition, which Valentina initiated in the late nineties, was ongoing, and she enlisted many of her students to gather and contribute photographs from the media, or from their own family collections.

Much of our discussion that day focused on Nashi. With Medvedev's succession to the presidency, the fate and future of youth policies were uncertain – the smooth transfer of power had been secured, hence, what further need would there be for state-run youth organizations? Indeed, in January of 2008 Nashi had been partly disbanded, and the media seethed with speculation about its future, including accounts of how it had "discredited" itself, and reported impatient statements by Kremlin insiders who (in another reformatting of the "problem of the crowd") referred to the organization as "a crowd of rowdy hooligans" (*likuiushchaia gopota*).

Leading the discussion were Yulia, Sergei, Lidiia, and Anton, four of the original research team members I had gotten to know when they were freshmen in 2005. As we discussed these shifts in state-youth policies, gender and patriotic pronatalism quickly emerged as a theme.

Yulia's research examined the attitudes of women activists toward state demographic policies. She was horrified by the rampant pronatalism – "All these 'Just give birth' [*Davaite rozhaite*] advertisements" – and was determined to explore the topic further. She explained that she had come to her research topic after reading an article in the Nashi newspaper, *Nashe vremia*. The article claimed that one in two girls has had an abortion, an extreme figure she was confident was exaggerated. Moreover, she told me, the article condemned contraception, claiming it was a US-led plot to lead to the nation's degeneration! Yulia took her studies and her profession very seriously. Objectivity mattered to her; schooled in the quantitative approach, she knew the value of a representative sample. Yet this issue touched her – she had been prompted to survey her own friends and dormmates as well.

Yulia reported more of the evidence of Nashi's pronatalist excesses she had located during her internet research: in addition to I Want Three, she had read about a Nashi campaign against thongs (ostensibly because they lead to sterility among women). "The whole internet is laughing at Nashi!" she said, commenting on how much the organization had discredited itself. "You might think that the enemy is a gay person in a thong!" she added exasperatedly, unwittingly echoing Brian Baer's (2009) analysis about the figure of the "global gay."

Debate over Nashi's pronatalism ensued – with most participants expressing strong disapproval of the "extreme and irresponsible" pronatalist elements (the love oasis, the pressure to begin family-making early) that took place at Seliger. Lidiia, who had come across similar materials in her own research on Nashi (including an article entitled "The Demographic Movement Nashi"), agreed. "Birth is a process, not an act," she said. "Why don't they put money into the provision of child care instead?" As she was the single mother of a two-year-old, Lidiia's comment carried weight. It is worth noting that her construction – like Valentina's – departed from the liberal package of citizen-state presumptions; like most people I spoke with, they had a roundly social democratic (socialist?) expectation that the state should provide support for child care. The students shared other horrors as well, including a banner they had seen in one neighborhood, Proletarian Region, which declared, "The happiness of the Tsar depends on the populousness of his people!"

What comes through in my field notes on the students' discussions is how this was all about a pondering of power. The students signaled their awareness of the state's tactics by discussing these demographic campaigns specifically as technologies. Moreover, they viewed them as absurd strategies that were based on mendacious claims (such as inaccurate abortion rates) and were inattentive to the realities of life. The students were offended simultaneously as sociologists, citizens (many of them had voted for the first time in 2008 and were newly engaged in the political process), and young men and women. The sexualization of politics offended them too, although they mostly responded to it with mirth (such as when Valentina jokingly quoted the refrain of the pop song "A Man like Putin" during one of our group discussions, prompting general laughter).

I had the chance to talk in greater depth with Yulia later one-on-one, and she told me more about the *Nashe vremia* article that had stimulated her research. "It was awful," she said. "It made me want to cry." Beyond its claims about abortion and contraception, she told me the article tried to entice young women to join the organization by claiming komissars make exemplary boyfriends! The article made an absurd comparison, she said, between a *gopnik* (a lout) and a clean-living komissar. While the komissar was flawless, the other young man was portrayed as a loser. There was another article that claimed that "girls who date *nashisty* have it good," she recalled, "while they run away from other [types of boys] and don't like them." It was such nonsense, she said. Indeed, she told me that one of her friends had just dumped her boyfriend upon discovering he was involved in Nashi!

More than most of the students I spoke with, Yulia was alive to the material contradictions of these state policies. She herself fit the profile of the archetypal provincial girl. She was from one of the rural settlements in Tver' region, and she lived in a student dorm and worked to support herself in tandem with her studies. She had been fortunate enough to get a job working as a sociologist in a small marketing center, which enabled her to use her skills. Her ambition was to enter graduate school and become a professional sociologist, maybe even, as her mentor Valentina encouraged her, to study abroad.

Yulia's research examined young women activists' views on specific policies – affordable housing (a new federal policy directed toward young couples and families), maternity capital (the controversial pronatalist program announced in 2006), and potential restrictions on abortion rights proposed by the Orthodox Church. She sought to examine the extent to which women activists' views corresponded with those of the parties they belonged to.[34] To her surprise, she discovered that her informants were as skeptical as she was.

One of the most eloquent testimonies came from a former Nashi activist. This young woman, whom Yulia wrote about in her research, recalled her negative reactions to Nashi materials she had seen, flyers depicting a young couple. "It was a scary picture," she had told Yulia.

> One child symbolized the country dying out, two children symbolized equality, and the ideal was three children, with bright sunshine and so on. I mean, on the one hand it is certainly good, so simple, to have a kid and all.... However, given our conditions of life, having children becomes a luxury. I recently heard on the Evropa Plus radio station ... one man said that having children was more expensive than maintaining a prestigious foreign car. It's kind of a male comparison [laughs], but it's true, indeed. A prestigious car is expensive but child-related costs are still higher.... Personally, I'm not ready and don't actually want to have

a baby at the age propagated by Nashi; to have three or more babies at such a young age . . . what would you do with them, then? Personally, I don't think that kind of propaganda is good for people at that age. . . . It could be a good message for the future, though.

This statement is very revealing. The radio discussion the student recalled portrays the large (*mnogodetnaia*) family as a luxury asset, equivalent to a car, a supposedly desirable accessory that proclaims political and economic capital at the same time that it represents a strategy for advancement. In drawing Yulia's attention to it and refuting the state's intended message, the student signaled her awareness that class-making processes were in motion.

Yulia ultimately elected to do her thesis research on gender equality and reproductive rights issues, based on her research and practicum at the local Department of Social Services. This brought her into contact with the official apparatus of social welfare that the state-run voluntarism-promoting campaigns I examined in the previous chapter were displacing (or officially sought to complement). The terrain she encountered and described to me was acutely gendered, yielding insight into the complex relationship between gender and the state. It is predominantly women who remain within the crumbling and underfunded areas of the public sector – social welfare and education – as teachers, doctors, nurses, and social workers. Her account backed up my own observations from earlier research (Hemment 2012b), which showed that public-sector employment (with its lower stakes and greater flexibility) serves as a niche for young women with small children, for elderly women who are near pension age, and for women who care for disabled family members. Indeed, she found that the boundary between these categories is fuzzy and that clients become employees.

As they undertook their research, members of the team reflected on their own identities and class-based opportunities as well. For her diploma research, Alisa, the "accidental activist" whom I introduced in chapter 3 (and who was an organizer at Seliger 2009), examined the influence of gender stereotypes on the career expectations of city officials. Alisa interviewed five women employees of different ranks and ages. Her commentaries on this research and these relatively privileged women (while the public sector crumbled, state administrative positions came with good salaries and benefits; in Russia such a career path is strongly dependent on family connections) reveal the extent to which this material prompted her to reflect on her own prospects.

When I interviewed her in May 2010 she told me she was "unpleasantly surprised" by her results. Going in, she had imagined she would find evidence of awareness of "progressive" European gender politics and some commitment to the principle of gender equality; on the contrary, she found that these women's consciousnesses were still "traditional and patriarchal." She explained, "These women ... are educated, smart – that is, they are on top of everything [*obladaiut vsem*] – all that's necessary to attain high-ranking positions. But in spite of that, they're ready to sit home, they are looking for husbands. So it's really a patriarchal orientation in their thinking. They used a lot of stereotypes. They said things like, 'The woman is the housewife, the man is the warrior.' That is, 'God made man, God made woman – they are different creatures, they live in different worlds.' I didn't expect to hear this. I was even a bit upset by my results."

Disconcertingly, she had found that this pattern held across generations; both the women who had grown up during the Soviet Union and the twenty-somethings who came of age in the post-Soviet period held the same views. "They spoke in absolutely identical phrases," she told me, "absolutely the same. I didn't see any difference." She gave a particularly concerning example of one young woman in her mid-twenties who was "very up-and-coming [*perskpektivnaia*]." She had won a lot of competitions, had a high rank, and looked like she was going places, but she told Alisa that her priority was to get married and have a family. "She's ready to refuse it all," Alisa told me. "That is, she won't feel like a full person until she's realized herself as a mother, as a wife. In spite of all that – I'll repeat – she's very promising, clever, and has already accomplished a lot!" Alisa was evidently quite perturbed by this – astonished that a woman who had made it would trade it all to have a family. She acknowledged, however, that these protestations should not be taken at face value. "Of course –" said Alisa.

I interjected, "She might say one thing and at once –"

"Do another," Alisa said, finishing my sentence.

Alisa's distress was inflected by her gender-studies training, which not only urged her to privilege the value of individual empowerment, but also cast a moralizing eye on "traditional" or "patriarchal" values. Her feminist response was a symbolic move to distinguish herself from her unenlightened interviewee, yet it betrayed her resentment toward her, too, as a representative of a privileged insider group whose ranks were closed to her. Fortunately, her own made-in-Seliger relationship did not threaten to disempower her in this way. Her boyfriend (whom she mentions in chapter 3) was one of the smart, talented, driven people she had encountered; far from being at odds with her self-development and studies, he elicited a similar drive in Alisa herself.

From the Participants' Point of View

But what of the gendered effects of participation in these state-run campaigns? It is important to note that while the controversial sexualized patriotic performances are prominent in the PR materials – and pumped up by a scandalized media – they were less manifest (and less relevant) on the ground. As we have seen, young people at Lake Seliger were kept busy with multiple projects – their educational program of workshops, lectures, and project design, and the leisure activities made available to them as well (sports, discos). In earlier chapters I have shown how this research reveals a complicated terrain, where young people may be highly skeptical and very sophisticated in their critiques of the workings of power and see campaigns, promotional items, and projects as authored materials (flawed, interested, etc.), yet are still sufficiently moved to participate. The same holds true here.

The young women we met that day at Seliger were propelled by diverse motivations, as were the young women described in other chapters. As we have seen, some young people like Marina and Masha were drawn to participate in Seliger by a gendered desire to "do good" and expressed "gendered compassion" (Read 2010) as a motivating force. They arrived to find voluntarism reformatted in state-run campaigns. The Technologies of Kindness session at Seliger 2009 contributed to some unexpected gendered realignments by bringing private-sector cultural expectations to voluntarism (Gal and Kligman 2000, 37–62); the new ideologies of volunteering that young people encounter encourage them to view volunteering as a professional, individual, and self-maximizing activity. This approach repels some young women, as we have seen, and a *do-*

brotekhnik (technologist of kindness) is more likely to be a young man than a young woman.

While state-run youth projects remain a male-dominated field, and while there were certainly instances of misogyny and sexism within them (Nashi founder Vasily Yakemenko was embroiled in numerous controversies regarding his conduct with young women at Seliger), they provided opportunities as well. Our research suggests that state-run youth campaigns and projects like Nashi and Seliger offered avenues for advancement and self-realization for girls, especially those living in rural areas where gender norms and expectations were rather limiting and oppressive. For girls like these, the promise of "social lift" held true to some extent. Sexualized patriotic performances notwithstanding, I suggest that in a social field dominated by the discourse of *glamur*, state-run youth projects and camps may have had particular appeal (Ratilainen 2012). Despite the beauty competitions and weddings it proclaimed, Seliger offered a model of relatively gender-neutral healthy, clean living (think bonfires, T-shirts, mass calisthenics, camping), not so very unlike the gender-egalitarian Komsomol before it. Indeed, its *lack* of glamour may have been part of its appeal. Several young women I spoke with reminisced happily about their camping experience; they loved the simplicity of it and the tight sociality it entailed. Our guide Olga who showed us around Seliger 2011 jokingly complained about the rain, the storms, and how she was "dying for a shower."

What of pronatalism? The projects that activists and participants in youth projects such as Seliger designed reveal them to be influenced by the neotraditional framings the state offers. As we have seen, many of the participants in the voluntarism session elected to do moralizing work on the family (understood to be heteronormative and procreative), premised on the notion that the family was in crisis and Russia was dying. Some projects exhibited both classist assumptions and demographic nationalism, that is, anxieties over the racial and cultural reproduction of the nation (Krause 2001; Rivkin-Fish 2005), insofar as they expressed concern about the "quality" not only of parenting, but of births and reproduction themselves – one student researcher picked up the construction "quality of reproduction" (*kachestvo rozhdaemosti'*) (Karmalskaia 2008). Many projects we encountered sought to educate (presumably marginal or lumpen) young families about how to raise children and instill family values.

Young women activists are clearly required to pay lip service to neotraditional values if they are to prosper, but they do not necessarily adhere to them. Indeed, confirming Valentina's hypothesis, our research suggests that despite the neotraditionalism they encounter, youth participants in state-run projects are shaped by feminist discourses and the liberalization of gender scripts. They do not support the erosion of abortion rights and they regard the idea of three children as patently absurd under Russian conditions, a luxury beyond their reach.

Our focus group held in July 2009 offered us the opportunity to analyze the gendered discourse among a group of activist women. Masha, Liuba, Lena, and Sveta were all former Nashi activists who had participated in the organization until it was restructured in 2008. Now students in different higher-education institutions in Tver', they had grown up – and participated in Nashi – in different cities, and were thus not acquainted with each other. When I asked them their views on what the most pressing issue facing young people was, Sveta stated firmly, "The problem of the young family." All the others appeared to agree, and a lively discussion followed. Young women are too independent, Sveta insisted; they think that they need to build a career first! Meanwhile, "young men are irresponsible and we can't rely on them," she added, invoking decades-old "crisis of masculinity" discourse.

Masha, the technologist of kindness and former Nashi activist introduced in chapters 2 and 4, was most vocal on this score and spoke most directly about her own life. Embracing the patriotic pronatalism of state policy, Masha declared her intention to have a large family: "I'd be ready to have a baby [*ia by tozhe rodila*]," she told us. "I have a plan – I want to have seven children. To give birth to five, and to adopt two. And in fact, I'd have already begun to have babies, but right now I don't have the material base." She was working on this part of the plan, Masha told us, adding that she had a steady boyfriend whom she had met at Seliger four years earlier. "It's just that – you have to take care of yourself first, like a bird builds its nest."

I met with Masha one year later in 2010. Both the substance of what she told me and the way she carried herself (her gender performance) totally defied my expectations. I had taken her to be an austere, clean-living (alcohol-abstaining, nonsmoking) adherent of the Putin project and felt slightly uncomfortable inviting her to meet with me in my hotel (which was lavish by my own standards, accustomed as I was to staying in the university hostel – my stay now was enabled by the NSF funding I had recently secured). The poised, self-assured young woman who knocked on my hotel room door, and the story she told, took me by surprise.

Masha told me that she was no longer involved in state-run youth projects and did not plan to attend Seliger 2010. Instead, she was pursuing an alternative plan for social mobility: the former dobrotekhnik was now a part-time manager at a local nightclub. Enjoying the look of astonishment on my face, she said that she had been offered the job by an old acquaintance of hers, Boris. He had called her up, she said proudly, and told her that none of the men he had tried to hire had what it took, adding that it was her organizational experience at Seliger that had impressed him.

From her account, it was clear that the work she did was part managerial, part social, and that she enjoyed it immensely. Her role, she explained, was to reach out to high-ranking clientele in the city and encourage them to come to the club (the governor and his wife had been there, she told me). Her job was to socialize with these clients, make them feel comfortable while they were there. The example she gave me defied any notion I might have started to form about the gendered or sexualized nature of this work. "There's one client," she said, "a woman in her fifties. She likes to smoke cigars and drink cognac and dance – sometimes she comes by herself, or with friends her own age but who don't want to dance, so I dance with her." She enjoyed the work, she told me, but beyond that, she was pursuing a goal: to make useful contacts who would help her establish her own social projects, the ones she had taken to Seliger.

We adjourned halfway through the interview so that she could smoke a cigarette in the lobby – she assured me, despite my protestations, that it was perfectly acceptable to smoke in the lounge of this nonsmoking hotel; she had done it before – and I asked her how she imagined herself in ten years' time. She told me that she needed to finish her medical degree, which would take another eight years. "My goal is to establish my independence," she said, using the very term that had been so contested during the focus group. She explained that she had broken up with her boyfriend. He had asked her to marry him, but she had refused, knowing it would mean a future of "washing, chores." He understood, she said, and they were still friends. She was pursuing other strategies to build her nest.

By 2011, when we last met, Masha had moved on once again. She had jettisoned the nightclub job to retrace the steps her doctor parents had taken and complete her medical degree. She told me – with a glint in her eye I am sure I did not imagine – that her ultimate professional destination was the decidedly unglamorous workplace of the psychiatric hospital. I found her trajectory revealing. Masha had picked her way through various gendered strategies for social mobility. She ended up discarding the technologies offered her by the state and happily shed her pronatalist commitments, ironically ending up with the tried and tested (if ambiguous) Soviet-era strategy for gendered empowerment: becoming a medical doctor.[35]

In the years that elapsed between our two collaborative projects, the terrain of Russia's gender politics changed considerably. I have suggested that the startling sexualized patriotic performances examined in this chapter become comprehensible if we place them in the context of a backlash against Western models and liberalism. We can view them in part as "geopolitical performances," self-conscious mocking assaults upon liberal democratic pieties as well as partial appropriations, ones that respond both to the decade of the 1990s and to the liberalizing interventions it entailed, including the ongoing project of global liberal governmentality that seeks to regulate conduct (Brown 2008).

Though orchestrated by the state, or undertaken in its name, they draw on a groundswell of support among the Russian people. They articulate both their inchoate discontents (anxieties about globalization, Western hegemony, and Russia's diminished place in the world, and concerns about the moral and physical health of the nation) and their desires. As we have seen, these performances are influenced and inflected by the ideology of *glamur* and postfeminist discourses that Russian women enthusiastically consume via pop-cultural texts and glossy magazines.

As with the other state projects I've examined, the outcomes of these campaigns are indeterminate. Via their participation in state-run youth projects, young women encounter new options and opportunities for advancement. Despite the lip service they might publicly pay to it, they do not blindly conform to the neotraditionalist agenda. Ironically, participation in these state-run campaigns may actually cause them to contest the state. Invoking a large family that young women know they can never afford (and do not necessarily desire) is a dangerous game and the outcomes are uncertain. My discussions with both research team members and other research participants reveal them to have a canny awareness of what matters: jobs, housing, and social welfare.

But what of the question we began with, the assumption that pervades so much of the Western literature that explores this topic: do these sexualized patriotic performances provide evidence of authoritarianism? The problem with seeing things this way is that it asserts a culturalist argument that fails to account for the political-economic and social processes these performances are situated within – global capital flows and the "post-Soviet commercialization of sexual discourse" (Heller 2007), and the peculiarities of what liberal oppositionists have referred to as "oil-and-gas glamour." It isolates and extricates Russia from processes that are very global and very shared.

If we shift our lens a little from the shock-and-awe quality of these startling campaigns, they begin to look a little less exotic. Beyond the hiss and fizz and rejection of Euro norms and cultural globalization, Putin-era pronatalist policies bear structural similarities to processes taking place elsewhere in Europe. There too, "the family" (heteronormative, procreative) is posited as the new site of social cohesion in the post-welfare state (Marchesi 2013; Yngvesson 2010). Looking comparatively enables us to see that these are distinctive shifts that have to do with the redrawing of the social. The contemporary resacralization of the family and propagandizing of family values has taken place at the same time as a neoliberal restructuring of social services, and marks the "moral authoritarianism" of the "moral neoliberal" regime (Muehlebach 2012). Russia's patriotic pronatalism bears traces not only of demographic nationalism (cf. Krause 2001), but also of neoliberal social and economic policies.[36] Meanwhile, the sexualized patriotic performances I have described strongly resemble postfeminist discourse globally.

A further problem is that the critique of sexualized Putiniana as evidence of authoritarianism is unreflexive; it fails to acknowledge how feminist knowledge operates as a mode of power.[37] As the formulation "neomasculinist semiauthoritarianism" (Johnson and Saarinen 2013) reveals, normative discourse links feminist principles to democracy, which implies a link between political practices, cultural competencies, and morality. Discussions that do not consciously resist these binarized modes of representation (liberal democracy versus authoritarianism) have the result of reinforcing liberal triumphalist discourses, becoming entangled in critiques of Russia as neoauthoritarian. These are problematic insofar as they are one-sided and fail to allow for points of commonality and broader trends, including the global alliances that permitted some of these illiberal policies to take shape. As Rivkin-Fish and Hartblay (2014) note, the Russian anti-gay and anti-abortion movements have been bolstered by international conservative activists, including US Christian Evangelicals.[38] I am not arguing that we should set aside "patriarchy" as an object of intellectual inquiry or political critique, or that neotraditional projects are benign; rather, I maintain that it is essential that we also examine the ways in which patriarchal projects are "deeply enmeshed with other systems of power" (Ortner 2014, 545). Our urgent task as feminists is surely to keep our eye on the global circulations and political economy we are all subject to, exploring, for example, authoritarianism's relationship to capitalism and neoliberalism and seeking ways to be good allies and achieve effective transnational feminist collaboration (Rivkin-Fish and Hartblay 2014, 108).

Finally, I have argued for the need to attend closely to the potential for play/stiob at the moment of production and reception. The sexualization of politics is very differently apprehended in Russia than it is in the United States, or in many Western European countries, as my colleagues' satirical responses reveal. It is neither taken at face value nor easily mapped onto the political field in the ways we might expect. Indeed, there is a marked instability of form.

CONCLUSION

ACCORDING TO THE COLD WAR BINARY LOGIC THAT CURRENTLY prevails in Western commentary about Russia, Putin-era state-run youth projects such as Nashi and Seliger 2009 mark the apotheosis of post-Bolshevik political culture. I have suggested that it is more profitable to consider them within a "broader political geography" (Gal and Kligman 2000, 4), that is, within the context of twenty-five years of development assistance in postsocialist states, and within global processes of neoliberal governance, welfare restructuring, and shifts in governmentality in the post-9/11 era.

Western observers who summarily dismissed state-sponsored civil-society organizations in Russia failed to acknowledge the very real problems with the civil society of NGOs brought into being by Western governments and agencies during the nineties. These critical commentaries also fail to acknowledge the depth of disenchantment many Russians experienced with the so-called transition period, an era that Western governments and international foundations helped usher in and legitimize. As has been well documented, the decade of the nineties was a period of intense economic and social dislocation. In addition to the material hardships people encountered, they grappled with a grave sense of loss in the aftermath of the Soviet Union's passing, leading in turn to disappointment and disillusionment with the promises of market democracy. Any analysis of contemporary Russian civil society must be mindful of these experiences and appreciative of the fact that this emotion is productive and capable of shaping political outcomes (Ost 2006; Oushakine 2009). Moreover, such analyses need to acknowledge the complex mutations that took place subsequently, in the post-9/11 era, and the power relations these were embedded within: civil society's militarization during the 2000s and its linkage to regime change by the United States government. Putin-era civil-society projects, exemplified by Nashi, responded to and channeled this sense of loss, indignity, and outrage.

This book has examined how during the Putin era (specifically, between 2005 and 2007), state policymakers and political technologists picked up and played with this complex cultural material, linking it to a widely shared sense of disillusion with and disappointment in liberal forms and institutions. They crafted policies and projects that responded to the needs raised by these expressions of loss. They were looking globally as they did so, drawing on an eclectic range of tools and diverse repertoires, including those of the liberal projects they had disparaged and the more statist, militarized version of civil society that took shape in the 2000s. The "revitalized" and "rebranded" patriotism manifest in the projects they crafted successfully appealed to many Russian young people.

True to the anthropological goal of "thick description," I have been interested in the multiple forces that propelled, inspired, and animated these projects. I took on the challenge of charting a representational path that neither disparaged the young people who participated in these projects, nor took their participation at face value, and which allowed for ambiguities within these projects as well.

The projects crafted by members of the "last Soviet generation" were more complex and unstable than most scholarly and media representations allow. Interpreting them is tricky; like nostalgic practices in general, they are slippery and combine complex motivations at the level of their design and enactment. I see these projects as animated by complex forms of disappointment and resentment about the processes of postsocialist change and the complex polyphonic forms of nostalgia these changes gave rise to (Cassiday and Johnson 2010; Greenberg 2014; Nadkarni and Shevchenko 2004). Further, they had uncertain effects, as we have seen. Young people claimed these spaces and experienced them as their own. There was no longer one unitary design center for these state-run projects, and authorship was opaque. Indeed, projects proliferated as youth activists spun and reformulated them with dizzying speed.

Although Nashi was undoubtedly a top-down project, the work of sophisticated political technologists, my research suggests that it did have considerable purchase on its participants. Beyond the controversial and belligerent campaigns that garnered most media attention, at the provincial level Nashi had a quite different profile and function. During 2006–2009 Nashi appeared to be a site where young people could imagine and envision their role and potential contribution to society, and position themselves as active agents vis-à-vis state authorities. Interviews with Nashi komissars revealed their passionate engagement in its stated goals; they viewed the movement (and themselves) as a force that had the capacity to cleanse Russian society of its dysfunctions – both those associated with the Soviet past and those associated with the market – and to bring about positive change. Kirill, Masha, and Igor, the three komissars I have profiled, all embraced Nashi both as a vehicle for self-improvement and as a site of ardent commitment (to the nation, to children, and to society).

Exemplifying the trends of global cultural borrowing I have discussed, Nashi was a Putin-era repackaging of the civil-society concept that proposed its own solution to the "problem" of the crowd and (youthful) bodies on streets. It illustrated most forcibly the Russian state's appropriation of democratic technologies (street control, direct action), yet, ironically, it was far weaker than its critics assumed. The portraits of Kirill, Masha, and Igor show that while Nashi may have framed activists' narratives, it was clearly not in control of them. Like many of the young people I spoke with, they engaged in the organization on a temporary basis, for career-building reasons or to pursue broader projects of self-realization; like US student volunteers (and their Soviet-era predecessors), they engaged in a complex choreography of doing good in the world and improving their own opportunities for upward mobility. Indeed, in ways that international foundations would surely approve of, many of the young people I interviewed gained skills, took what they wanted from Nashi, and moved on.

We have seen that the Putin-era youth projects Nashi and Seliger 2009 were not solely Putin's projects (or Surkov's projects, or Yakemenko's), but a more diffuse and uncertain project of governing that did not emanate exclusively from a unified state. Although in sync with state policy discussions, Seliger 2009 (like "new youth policies" more broadly) was less a "systematic platform" than a site of chaotic productions and improvisations made by middle-ranking officials and the *proektirovshiki* (project designers) they created. As we have seen, the Federal Youth Affairs Agency (Rosmolodezh) and its "project approach" spawned new agents with multiple and complex motivations (c.f Rogers 2015).

These were tiered projects that catered to different crowds. Seliger's diverse sessions – on leadership, voluntarism, and entrepreneurship, and the eroticized pro-Putin performances described in the previous chapter – were niche-marketed to different kinds of young people in recognition of the fact that the one-size-fits-all model no longer worked. We have seen as well that there was more going on within the projects than was widely assumed. Seliger 2009 was about "prevention" as much as it was about producing loyal patriots – it was oriented toward provincial youth, who lacked connections and who were anxious about their future prospects and uncertain of the benefits formal education provided. From this perspective, it appears to have been a "weak state" technique rather than a tool of authoritarianism.

The portraits I have drawn of youth participants at Seliger 2009 reveal that they did not take the state's pledges at face value. But they did not completely refuse them, either. As the cases of Alisa and Igor illustrate, young people engaged selectively in Seliger 2009, reaping unexpected rewards. The "horizontal" connections Alisa encountered reenergized her; her story shows that the innovation incubator Seliger did not displace, but rather reformulated, the tight forms of intimate *obshchenie* between students (c.f. Matza 2009). These state-run projects intersected with and stimulated other forms of sociality – channels of student governance and networks of acquaintance. Indeed, they intersected with our research team as well, the cell of active and engaged students who gathered around Valentina and her colleagues, nourishing our alternative educational project on occasion.

Across the board, we have seen evidence of these projects' uncertain effects. Young people's participation in these state projects didn't lead any one particular way; indeed, in some cases it had what the Russian authorities would view as adverse effects, encouraging young people to be more critical of the state than slavishly devoted to it. Neither was our collaborative research project a one-way street; students' participation in it played out in similarly unpredictable ways, as we have seen. In detailing the ways the two projects rubbed up against each other and the entanglements between them, I have sought to emphasize this complex and multidirectional flow and movement.

Our collaborative research project brought into view not only difference, but also commonality. It is not just in Russia that young people are targeted; as a great deal of recent anthropological scholarship attests, "youth" has emerged as a charged category in many "neoliberal nation states in difficulty" (Comaroff and Comaroff 2006). In the United States and Western Europe as well, civil-society discourse is implicated in shifting disciplinary tactics. Here too, youth empowerment projects unfold as welfare states unravel, and they intersect with discussions about national sovereignty and security. Throughout this project, I have been struck not by what divides Russia from Europe and the United States but by what they have in common: a shared set of concerns and anxieties about politics, citizenship, and social responsibility in times of globalizing neoliberalism. Our project, with its long duration and rhythms of departure and return, gave me ample space to ponder this. As I have shared the results of this research with my US students I have realized the extent of its resonance with many of their concerns. They too are worried about their own precarity, the value (and cost) of their education and its capacity to serve them; they are sick of "lies" and deception and troubled by the tight relations between political and economic elites and the narrowing of liberal democracy (c.f. Razsa and Kurnik 2012).

My purpose in flagging these points of commonality is not to rehabilitate the unsavory Putin administration; rather, against the tide of a reenergized "binary socialism" (Yurchak 2006, 4), where Cold War metaphors abound and politicians and media commentators attribute complex structural processes to "Putin," my task is to insist that we need to locate it within an unstable field. Especially at this time of austerity, citizens of the EU and the United States grapple with their own series of "post"s – postwelfare, post-Fordism, postsocial (Rose 1996, 331) and with disillusion, disenchantment, and nostalgia as well (Muehlebach 2012). They engage in robust forms of contestation about liberal democracy's limitations, as the 2011–2012 protests and uprisings associated with the

Occupy movement most clearly exemplified (Butler 2011; Hardt and Negri 2011; Juris and Razsa 2012). Failure to acknowledge these instabilities and forms of contestation – as Russia's unreflexive critics of the West fail to acknowledge them – does not serve us. We need to view Putin-era youth movements (and other projects) in the context of shifting relationships between state/society and capital globally and in the context of emergent authoritarianisms.[1]

Subsequent events – including the repressive turn of the third Putin presidency and the sharp deterioration of relations between Russia and the West following the 2014 Ukraine conflict – make this more important than ever. The stakes are high and we must not give up on stories of complexity.

Valentina visited me in Amherst in November 2014 as I was bringing this book to a close. As usual, we presented on our research to my University of Massachusetts students. This "feminist talk show" – as she refers to our co-presentations – was more somber and less playful than the ones we had delivered in the past. The troubling events of 2014 and the "reductive, dichotomizing" discursive violence that accompanied them (Ries 2014) cast a pall.[2] As I showed images of Nashi campaigns and our trips to Seliger, and our encounters with young people at Seliger, she spoke about the newly virulent anti-Western discourse of Russian politicians and media commentators, and the emergence of a new binary: "patriot"/"traitor." The Nashi constructions it seemed most Russian people had regarded as exotic and extreme (charges of "fascism" to describe and discredit political opponents, invoking Naziism) had been mainstreamed and were now the stuff of everyday political commentary (Yurchak 2014). As we exchanged observations on how this played out, I realized we were both struggling to orient ourselves.

Later, over coffee, Valentina spoke more about these discursive shifts. Beyond "patriot"/"traitor" she had just picked up a new phrase in the lexicon of Russian political leaders: *antinarodnoe myshlenie* (anti-people thinking). "In the Soviet period it was 'anti-Soviet thinking,'" she mused. "But who is the *narod*? And am I not a patriot?" She spoke with concern about the gendered dimensions of this discourse as well, such as the celebration of militarized forms of masculinity (the figure of the separatist fighter, or the *muzhik*). This climate marked a new threat to

the spirit of the university she was committed to. Indeed, she reported
that one nationalist politician had declared at the Seliger 2014 summer
camp, "We must shut down [*nado prikhlopnut'*] the university!" But, she
reported with a wry smile, it hadn't happened yet. Her classes remained
her own. As ever, she used them as an opportunity for the dialogue and
engagement with her students that she thrived on, as an opportunity
to disrupt the narrow constructions they were offered and to challenge
them to think critically about what they saw on TV. "There's such disinformation [about the West]," she told me. "Young people just don't know
how it is." According to recently published data, she said, only 14 percent
of Russian citizens have foreign passports. Those who do travel mostly
go on tours to Egypt or Spain; very few of her own students had been
outside the country. "That's why I don't leave the university," she said,
simply. Indeed, she was gathering material for this project of discursive
disruption while in the United States. In New York City and Amherst
she had taken photos of sites of sociality and public space – parks, streets,
the 9/11 Memorial, the UMass library, campus cafés, the student union,
and student-run cooperatives. She planned to make a video montage to
share with her students. It was an ethnographic project that sought to
portray the United States beyond the headlines, to displace anti-Western
stereotypes with images of civic participation and everyday civility, and,
in so doing, to stimulate the forms of engaged university-based dialogue
it was her life's project to effect.

It is for moments like these that I advocate for continued forms of
collaboration. The polarizing times we find ourselves in present a set of
political, ethical, and representational challenges that scholars of the
region struggle with. In this context of heightened tension between Russia and the West, there is a strong – and often problematic – impulse to
assume bold stances and take sides, a tug toward moral and political
certainty (Pisano 2014; Ries 2014; Yurchak 2014).[3] In the face of this
logic and the resulting calls to cut off, divest from, isolate, and boycott
Russia, I remain committed to anthropology and its methodologies – to
its determination to see complexity and keep an eye on context, and
to ethnography's potential to contribute to a different kind of politics
(c.f. Razsa and Kurnik 2012; Ries 2014; Rivkin-Fish and Hartblay 2014;
Yurchak 2014).[4]

I have argued for collaboration as a method that is uniquely well suited to these polarized times. Collaboration, and the dialogic engagement it entails, brings diverse perspectives, analytic frameworks, and priorities to the fore. Insofar as it does not permit a retreat to certainty and conviction, this approach is extremely appropriate. I advocate for collaboration in ethnography and the use of ethnography to enhance collaborations with Russian scholars and activists as well. Across this polarized terrain we need to maintain, not cut off, connections. If we are to be good allies we need to embrace a mode of collaboration that is reflexive and acknowledges the existence of competing frames, and that is open to divergence, incoherence, and the possibility of novel coalitions and spaces (c.f. Rivkin-Fish and Hartblay 2014; Gibson-Graham 2006, xxxi).

As this book closes, Valentina and I continue to devise new modes of collaboration. As we spoke in Amherst about the final chapters of this research and the book I was writing, we expressed sorrow that the form of collaborative research we had engaged in could likely not be repeated – yet we were determined to figure out something new. Across this shifting geopolitical field, our plan is to forge a new project that will enable us to continue working together and with her students, the young people who inspire her, to enact our solidarity and maintain the bridges we have built.

NOTES

INTRODUCTION

1. The term *kontrolno-propusknoi punkt* has a police or security connotation, and is usually used to indicate form of identity or passport checkpoint.

2. According to media reports, a total of two hundred million rubles ($6.8 million) was spent on the 2009 forum, including seventy-five million rubles ($2.6 million) from the federal budget. Because the forum was organized by the Federal Youth Affairs Agency (Rosmolodezh) instead of the pro-Kremlin Nashi movement, it had state status and was eligible for financing from the state budget for the first time. "Russian Billionaire Prokhorov to Finance Kremlin's Youth Forum—Newspaper," *Sputnik News*, March 15, 2010, http://en.rian.ru/russia/20100315/158199960.html.

3. See for example Gillis (2007); Lucas (2008); and Myers (2007). On "black PR," see Wilson (2005).

4. NEET is a new term in European policy circles, prompted by concerns about the global recession's disproportionate impact on young people (i.e., those under thirty years old). In these discussions, youth who lack higher education, or who have an immigrant background, are considered most "at risk" for attaining NEET status. "Young People and 'NEETS,'"

Eurofound, December 13, 2013, http://www.eurofound.europa.eu/emcc/labour market/youth.htm.

5. Rupert Neate and Graeme Wearden, "Euro Leaders Unite to Tackle Soaring Youth Unemployment Rates," *Guardian*, May 28, 2013, http://www.theguardian.com/business/2013/may/28/european-youth-unemployment-francois-holland.

6. The issue was high on the agenda at the World Economic Forum in Davos on May 2013. Ibid.

7. Eliasoph's study tracks US-based civic and community-based volunteer programs, but her characterization holds true for the diverse empowerment projects I consider and which continue to proliferate globally.

8. Education Minister Andrei Fursenko made similar pronouncements, once proclaiming, "Our goal is to educate qualified consumers!"

9. Yurchak's (2005) formulation offers an analytic lens through which to examine these architects, and clues as to how we might interrogate the projects they have created. Putin-era youth projects are shaped by this generation's memories of the past and its particularly agentive relationship with the state.

10. Consider two of the key ideologues of Putin's youth policies: Vasily Yakemenko, founder of Nashi, born in 1971; and Vladimir Surkov, Putin's "gray cardinal," who is widely regarded as the key architect behind Putin's youth policies, born in 1964.

11. As Jessica Greenberg (2012, 376) notes, there has been a highly productive relationship between indigenous activists and foreign policymakers and funders. In the mid-2000s, former Serbian pro-democracy activists became globally mobile "resistance consultants," signing on to support some of the color revolutions that upset the Russian state, and, later, those that rocked the Middle East as well. Others joined the ranks of the reenergized left, participating in some of the radical anti-globalization uprisings associated with the Occupy movement (Razsa 2013).

12. To quote Margaret Carullo, there's a need to study "innovations in dominance in conjunction with innovations in resistance," rather than seeing them separately. The tech-enabled "perverse reconfigurations of power" that propel recent antistate oppositional movements such as the Occupy movement are enabled by the same technology and global flows that repress this protest. Remarks delivered to the On Protest Research Symposium, University of Massachussets Amherst, April 13, 2013.

13. Alexei Yurchak (1999, 2005) defines *stiob* as a form of irony that is performed through overidentification with the object of irony such that it becomes impossible to distinguish between complete sincerity and ridicule. In his analysis, people can apply this "stiob-based" set of relations to any kind of dominant discourse to which they become exposed, including market reforms or Western feminism (1999, 92).

14. Following anthropological conventions, I use pseudonyms for most research participants, except for my colleagues Valentina Uspenskaya and Dmitry Borodin.

15. As Urla and Helepololei (2014, 434) put it, drawing on Ortner (1997), thick descriptions are those that explore "the internal politics and tensions of subaltern groups, the heterogeneity of perspectives within them, as well as asymmetries and hierarchies that characterize their social groupings."

16. Vladimir Zhirinovsky is the clownish and controversial founder and leader of the nationalist Liberal Democratic Party of Russia, founded in 1990.

17. When we later conferred, Valentina told me she interpreted their reaction to the video as *sniskhozhdenie* (condescension).

18. Yurchak (2008, 262) finds evidence of an aesthetic turn that took place in Russia during the mid-2000s that is particularly manifest among youth: "a growing fascination in contemporary Russian youth culture, media and art with the alleged Soviet traits of idealism, sincerity and futurism."

19. In the early revolutionary period, the Bolsheviks created two key institutions to reshape the new society and culture: the Women's Council (Zhenotdel, established 1919) and the Communist Youth League (Komsomol, established 1918). They were conceptualized as institutions that would "reform and refashion sexual behavior and morality" (Stites 1989, 48).

20. The Komsomol peaked in size during the 1970s, when it had tens of millions of members; about two-thirds of the present adult population of Russia is believed to have once belonged.

21. The insistence on the mutual constitution of "East" and "West" during the Cold War was one of anthropology's most foundational contributions to the study of postsocialist states (Borneman 1992;

Gal and Kligman 2000). A burgeoning field of scholarship now grapples with the challenge of making sense of the complex social and cultural forms that characterize contemporary life both in the former Eastern bloc and in "late socialist" China. These scholars have pointed to moments of resonance, fusion, or mutation between socialist and liberal formations that confound exclusionary models and challenge the notion of liberalism and socialism as mutually exclusive and incommensurate (see for example Yurchak 2003; Boyer and Yurchak 2010; Hoffman 2006, 2010; Kipnis 2008; Song 2009). This scholarship suggests that we can view neoliberalism and socialism as utopian projects that have substantial points of commonality and overlap (Buck-Morss 2002; see also Bockman and Eyal 2002; Chari and Verdery 2009).

22. Yurchak's (2003) analysis of magazines targeting Russia's new business elite shows that these nineties-era journals beckoned forth new forms of personhood, the "true careerist," a neoliberal entrepreneurial subject.

23. Between 2003 and 2004 the Putin administration introduced new legislation that threatened to have profound implications for NGOs. One bill proposed amending the tax code; another sought to give authorities increased powers to monitor the activities and finances of NGOs. While the legislation influenced all NGOs, foreign NGOs were disproportionately targeted.

24. The concept of "sovereign democracy" articulates an argument about Russia's own distinct path and approach to governance. Crucially to my arguments, the concept signifies Putin's determination to seize control of Russia's path to democracy, and not to be guided or dictated to by foreign states.

25. Russian literary scholar Eliot Borenstein (2005) has discussed *bespredel* as a key term of nineties-era Russian discourse. Not static, the term picks up new inflection via its use, but always signals something to be lamented. In his account, the term has a generational component; it communicates great power nostalgia and is linked to anxieties about youth.

26. The Russian Governmental Decree No. 1760-r of December 18, 2006, confirmed the strategy for state youth policy in the Russian Federation. The conception (*konseptsiia*) "of long-term socioeconomic development of the Russian Federation through the year 2020," which included a discussion of youth policies, was approved by the federal Parliament in November 2008.

27. The Ministry for Education and Science, the Ministries of Culture and Media, and Russia's "power ministries," the Ministry of Defense, the Federal Security Service (FSB), and the Foreign Intelligence Service. A new federal agency, the Russian State Military Historical-Cultural Center (*Rosvoentsentr*), was founded to coordinate initiatives (Sperling 2009).

28. In his analysis of blockbusters, Stephen Norris (2012) examines the "memory work" that is undertaken via the new Hollywood-inspired yet Russia-specific form of cinema and its shifting use of the past.

29. Helena Goscilo (2013a, 2013b) has mapped the contours of this terrain. As she notes, the media, popular culture, and new technologies have played an important role in the crafting of Putin's public persona, which is the creation of an alliance between "the Kremlin, the state-controlled media, wily entrepreneurs, sycophantic celebrity figures, the citizenry and Putin himself" (2013a, 2).

30. Rogers's ethnography traces Russia's "oil culture" and its role in the

production of the new Russian state, examining the distinctive corporate-state formations that unfolded in the Putin era.

31. Recent scholarship has tracked the effects of the "boom" of glamour discourse in Russia since the mid-2000s (Ratilainen 2012) and its highly ambiguous (gendered) effects.

32. The Russian state recognized that highly educated youth had the greatest potential to contribute creative and technical skills to the nation but were among the most politically disengaged and skeptical of "the system" (Lassila 2012). Hence, it sought to target them for these programs.

33. Indifference (*bezrazlichie*) is a key word of the new youth campaigns. In a focus group, Marina, a twenty-one-year-old Nashi activist, named it as the greatest problem facing youth today.

34. "Contemporary Youth Policy in Russia—A Conscious Policy of Degradation?," September 1, 2010, http://www.yabloko.ru/2010/09/01_0.

35. See for example K. Brown (2006); Burawoy and Verdery (1999); Ghodsee (2004); Hann and Dunn (1996); Ishkanian (2008); Richter (2002); Rivkin-Fish (2005); Sampson (1996); Wedel (1998).

36. I would like to acknowledge the work of Michele Rivkin-Fish, with whom I have long pondered these dilemmas, including in the context of a 2013 conference panel we co-organized ("Where Is Feminist Analysis after the Critique of Dualisms? Interrogating Russia's Gender Politics, Mapping Feminist Interpretation," at the Annual Meeting of the Association for Slavic, East European, and Eurasian Studies, Boston, November).

1. COLLABORATIVE POSSIBILITIES, NEW COLD WAR CONSTRAINTS

1. Participatory action research (PAR) is a social-change methodology that has its roots in popular struggles in the global South. It recasts research as a collaborative endeavor between outside researcher and community group. As such, it offered appropriate tools for the transnational feminist collaboration Valentina and I sought to undertake (Hemment 2007b).

2. J. K. Gibson-Graham is the pen name of feminist economic geographers Katherine Gibson and Julie Graham.

3. Our joint presentation was entitled "The Rise of State-Run Youth Organizations in Putin's Russia: A Report from a Second-Generation Post-Socialist (East-West) Feminist Collaboration."

4. The NEWW was set up in 1991 as an informal coalition of feminist scholars and activists from the United States and former Eastern Bloc countries, and stimulated some of the first "East-West" feminist exchanges of the postsocialist era. With funding from various US-based agencies, including the MacArthur and Ford Foundations, it launched the NEWW On-Line project, which offered small grants to women's groups in the region and enabled them to buy computers, connecting thirty-five locales throughout Central Eastern Europe and the Newly Independent States of the former Soviet Union. Ann Snitow, Nannette Funk, and Sonia Jaffe Robbins were founding members. For a firsthand account of NEWW's origins and history, see Sonia Jaffe Robbins, "Opening the Electronic Curtain: The Network of East-West Women," accessed November 23, 2014, http://www.inch.com/~shebar/neww/neww1.htm.

5. Some of the dynamic community-based projects of that optimistic period (also inspired by East-West feminist collaboration) include women's crisis centers.

6. Loyalty has emerged as a key word of the Putin era. I first noted it in the lexicon of my TGU colleagues in 2004, as

they ironically told me about some of the decisions made by university administrators (for example, my colleagues were "insufficiently loyal" to be invited to various bureaucratic meetings).

7. The Bologna Process (or Bologna Accords) was signed in 1999 by twenty-nine European states. Its purpose is to create a European Higher Education Area, by making academic degree and quality assurance standards more comparable and compatible, or to "harmonize" the architecture of the European higher education system. Russia has been a full member of the Bologna Process since 2003. See the official website, http://www.ond.vlaanderen .be/hogeronderwijs/Bologna/.

8. Students worked at the crisis center as volunteer interns, gaining valuable experience with computers, counseling, and working with members of the public. Several sociology students wrote undergraduate theses on domestic violence, offering socially useful research to the city and the center. And the traffic moved in both directions: crisis center staff gave lectures at the Gender Studies Center on domestic violence and some of the counselors subsequently entered the university to undertake graduate studies based on their applied work.

9. Thirteen teachers and activists attended the seminar: core faculty of the Center for Women's History and Gender Studies and some former staff members of the Gortensia crisis center. The four texts were Hyatt (2001b), Benson, Harkavy, and Puckett (1996), Stanton, Giles, and Cruz (1999), and Strand (2000). I have written about this early phase of our collaboration elsewhere (Hemment 2008).

10. Students interned at Vazhnoe Delo, the regional administration, and in the offices of the regional Social Defense Agency.

11. Youth voluntarism has long been promoted on college campuses in the United States under the auspices of "service learning." Over the last decade, service learning has increased exponentially; indeed, it has won mainstream acceptance that causes many of its practitioners disquiet. Rather than engaging in the critical thinking that its proponents envisaged, students are directed into docile forms of charity work, and in this way depoliticized (Harvey 2005; Hyatt 2001b). Via service learning, student volunteers take on the responsibilities of the retreating welfare state.

12. Holmes and Marcus (2008, 83) address the "profoundly altered" context that has brought about and requires changes in the ways fieldwork is conducted today. They coin the term "paraethnographer" to refer to the reflexive subjects ethnographers increasingly engage, as they work with existing "epistemic communities."

13. Some student work was published in Valentina Uspenskaya, ed., *Sbornik: Molodezhnye organizatsii, dobrovol'chestvo I restrukturizatsiia program sotsialnoi pomoshchi v Rossii* [Youth organizations, voluntarism and the restructuring of social welfare in Russia] (Tver': Feminist Press, 2010). Student research also appeared in a special issue of the *Anthropology of East Europe Review* under my editorship (see Karmalskaia 2008, Belov 2008, and Artiushin 2008).

14. During this period, Valentina was undertaking a research project on gender equality policies in EU countries, as well as finishing two books: *Muzhskie otvety na zhenskii vopros v Rossii* [Men's answers to the woman question in Russia] (Tver': Feminist Press, 2005) and *Feministskie otvety na zhenskiii vopros v Rossii* [Feminist answers to the woman question in Russia] (Tver': Feminist Press, 2012).

15. This was a very different collaboration from the pattern established and
endorsed. I have collected many grumbles
from Europe-based colleagues who find
themselves overstretched, required to spin
"projects"; many of us have encountered
requests to collaborate (where "collaboration" is often little more than a bureaucratic requirement for funding applications
and can be signaled with the lightest of
touches and commitments, only minimal
acquaintance required).

16. In spring 2008, members of the international academic community received
an impassioned plea from the rector of European University, concerning the politically motivated closure of the university
(on the pretext of a fire code violation).
This led to a well-coordinated protest by
professors and students, captured on Illia
Utekhin's blog and later in the 2009 documentary film *Pugovka* (Button). Finally,
compliance with fire regulations was
deemed sufficient by the court, and the
university reopened six weeks later.

17. Elena L. Omel'chenko and Anna
Zhelnina, "Sociology under Threat? ...
Or Who Is on the Lookout for New Enemies of Russia, and Why ... ," *MYPLACE*
(blog), November 6, 2012, http://myplace
fp7.wordpress.com/2012/11/06/sociology
-under-threat-or-who-is-on-the-lookout
-for-new-enemies-of-russia-and-why/.

18. The Order of the Red Star was originally a military honor; it was also awarded
for outstanding achievements in peace-
time during the Soviet period.

19. The cartoon was provided to me
by Roberta Garner (sociologist, DePaul
University).

20. The Moscow-based Democratic
Union, founded in 1988 out of a cluster of
informal groups, was the first organization to claim opposition to the USSR. It
called for a multiparty system and the
withdrawal of Soviet troops from Eastern

Europe, Western Ukraine, and the Baltic
states (Tolz 1990, 56).

21. Organizations that refused to
register under the law were subject to enforced audit; since 2012 law enforcement
officers in Russia have raided the offices of
numerous NGOs, including the renowned
Levada public opinion research center and
Memorial, as well as international organizations like Human Rights Watch and
Amnesty International. The legislation
gave rise to forms of harassment as well. In
2012 (shortly after the "foreign agent" legislation went into effect), an anonymous
blogger posted an article denouncing the
Ulianovsk-based Region research center,
making reference to its involvement in a
major EU-funded multicountry research
project on historical memory and contemporary youth and political activism.
The blogger's hostile post was entitled,
"Does USU [Ulianovsk State University]
Need a 'Foreign Agent'?" For discussion,
including Region's response to this, see
Omel'chenko and Zhelnina, "Sociology
under Threat?"

22. US-based anthropologists have
long been concerned about the US government's use of anthropology. See for
example contemporary concerns about the
"weaponizing" of social science and the
security-driven goals of infiltrating social
movements (Price 2011; Network of Concerned Anthropologists 2009).

23. Many versions of this story circulate, but the gist is that the lion may think
he is the king of the jungle, but the monkey
is smarter and outwits him.

24. Their project in *A Postcapitalist Politics* was prompted primarily by the trials of
collaboration, or what the authors call "the
comforts and discomforts of collectivism,
the bounds and liberties of (joint) identity,
the struggle to make collaboration work,
not just for itself, but for its participants"
(Gibson-Graham 2006, xi).

2. NASHI IN IDEOLOGY AND PRACTICE

1. Grandfather Frost, the mythical character of fairy tales, was "unmasked as an ally of the priest and the kulak" by the Bolsheviks during the 1920s as part of their assault upon religion (Stites 1989, 231). He was subsequently rehabilitated and was a beloved figure for children during later Soviet periods.

2. Nashi claimed to be an independent political movement, supported by private donations; however, the support of the presidential administration played an important role. Nashi founder Vassili Yakemenko boasted of the Kremlin's support and of the leverage it gave the organization, effectively guaranteeing it the financial support of businesses (Atwal 2009, 743).

3. In his rich analysis of Nashi's political communication, Jussi Lassila (2011, 2012) accounts for this complex play of logics, casting it as a tactic via which state actors seek to mobilize youth. He attributes the diverse logics and symbols it draws on to the central tension between what he calls "didactics" and "stimulation," itself the result of Nashi's challenging and paradoxical goal: to appeal to and mobilize apolitical youth who are skeptical about official power, while advancing a pro-regime orientation.

4. Nashi had a rogue energy about it that occasionally led it into trouble. See note 27.

5. Nelli Monastyrskaia, "'Nashi' milliony" ["Our" millions], *Moskovskie novosti*, July 22–28, 2005, http://www.edu.ru/db /mo/Data/d_02/393.html.

6. Peter Finn, "Another Russian Revolution? Youth Movement Adopts Spirit of Uprisings Nearby," *Washington Post*, April 9, 2005, http://www.washingtonpost.com /wp-dyn/articles/A38431-2005Apr8.html.

7. They mobilized as well against the 2006 G8 summit, held in Saint Petersburg.

8. *Ekspert*, April 5, 2005, quoted in Jeremy Bransten, "Russia: Kremlin Chief of Staff Warns of Potential Disintegration," *Radio Free Europe*, April 5, 2005, http:// www.rferl.org/content/article/1058279 .html.

9. Paul Manning's work examines the ways "revolution" can be reframed for different audiences (2007).

10. Reported by the Russian News Agency, ITAR-TASS, May 18, 2006.

11. It introduced one bill that proposed amendments to the tax code, and another that sought to give authorities increased powers to monitor the activities and finances of NGOs. While the legislation influenced all nongovernmental organizations, foreign NGOs were disproportionately targeted.

12. Rogers locates these social and cultural projects as components of a new kind of state-corporate field that emerged after the economic crisis of 1998.

13. *The Strategy of State Youth Policy in the Russian Federation, 2006–2016* emphasizes the import of the development of civil society as a yardstick for the development of Russia.

14. Until his imprisonment in 2005, Mikhail Khodorkovsky's Open Russia Foundation disbursed funds to a number of liberal-oriented organizations and collaborated with foreign foundations.

15. This vision as laid out by its architect, Surkov, emphasized the collective nature of Russian national identity. As Richter and Hatch (2013, 335) explain, Surkov's argument is that "the individual is most free . . . when the nation as a whole is strong."

16. Jessica Greenberg (2014) traces democracy promotion through this phase, pursuing its legacies and aftermath from the vantage point of postrevolutionary

Serbia. As she shows, shifts in civil society's resonance were accompanied by the shifting meanings of streets, crowds, and crowds on the streets, which often had a youth angle.

17. The Time of Troubles, or *Smutnoe vremya*, refers to the turbulent period during the late sixteenth and early seventeenth centuries when Russian statehood was compromised.

18. *Fascists Today, Tomorrow.* For an analysis of this booklet, see Belov (2008).

19. I quote here from the original published version of the manifesto that Kirill gave me (*Manifest molodezhnogo demokraticheskogo antifashistskogo dvizheniia "Nashi"* [Manifesto of the youth democratic antifascist movement "Nashi"], also available at http://Nashi.su/manifest). The manifesto was subsequently updated, as my visits to the Nashi website revealed.

20. In his rich ethnography of postsocialist Russian life, Oushakine (2009) presents the interpretive frameworks used by marginalized provincial subjects and the nationalist-oriented scholarship they draw on. One of the authors he profiles specifically discusses the civil-society concept, arguing that it functions in a form of imperceptible domination ("programming") to accomplish the atomization of people, or "atomization of the crowd" (42–43).

21. Note the diverse ideological orientation of these authors. Bredemaier is a "top executive coach and communication strategist" who runs regular seminars on project management; Tarasov is a left-oriented sociologist; Amin is an Egyptian Marxist economist.

22. I owe these insights to my engagement with the work of Sonia Alvarez, Barbara Cruikshank, and their colleagues associated with the Theorizing the Tahrir Moments Research Group and the Mellon-LASA workshop "On Protest":

Latin America in Comparative and Transnational Perspective.

23. Nashi campaigns exhibited some classic examples of stiob, but, like Lassila (2012, 196), I see them as an adaptation of stiob. Stiob's deployment for pro-regime purposes unsettles and disturbs its meaning, insofar as it signals a clear political orientation; the campaigns may "fail" politically as a result (161).

24. *Putin's Kiss* is a Danish documentary film, directed by Lise Birk Pedersen, that focuses on the trajectory of one Nashi komissar, Masha Drokova, a provincial activist who shot from obscurity to fortune via the organization and ultimately quit, disenchanted.

25. *Manifest s kommentariami* [Manifesto with commentaries], accessed July 10, 2010, http://Nashi.su/manifest /comments.

26. Natsional'nyi Institut Vyshaya Shkola Upravleniya (the National Institute of Administration), accessed May 19, 2011, http://www.vshu.ru/ru/.

27. In 2006 Nashi began a campaign against the British ambassador in Moscow, Tony Brenton, objecting to his attendance at an oppositional event organized by the group Another Russia. In 2007, it harassed the Estonian ambassador in protest against the Estonian decision to relocate the Bronze Soldier war memorial in Tallinn, which depicted Soviet losses in World War II. These actions were condemned in a series of statements by representatives of the EU and NATO (Mijnssen 2014, 117).

28. Lassila's (2012, 89) three komissars come across very similarly: they also do not read as "joiners," but see themselves as different from other Nashi activists.

29. The deaths of two Russian men in a brawl at a Chechen-owned bar was followed by days of intense violence, where mobs of ethnic Russian youths attacked Chechen-owned properties and

businesses. The violence captured national attention after city residents—supported by ultranationalists—called for the immediate deportation of people from the Caucasus.

30. Here we see how Nashi is implicated in the appropriation and displacement of existing civic organizations. The Tver' oblast human rights commission, which was set up in the 1990s by one of Valentina's colleagues, was shut down in the early 2000s.

31. The book, subtitled *What the Rich Teach Their Kids about Money—That the Poor and Middle Class Do Not!*, written by Robert T. Kiyosaki and Sharon L. Lechter, is a *New York Times* bestseller that offers individuals strategies for achieving financial independence in the new millennium via investing, real estate, owning businesses, and the use of finance protection tactics.

32. Starikov is a very vocal nationalist neo-Stalinist author and blogger who has published a number of historical and political novels. He is the organizer of the (ironic) "Goebbels Award," which is given to those who purportedly lie about, slander, or vilify Russia.

33. Igor's constructions recall Pilkington et al.'s (2002) findings, where young people embrace the "West" in terms of what it offers them in lifestyle or material well-being, but reject it in terms of "being"—i.e., morally, spiritually.

34. At the time of this writing, Nashi still nominally exists (its website is up, but rarely updated); however, it was perhaps fatally wounded by its participation in efforts to discredit the oppositional protests of 2011–2012.

3. SELIGER 2009

1. Nadia Popova, "Rusnano Pledges to Fund Youth Projects," *Moscow Times,* July 7, 2009.

2. President Dmitry Medvedev was quick to embrace the civil-society concept. His early statements were seized upon by journalists as evidence of his inclination to support a more liberal-democratic vision of civil society, where organizations play an oppositional role vis-à-vis the state.

3. In June 2009 Medvedev announced a new Presidential Award for young scientists, worth 2.5 million rubles each (approximately $80,000), as well as increased presidential grants for young PhD and ScD degree holders.

4. Chubais served in the Yeltsin administration of the early 1990s and was responsible for effecting the introduction of market reforms. Reviled in the late 1990s and early 2000s, he was appointed director general of RUSNANO, a joint-stock company created and owned by the government of Russia and aimed at commercializing developments in nanotechnology by Medvedev in 2008.

5. These policy shifts had broad support from—and may have been prompted by—academics and professional educators as well. On October 2, 2009, the *Vedomosti* daily carried an open letter to Medvedev and Putin, signed by more than forty top Russian scientists working in leading universities and research centers in Europe and the United States, decrying the "catastrophic situation of basic science in Russia," caused by low levels of state funding.

6. Federal Youth Affairs Agency mission statement, accessed January 15, 2015, http://www.fadm.gov.ru/about/mission.

7. Yakemenko was first appointed head of an RF state committee on youth affairs (by presidential decree in 2007); it was later relaunched and renamed the Federal Youth Affairs Agency, its status as an agency affirmed by presidential decree in May 2008.

8. The conception (*konseptsiia*) was approved by RF Parliament in November 2008.

9. Asset-based mapping is a technology that has become extremely influential in development circles over the last decade, both in the United States and globally. This approach is in essence a form of positive thinking for community development. It maps community resources by emphasizing a community's positives (such as "loving grandmothers" and strong families), rather than its "deficits" and "needs." The technology is highly controversial; while its proponents claim it empowers and dignifies communities, critics point to its political effects—it screens out structural forces that propel social inequalities and quells political protest and action (Hyatt 2011). See Eliasoph (2011, 243–245).

10. The "project design" materials and booklet were commissioned by Romolodezh especially for the 2009 camp, and produced and delivered by the Moscow-based Sholokhov Humanitarian Institute. The definition of "project" they offer is attributed to Joseph Juran, a Romanian-born US management consultancy guru.

11. My point here isn't merely that social welfare/empowerment projects become neoliberalized, but that in the neoliberal moment corporate activity and entrepreneurship become sanitized and dressed up as social activism. To that extent, Seliger superficially resembled the Silicon Valley high-tech innovation boot camps and "mash-ups" it modeled itself on; these too hold utopian promise and make bold claims to improve the world (Packer 2013).

12. Brin left the Soviet Union for the United States as a child in 1979 with his family, fleeing antisemitic discrimination. Vladimir Zvorykin's flight had to do with

the political turmoil of the early twentieth century; he fled the Soviet Union during the Civil War in 1918 and settled permanently in the United States.

13. "Putin Gives New Definitions to 'Russia's Defensibility and Competitiveness' at the Seliger-2009 Forum," *Russia Corporate World*, July 31, 2009, http://www.trcw.ru/en/news/detail.php?print=yes&ID=1089.

14. Both the material and Vitaly's handling of it recall Mark Lipovetsky's (2004) discussion of Post-Sots (a postmodern sensibility that took root in the 2000s and with which contemporary cultural production in Russia is infused). Lipovetsky defines Post-Sots as the postmodern redeployment of socialist-realist models and myths, which he locates as "one of the most distinctive trends in Russian mass culture over the last five years" (357). This implies that a kind of postmodernist sensibility is something encoded into Nashi's training programs ("political PR").

15. Here, she is implicitly referencing the Seliger session on leadership, whose promotional materials bluntly ask, "Will you be a leader, or a horse?"

16. This is an odd claim, since workbooks (which indicate past employment, reasons for terminating employment, etc.) are still used and required by employers who wish to hire people officially.

17. Our conversations about Seliger took place against a backdrop of increased concern about cutbacks in higher education. In 2010, I found students up in arms due to the sharp reduction in state-funded (*budgetniky*) places for graduate school.

18. Federal Youth Affairs Agency materials communicated the critique encoded into policy discussions of higher education since 2001; however, instead of tackling issues systematically, its funds went into glossy projects.

19. I picked up similar accounts from other komissars that summer. A couple of these Nashi activists referred to the "komissar's society," a term I had never heard previously.

20. Surkov served as first deputy of the chief of the Russian presidential administration from 1999 to 2011. In December 2011—in a move widely interpreted as a consequence of the fallout from the elections that month—he was reassigned to the post of deputy prime minister for economic modernization. Vasily Yakemenko quit his post as the head of the Federal Youth Affairs Agency in June 2012, after founding a new political party designed to attract the young, disaffected, middle-class voters who were drawn to 2011 opposition protests.

21. The organizers invited Dmitry Ternovsky, a young anticorruption blogger, to run the session. According to the website, the goal was "to convert the energy of those who went to Bolotnaya Ploshchad and those who today are called the 'creative class' into something useful for the country."

4. FROM KOMSOMOL'TSY-DOBROVOL'TSY TO ENTREPRENEURIAL VOLUNTEERS

1. The word for kindness is *dobrota*. *Dobrinka* is a childish-sounding version of the word that appears to have been especially coined by the designers of this campaign.

2. In Yurchak's (2006, 159) account, the Imaginary West was a late Soviet cultural and discursive formation, an imaginary "outside" that was "produced locally and could be experienced only at the time when the real West could not be encountered."

3. This Foucauldian scholarship has brought a governmentality lens to analyze social welfare contexts in the United States. It examines how neoliberal logics have been inculcated in volunteering subjects, caseworkers, and the clients they serve.

4. The *subbotnik* was a form of state-mandated voluntarism, in which citizens gave up their Saturdays to engage in neighborhood cleanup or maintenance projects, or to undertake agricultural work such as picking potatoes.

5. "Komsomol'tsy-Dobrovol'tsy," accessed January 4, 2013, http://www.karaoke.ru/song/2731.htm.

6. This is distinct from the forms of voluntarism undertaken during the Soviet period. Then, voluntary activities were articulated not as a way of serving the needy (officially, there *was* no social inequality), but rather as a form of societal work, or contribution to the collective. In the Soviet period, social welfare was defined as a set of entitlements that were guaranteed by the state; education and health care were constituted as rights that were free to all citizens (Cook 1993).

7. The decision was made by the United Nations General Assembly in 1997. A new body, the United Nations Volunteers (UNV), was designated the international focal point. Like Russia's Year of Youth, the UN's Year of Volunteers operated as a campaign to propagandize, encourage, and campaign to stimulate volunteer activities globally. "International Year of Volunteers 2001," World Volunteer Web, accessed January 28, 2013, http://www.worldvolunteerweb.org/tools/about-us/iyv-2001.html.

8. "About Us," United Nations Volunteers, accessed December 2, 2014, http://www.unv.org/about-us.html.

9. Russian policy documents (the Conception and the Strategy) make clear that voluntarism is conceptualized as part of a civic and patriotic education program to create legal, moral, and cultural values among youth. For additional information, see note 25 of the introduction.

10. Vazhnoe Delo benefitted from the new system of grants and funding established by the Putin administration; the money was distributed by both federal ministries and the federal Public Chamber (Hemment 2009).

11. This center and its rising fortunes illustrate the reintegration of the psychological profession into public establishments in post-Soviet Russia (Matza 2012).

12. The center collaborated closely with the local, regional, and federal governments; it was an agent of the Ministry of Sports, Tourism, and Youth Policy and the Ministry of Education.

13. *Pafos* was a word I heard frequently in interviews with young people. It directly translates as "pathos," but can more accurately be understood as meaning "pomp."

14. Read (2010) notes a similar dichotomy between real and false voluntarism in the Czech Republic, where "inauthentic" voluntarism is associated with the socialist state.

15. International adoption, especially to the United States, has been controversial in the postsocialist period. In 2012, the Putin administration signed into law a measure banning US adoption of Russian children.

16. The Potanin Foundation utilizes technologies similar to those of Seliger 2009. Students compete in tests and role-playing games, oriented toward identifying personal characteristics.

17. Though I found her listed on the Year of Youth website as a dobrovoller,

or team leader, her project failed to score high enough to be in the top hundred projects presented at Seliger, and thus was ineligible for formal sponsorship.

18. I am grateful to Suvi Salmenniemi for helping me advance this analysis.

5. "AROUSING" PATRIOTISM

1. The song can be heard on YouTube, accessed November 17, 2013, https://www.youtube.com/watch?v=4OCnygmuf7U.

2. Different versions of the film exist; it was screened at least once on REN TV.

3. Valerie Sperling's recent work documents the political use of gender, sexuality, sexism, and homophobia by political youth groups such as Nashi (for example, where claims of sexual inadequacy or deviance are used to disparage political opponents).

4. Edward Lucas, "Sex for the Motherland: Russian Youths Encouraged to Procreate at Camp," *Daily Mail,* July 29, 2007.

5. The fashion line was described as being distinguished by its "original, intellectual, patriotic and socially useful [*sotsial'no poleznym*] design" (quoted in Lassila 2011, 236).

6. Although not officially launched by Nashi, the organization publicized and endorsed the calendar, and the group's spokeswoman, Kristina Potupchik, posted the images on her blog.

7. "Who else if not you?" later became a slogan for the 2012 presidential election.

8. The online campaign was posted on the Russian social-networking site VKontakte (Russia's version of Facebook) and caused a sensation in the domestic and foreign media.

9. "Women Urged to Strip to Support Putin as President," July 18, 2011, http://www.reuters.com/article/2011/07/18/us-putin-girls-odd-idUSTRE76H3TU20110718.

10. Lucas, "Sex for the Motherland."

11. Survey data has shown that the Russian Orthodox Church was one of the few institutions young Russians had trust in during the late 2000s (Omel'chenko 2006; cited in Lassila 2012, 121).

12. The benefit, which came into effect in January 2007, was worth the equivalent of ten thousand dollars and could be used for any of three purposes: to purchase an apartment or to contribute to the child's education or the mother's pension savings. Critics soon lambasted it for its inadequacy (Rivkin-Fish 2010).

13. The power vertical was a concept introduced by Putin to explain the recentralization of the power of the presidency and federal center.

14. Not that International Women's Day ever played out in the way I expected. As a young English-language teacher in Russia in March 1990 I was surprised by a visit from two of my students—middle-aged army colonels—who arrived at my far-flung Moscow high-rise apartment in a chauffeur-driven car to congratulate me on International Women's Day and deliver gifts. As I contemplated the flowers and garish palette of the Polish-manufactured makeup compact they left me, I realized all was not as it seemed in the gender-egalitarian Union of Soviet Socialist Republics!

15. Patriarch Kirill is a controversial figure, embroiled in many media controversies surrounding his fabulous wealth and embrace of a luxurious, glamorous lifestyle. In 2012 he was given the satirical Silver Shoe Award (announced annually for the "most dubious achievements in show business") by the oppositional radio show *Rain*. The dubious achievement in question was the clumsy Photoshop attempt to retroactively erase traces of a luxury watch from his wrist in a photograph that had already been released by his publicists.

16. Salmenniemi and Adamson (2015) explore how the globally circulating discourse of postfeminism transforms as it arrives in postsocialist Russia via popular psychology texts.

17. Yelin's ambivalent position vis-à-vis the song and its political use has been well documented, for example in the PBS documentary *Sound Tracks*. The song was commissioned by an ideologist, but written by Yelin on a three-hundred-dollar bet, to prove he could write a hit song on a low budget. He chose to write about Putin, as this seemed the most commercially viable option ("All I needed was the right message. I approached the project as a technical problem," he said). Yelin went on to write anti-Putin songs.

18. The erotic calendar produced by Moscow State University journalism students was highly controversial. One of the most critical responses came from a group of women students in the same department: a counter-calendar, depicting young women dressed in black with tape across their mouths and posing critical questions to the president (addressing the repressive practices of the Putin administration and limitations on freedom of assembly). See also Sperling (2014).

19. The song was featured in the popular Soviet-era film *Sword and Shield* (1968).

20. On January 21, 2011, Chapman began hosting a weekly TV show in Russia called *Secrets of the World* for REN TV. Her state service continued through the spring 2012 presidential election season, as the media reported rumors of an affair with Putin himself.

21. With Lassila (2012), I see Nashi's use of stiob as an adaptation; within Nashi campaigns it is deployed for pro-regime purposes to discredit the political opposition, here "liberalism" more broadly.

22. My discussion here draws on Dana Heller's analysis of another case where young women's bodies were deployed to deliberately unsettle European liberal audiences: the faux-lesbian pop duo t.A.T.u, who represented Russia at Eurovision in 2003 (see Heller 2007).

23. See "Help Us, America," accessed May 20, 2011, http://www.Nashi.su/usa.

24. Lipovetsky (2004, 360) writes, "In the Russian cultural context, 'political correctness' is invariably viewed as a 'hypocritical' norm of censorship that limits free self-expression."

25. The contours of liberalism's disparagement has shifted over the course of the last decade. I was recently made aware of the neologism *liberast*, a highly pejorative term embraced by those who seek to disparage liberalism and the reforms of the 1990s. Note that it combines two words— "liberal" and "pederast"—and simultaneously expresses hostility to liberal reforms and homophobic hostility to those who permitted them.

26. Members of Pussy Riot were celebrated in the West as feminists and LGBT rights crusaders, but they met with a highly ambivalent reaction in Russia. In a provocative article, Elena Gapova (2015) persuasively argues that the Pussy Riot controversy as it played out in Russia can be read as "a displaced conversation about class relations and subjectivites in a media-saturated information society." Crucially, the incident was not seen as a "feminist" issue. The group's actions were depoliticized in the mainstream media, liberal publics initially mocked them, and Russian feminists were deeply ambivalent about Pussy Riot, its strategies, and the "feminism" it claimed to espouse.

27. One contributor to the site (a thirty-seven-year-old mother of four living in Moscow) quoted the response of various (Orthodox) parents' organizations, which viewed the draft legislation as a "threat to demographic security" that would "destroy the family and basic cultural-moral values." She went on to state, "The law represents the duplication of the most radical feminist laws of North Europe" ("New Gender Law Will Harm Birthrate," online forum, February 2, 2012, http://mnogo detok.ru/viewtopic.php?f=17&t=33122).

28. Wendy Brown (2008, 6) has critiqued the liberal project of tolerance, discussing it as a mode of late modern governmentality that "emerges as a part of a civilizational discourse that identifies both tolerance and the tolerable with the West, marking nonliberal societies and practices as candidates for an intolerable barbarism that is itself signaled by the putative intolerance ruling these societies."

29. Gapova (2009a) argues that popular hostility to liberalism, feminism, and LGBT rights in Russia has a class character insofar as feminism is associated with "globalized, urban, cosmopolitan elites."

30. Gender-equity legislation, which was initiated in the 1990s, has languished during the 2000s and has failed to gain ground.

31. The USSR ratified CEDAW in the early eighties. Feminist scholars found themselves in demand, because of the need to collect data (Sperling 1999, 111). This document was evidently an artifact of the region's UN-mandated gender accounting.

32. Although Sweden is frequently invoked (as it is here) as an exemplar of progressive gender policies, feminist critiques of Swedish familialism proliferate (Barbara Yngvesson, in conversation with the author, June 2013).

33. As Sperling (2012, 246) notes, skeptical intelligentsia critiques of state-run youth organizations and their participants

include disparaging sexualized imagery. For example, liberal intellectuals have described participants as "sluts."

34. Her diploma research examined the attitudes of young activists in three organizations toward state demographic policies. She interviewed nine people: three members each of Nashi, a municipal organization called the Active Youth Union, and the local branch of a Communist Youth organization.

35. The decision to become a doctor represented an ambivalent empowerment strategy, due to the feminized status of the medical profession during the Soviet period. Doctors had tremendous cultural capital, but were poorly remunerated; regarded as agents of the state, they did not experience the professional authority enjoyed by their Western peers (Rivkin-Fish 2005, 141).

36. See also Barbara Yngvesson's (2010, 50–52) discussion of the politics of adoption in Sweden, another welfare state under reconfiguration.

37. Feminist anthropologists and scholars have done extensive work on this topic, issuing their own critiques of Western secular liberalism. See, for example, Abu-Lughod (2002); Mohanty (1984); Ong (2003); and Brown (2008).

38. US Evangelical activists claimed to have played a significant role in producing Russia's 2013 anti-gay legislation, and have influenced Russian anti-abortion activism as well. See Federman (2014).

CONCLUSION

1. This goal animates much recent anthropological scholarship on postsocialism, and the emergent anthropology of

democracy as well (Greenberg 2010, 2012, 2014; Nugent 2008; Razsa and Kurnik 2012; Paley 2008).

2. As Nancy Ries (2014) writes, the conflict in Ukraine comprises forms of discursive as well as military violence. Russian and Ukrainian politicians and media commentators have taken the lead, but scholars contribute as well. In this context, "nuance and diversity fall victim to the polarizing demands of war."

3. See contributions by Pisano, Yurchak, Ries, and others to the *Cultural Anthropology Online—Hot Spots* section "Ukraine and Russia: The Agency of War," edited by Nancy Ries (http://www.culanth.org/fieldsights/610-ukraine-and-russia-the-agency-of-war). As Yurchak (2014) notes, both state-authorized Russian commentators and Western liberal media accounts reproduced Cold War binaries in their reporting of the Ukraine conflict. While Russian accounts portrayed it as a "fascist" coup with US imperialist backing, Western liberal accounts portrayed it as a democratic uprising against (Soviet-style) authoritarianism.

4. Rivkin-Fish and Hartblay (2014) track the urgent mobilization by US-based activists that took place in response to the Russian Duma's "anti-gay" law and document its regrettable outcomes and costs. Passage of this legislation in 2013 led to a crescendo of calls for the United States to boycott the Sochi Olympics. In Chapel Hill, North Carolina, the call to boycott resulted in the dismantling of a painstakingly crafted form of citizen-to-citizen exchange between Russia and the United States—Chapel Hill's sister-city scheme with Saratov.

REFERENCES

Abu-Lughod, Lila. 2002. "Do Muslim Women Really Need Saving? Anthropological Reflections on Cultural Relativism and Its Others." *American Anthropologist* 104 (3): 783–790.

———. 2008. *Dramas of Nationhood: The Politics of Television in Egypt.* Chicago: University of Chicago Press.

———. 2013. *Do Muslim Women Need Saving?* Cambridge, MA: Harvard University Press.

Aivazova, Svetlana. 1998. *Russkie zhenshchiny v labirinte ravnopraviia* [Russian women in the labyrinth of equality]. Moscow: RIK Rusanova.

Alcoff, Linda. 1994. "The Problem of Speaking for Others." In *Feminist Nightmares: Women at Odds; Feminism and the Problem of Sisterhood,* edited by Susan Ostrov Weisser and Jennifer Fleischner, 285–309. New York: NYU Press.

Allison, Anne. 2013. *Precarious Japan.* Durham, NC: Duke University Press.

Alvarez, Sonia E. 2008. "Beyond the Civil Society Agenda? 'Civic Participation' and Practices of Governance, Governability and Governmentality." Paper presented at the Watson Institute, Brown University, September 17.

———. 2009. "Beyond NGO-ization? Reflections from Latin America." *Development* 52 (2): 175–184.

Alvarez, Sonia E., Evelina Dagnino, and Arturo Escobar, eds. 1998. *Cultures of Politics, Politics of Cultures: Re-Visioning Latin American Social Movements.* Boulder, CO: Westview.

Amar, Paul. 2014. "The Street, the Sponge and the Ultra in Egypt: Queer Logics of Twenty-First-Century Children's Rebellion at the Intersections of Violent Securitization and Political Infantilization." Paper presented at the Mellon-LASA Workshop "On Protest: Latin America in Comparative and Transnational Perspective," University of Massachusetts Amherst, October 10.

Arsen'eva, T. N., N. V. Vinogradova, I. M. Pelevina, and A. A. Sokolov. 2009. *Innovatsionnye proekty sistemnoi podderzhki molodezhnogo dobrovol'chestva: Nauchno metodogicheskoe posobie* [Innovative projects of systematic support for youth voluntarism: Scientific-methodological assistance]. Saint Petersburg–Tver'.

Artiushin, Evgenii. 2008. "Football Fans in Russia as a Would-Be Youth Movement." Translated by Dmitry Borodin. *Anthropology of East Europe Review* 26 (2): 68–72.

Attwood, Lynne. 1990. *The New Soviet Man and Woman: Sex-Role Socialization in the USSR.* Bloomington: Indiana University Press.

Atwal, Maya. 2009. "Evaluating Nashi's Sustainability: Autonomy, Agency and Activism." *Europe-Asia Studies* 61 (5): 743–758.

———. 2011. "Вперёд! Exploring the Dialectic between Continuity and Transformation in the Development of the Pro-Regime Russian Youth Organisation Nashi." In *Perpetual Motion? Transformation and Transition in Central and Eastern Europe and Russia*, edited by Tul'si Bhambry, Clare Griffin, Titus Hjelm, Christopher Nicholson, and Olga G.Voronina, 86–99. London: School of Slavonic and East European Studies, University College London. http://discovery.ucl.ac.uk/1322705/1/SSEES%209th%20PG%20Conf%20.pdf.

Baer, Brian James. 2009. *Other Russias: Homosexuality and the Crisis of Post-Soviet Identity*. Basingstoke: Palgrave Macmillan.

Baker, Peter, and Susan Glasser. 2005. *Kremlin Rising: Vladimir Putin's Russia and the End of Revolution*. New York: Scribner.

Balibar, Etienne. 1991. "Racism and Nationalism." In *Race, Nation, Class: Ambiguous Identities*, edited by Etienne Balibar and Immanuel Wallerstein, 37–68. London: Verso.

Belov, Oleg. 2008. "Nashi vs. Nazi: Anti-Fascist Activity as a Means of Mass Youth Mobilization in Contemporary Russia." *Anthropology of East Europe Review* 26 (2): 48–55.

Benson, Lee, Ira Harkavy, and John Puckett. 1996. "Communal Participatory Action Research as a Strategy for Improving Universities and the Social Sciences: Penn's Work with the West Philadelphia Improvement Corps as a Case Study." *Educational Policy* 10 (2): 202–220.

Berdahl, Daphne. 1999. *Where the World Ended: Reunification and Identity in the*

German Borderland. Berkeley: University of California Press.

Blum, Douglas W. 2006. "Russian Youth Policy: Shaping the Nation-State's Future." *SAIS Review* 26 (2): 95–108.

Bockman, Johanna. 2011. *Markets in the Name of Socialism: The Left-Wing Origins of Neoliberalism*. Stanford, CA: Stanford University Press.

Bockman, Johanna, and Gil Eyal. 2002. "Eastern Europe as a Laboratory for Economic Knowledge: The Transnational Roots of Neoliberalism." *American Journal of Sociology* 108 (2): 310–352.

Borenstein, Elliot. 2005. "Gratuitous Violence and Gratuitous Acts: Defining Bespredel." Paper presented at the Annual Meeting of the American Association of Teachers in Slavic and East European Languages, Washington, DC, December 27–30.

———. 2008. *Overkill: Sex and Violence in Contemporary Russian Popular Culture*. Ithaca, NY: Cornell University Press.

Borneman, John. 1992. *Belonging in the Two Berlins: Kin, State, Nation*. Cambridge: Cambridge University Press.

———. 1998. *Subversions of International Order*. Albany: SUNY Press.

Boyer, Dominic, and Alexei Yurchak. 2010. "American Stiob: Or, What Late-Socialist Aesthetics of Parody Reveal about Contemporary Political Culture in the West." *Cultural Anthropology* 25 (2): 179–221.

Brown, Keith, ed. 2006. *Transacting Transition: The Micropolitics of Democracy Assistance in the Former Yugoslavia*. Bloomfield, CT: Kumarian.

Brown, Wendy. 2006. "American Nightmare: Neoliberalism, Neoconservatism, and De-Democratization." *Political Theory* 34 (6): 690–714.

———. 2008. *Regulating Aversion: Tolerance in the Age of Identity and Empire*. Princeton, NJ: Princeton University Press.

Buck-Morss, Susan. 2002. *Dreamworld and Catastrophe: The Passing of Mass Utopia in East and West.* Cambridge, MA: MIT Press.

Burawoy, Michael, and Katherine Verdery. 1999. "Introduction." In *Uncertain Transition: Ethnographies of Change in the Postsocialist World,* edited by Michael Burawoy and Katherine Verdery, 1–17. Lanham, MD: Rowman & Littlefield.

Butler, Judith. 2011. "Bodies in Public." In *Occupy! Scenes from Occupied America,* edited by Keith Gessen, Carla Blumenkranz, Mark Greif, Sarah Leonard, Sarah Resnick, Nikil Saval, Astra Taylor, and Eli Schmitt, 192–195. London: Verso.

Caldwell, Melissa. 2004. *Not by Bread Alone: Social Support in the New Russia.* Berkeley: University of California Press.

Carothers, Thomas. 2004. *Critical Mission: Essays on Democracy Promotion.* Washington, DC: Carnegie Endowment for International Peace.

———. 2006. "The Backlash against Democracy Promotion." *Foreign Affairs* 85 (2): 55–68.

Cassiday, Julie A., and Emily D. Johnson. 2010. "Putin, Putiniana and the Question of a Post-Soviet Cult of Personality." *Slavonic and East European Review* 88 (4): 681–707.

Chandler, Andrea. 2009. "Gender, Political Discourse and Social Welfare in Russia: Three Case Studies." *Canadian Slavonic Papers* 51 (1): 3–24.

———. 2013. *Democracy, Gender, and Social Policy in Russia: A Wayward Society.* Basingstoke: Palgrave Macmillan.

Chari, Sharad, and Katherine Verdery. 2009. "Thinking between the Posts: Postcolonialism, Postsocialism, and Ethnography after the Cold War." *Comparative Studies in Society and History* 51 (1): 6–34.

Cohen, Stephen F. 2006. "The New American Cold War." *The Nation,* July 10.

———. 2011. *Soviet Fates and Lost Alternatives: From Stalinism to the New Cold War.* New York: Columbia University Press.

———. 2012. "Stop the Pointless Demonization of Putin." *The Nation,* May 7.

Coles, Kimberley. 2007. *Democratic Designs: International Intervention and Electoral Practices in Postwar Bosnia-Herzegovina.* Ann Arbor: University of Michigan Press.

Collier, Stephen J. 2011. *Post-Soviet Social: Neoliberalism, Social Modernity, Biopolitics.* Princeton, NJ: Princeton University Press.

Comaroff, Jean, and John L. Comaroff. 2001. "Millenial Capitalism: First Thoughts on a Second Coming." In *Millenial Capitalism and the Culture of Neoliberalism,* edited by Jean Comaroff and John L. Comaroff, 1–56. Durham, NC: Duke University Press.

———. 2006. "Reflections on Youth, from the Past to the Postcolony." In *Frontiers of Capital: Ethnographic Reflections on the New Economy,* edited by Melissa S. Fisher and Greg Downey, 267–281. Durham, NC: Duke University Press.

Cook, Linda J. 1993. *The Soviet Social Contract and Why It Failed: Welfare Policy and Workers' Politics from Brezhnev to Yeltsin.* Cambridge, MA: Harvard University Press.

———. 2007. *Postcommunist Welfare States: Reform Politics in Russia and Eastern Europe.* Ithaca, NY: Cornell University Press.

Cruikshank, Barbara. 1999. *The Will to Empower: Democratic Citizens and Other Subjects.* Ithaca, NY: Cornell University Press.

Darian-Smith, Eve. 2002. "Beating the Bounds: Law, Identity, and Territory in the New Europe." In *Ethnography in Un-*

stable Places: Everyday Lives in Contexts of Dramatic Political Change, edited by Carol Greenhouse, Elizabeth Mertz, and Kay Warren, 249–275. Durham, NC: Duke University Press.

Dunn, Elizabeth C. 2004. *Privatizing Poland: Baby Food, Big Business, and the Remaking of Labor.* Ithaca. NY: Cornell University Press.

Edmondson, Linda. 1984. *Feminism in Russia, 1900–17.* Stanford, CA: Stanford University Press.

Edwards, Bob, and Michael W. Foley. 1998. "Civil Society and Social Capital beyond Putnam." *American Behavioral Scientist* 42 (1): 124–139.

Eliasoph, Nina. 2011. *Making Volunteers: Civic Life after Welfare's End.* Princeton, NJ: Princeton University Press.

Federman, Adam. 2014. "How US Evangelicals Fueled the Rise of Russia's 'Pro-Family' Right." *The Nation,* January 7.

Ferguson, James. 2002. "Spatializing States: Toward an Ethnography of Neoliberal Governmentality." *American Ethnologist* 29 (4): 981–1002.

Fischer, Michael M. J. 2003. *Emergent Forms of Life and the Anthropological Voice.* Durham, NC: Duke University Press.

Fournier, Anna. 2012.*Forging Rights in a New Democracy: Ukrainian Students between Freedom and Justice.* Philadelphia: University of Pennsylvania Press.

Funk, Nanette, and Magda Mueller, eds. 1993. *Gender Politics and Post-Communism: Reflections from Eastern Europe and the Former Soviet Union.* London: Routledge.

Gal, Susan, and Gail Kligman. 2000. *The Politics of Gender after Socialism.* Princeton, NJ: Princeton University Press.

Gapova, Elena. 2009a. "'Itogi s'Ezda': Eshche raz o klassovom projecte Post-

Sovetskogo feminism" ["The Outcome of the Congress": Once more on the class project of Post-Soviet feminism]. *Zhurnal issledovanii sotsial'noi politiki* 7 (4): 465–484.

———. 2009b. "Post-Soviet Academia and Class Power: Belarusian Controversy over Symbolic Markets." *Studies in East European Thought* 61 (4): 271–290.

———. 2012. "Delo 'Pussy Riot': Feministskii protest v kontekste klassovoi bor'by" [The "Pussy Riot" affair: Feminist protest in the context of class war]. *Neprikosnovennyi zapas* 85 (1): 10–21.

———. 2015. "Becoming Visible in the Digital Age: The Class and Media Dimensions of the Pussy Riot Affair." *Feminist Media Studies* 15 (1): 18–35.

Garton-Ash, Timothy. 1990. *The Uses of Adversity: Esssays on the Fate of Central Europe.* New York: Vintage Books.

Ghodsee, Kristen. 2004. "Feminism-by-Design: Emerging Capitalisms, Cultural Feminism, and Women's Nongovernmental Organizations in Postsocialist Eastern Europe." *Signs* 29 (3): 727–753.

Gibson-Graham, J. K. 1994. "'Stuffed If I Know!' Reflections on Post-Modern Feminist Social Research." *Gender, Place and Culture* 1 (2): 205–223.

———. 2006. *A Postcapitalist Politics.* Minneapolis: University of Minnesota Press.

Gill, Rosalind. 2007. "Postfeminist Media Culture Elements of a Sensibility." *European Journal of Cultural Studies* 10 (2): 147–166.

Gillis, Charlie. 2007. "Putin the Terrible." *Maclean's,* September 3.

Goldman, Wendy. 1991. "Working-Class Women and the 'Withering Away' of the Family: Popular Responses to Family Policy." In *Russia in the Era of NEP,* edited by Sheila Fitzpatrick, Alexander Rabinowitch, and Richard Stites, 125–

143. Bloomington: Indiana University Press.

Goode, Judith, and Jeff Maskovsky, eds. 2001. *New Poverty Studies: The Ethnography of Power, Politics, and Impoverished People in the United States*. New York: NYU Press.

Gordon, Colin. 1991. "Governmental Rationality: An Introduction." In *The Foucault Effect: Studies in Governmentality*, edited by Graham Burchell, Colin Gordon, and Peter Miller, 1–52. Chicago: University of Chicago Press.

Gorsuch, Anne E. 2000. *Youth in Revolutionary Russia: Enthusiasts, Bohemians, Delinquents*. Bloomington: Indiana University Press.

Goscilo, Helena. 2013a. "Introduction." In *Putin as Celebrity and Cultural Icon*, edited by Helena Goscilo, 1–5. London: Routledge.

——. 2013b. "Russia's Ultimate Celebrity: VVP as VIP Objet d'Art." In *Putin as Celebrity and Cultural Icon*, edited by Helena Goscilo, 6–36. London: Routledge.

Goscilo, Helena, and Vlad Strukov, eds. 2011a. *Celebrity and Glamour in Contemporary Russia: Shocking Chic*. London: Routledge.

——. 2011b. "Introduction." In Goscilo and Strukov, *Celebrity and Glamour in Contemporary Russia*, 1–26.

Gradskova, Yulia. 2014. "Group-Work on Gender Equality in Transnational Cooperation:Raising Feminist Consciousness or Diminishing Social Risks?" In *The Sea of Identities:A Century of Baltic and East European Experiences with Nationality, Class, and Gender*, edited by Norbert Götz, 247–268. Stockholm: Elanders.

Greenberg, Jessica. 2010. "'There's Nothing Anyone Can Do about It': Par-ticipation, Apathy, and 'Successful' Democratic Transition in Postsocialist Serbia." *Slavic Review* 69 (1): 41–64.

——. 2012. "Gaming the System: Semiotic Indeterminacy and Political Circulation in the New Age of Revolution." *Language & Communication* 32 (4): 372–385.

——. 2014. *After the Revolution: Youth, Democracy, and the Politics of Disappointment in Serbia*. Stanford, CA: Stanford University Press.

Greenberg, Jessica, and Andrea Muehlebach. 2007. "The Old World and Its New Economy: Notes on the 'Third Age' in Western Europe Today." In *Generations and Globalization: Youth, Age, and Family in the New World Economy*, edited by Jennifer Cole and Deborah Durham, 190–214. Bloomington: Indiana University Press.

Grewal, Inderpal, and Caren Kaplan, eds. 1994. *Scattered Hegemonies: Postmodernity and Transnational Feminist Practice*. Minneapolis: University of Minnesota Press.

Guillory, Sean. 2008. "Nashi: Is It Really the End?" *The eXile*, April.

Hall, Stuart. 1996. "Who Needs Identity." *Questions of Cultural Identity* 16 (2): 1–17.

Haney, Lynne A. 2002. *Inventing the Needy: Gender and the Politics of Welfare in Hungary*. Berkeley: University of California Press.

Hann, Chris, ed. 2002. *Postsocialism: Ideals, Ideologies and Practices in Eurasia*. London: Routledge.

Hann, Chris, and Elizabeth Dunn, eds. 1996. *Civil Society: Challenging Western Models*. London: Routledge.

Hann, Chris, Caroline Humphrey, and Katherine Verdery. 2002. "Introduction: Postsocialism as a Topic of Anthropological Investigation." In Hann, *Postsocialism*, 1–28.

Haraway, Donna. 1991. *Simians, Cyborgs and Women: The Reinvention of Nature.* New York: Routledge.

Hardt, Michael, and Antonio Negri. 2011. "The Fight for 'Real Democracy' at the Heart of Occupy Wall Street." *Foreign Affairs,* October 11.

Harvey, David. 2005. *A Brief History of Neoliberalism.* Oxford: Oxford University Press.

Heller, Dana. 2007. "t.A.T.u. You! Russia, the Global Politics of Eurovision, and Lesbian Pop." *Popular Music* 26 (2): 195–210.

Hemment, Julie. 2004a. "Global Civil Society and the Local Costs of Belonging: Defining 'Violence against Women' in Russia." *Signs: Journal of Women in Culture and Society* 29 (3): 815–840.

———. 2004b. "The Riddle of the Third Sector: Civil Society, International Aid, and NGOs in Russia." *Anthropological Quarterly* 77 (2): 215–241.

———. 2004c. "Strategizing Gender and Development: Action Research and Ethnographic Responsibility in the Russian Provinces." In *Post-Soviet Women Encountering Transition: Nation Building, Economic Survival, and Civic Activism,* edited by Kathleen Kuehnast and Carol Nechemias, 313–333. Washington, DC: Woodrow Wilson Press.

———. 2007a. *Empowering Women in Russia: Activism, Aid, and NGOs.* Bloomington: Indiana University Press.

———. 2007b. "Public Anthropology and the Paradoxes of Participation: Participatory Action Research in Russia." *Human Organization* 66 (3): 301–314.

———. 2008. "Who's Serving Whom? Community Service Learning as Critical Pedagogy at a Time of Neglasnost' (Non-Transparency) in Russia." *Anthropology of East Europe Review* 26 (2): 36–47.

———. 2009. "Soviet-Style Neoliberalism?" *Problems of Post-Communism* 56 (6): 36–50.

———. 2012a. "Nashi, Youth Voluntarism, and Potemkin NGOs: Making Sense of Civil Society in Post-Soviet Russia." *Slavic Review* 71 (2): 234–260.

———. 2012b. "Redefining Need, Reconfiguring Expectations: The Rise of State-Run Youth Voluntarism Programs in Russia." *Anthropological Quarterly* 85 (2): 519–554.

Herzfeld, Michael. 2005. *Cultural Intimacy: Social Poetics in the Nation-State.* 2nd ed. New York: Routledge.

Hoffman, Lisa M. 2006. "Autonomous Choices and Patriotic Professionalism: On Governmentality in Late-Socialist China." *Economy and Society* 35 (4): 550–570.

———. 2010. *Patriotic Professionalism in Urban China: Fostering Talent.* Philadelphia: Temple University Press.

Holmes, Douglas R. 2000. *Integral Europe: Fast-Capitalism, Multiculturalism, Neofascism.* Princeton, NJ: Princeton University Press.

Holmes, Douglas R., and George E. Marcus. 2008. "Collaboration Today and the Re-Imagination of the Classic Scene of Fieldwork Encounter." *Collaborative Anthropologies* 1 (1): 81–101.

Hulme, David, and Michael Edwards, eds. 1997. *NGOs, States and Donors: Too Close for Comfort?* New York: St. Martin's, in association with Save the Children.

Humphrey, Caroline. 2002. "Does the Category 'Postsocialist' Still Make Sense?" In Hann, *Postsocialism,* 12–15.

Hyatt, Susan Brin. 2001a. "From Citizen to Volunteer: Neoliberal Governance and the Erasure of Poverty." In Goode and Maskovsky, *New Poverty Studies,* 201–235.

——. 2001b. "'Service Learning,' Applied Anthropology and the Production of Neo-Liberal Citizens." *Anthropology in Action* 8 (1): 6–15.

——. 2011. "What Was Neoliberalism and What Comes Next?" In *Policy Worlds: Anthropology and the Analysis of Contemporary Power,* edited by Cris Shore, Susan Wright, and Davide Però, 105–123. New York: Berghahn Books.

Ishkanian, Armine. 2003. "Importing Civil Society? The Emergence of Armenia's NGO Sector and the Impact of Western Aid on Its Development." *Armenian Forum* 3 (1): 7–36.

——. 2008. *Democracy Building and Civil Society in Post-Soviet Armenia.* London: Routledge.

Ivanova, Natalia. 1999. "(Now)Stalgia: Retro on the Post-Soviet Television Screen." *Harriman Review* 12 (2–3): 25–32.

Jeffrey, Craig. 2010. *Timepass: Youth, Class, and the Politics of Waiting in India.* Stanford, CA: Stanford University Press.

Johnson, Janet Elise, and Aino Saarinen. 2013. "Twenty-First-Century Feminisms under Repression: Gender Regime Change and the Women's Crisis Center Movement in Russia." *Signs: Journal of Women in Culture and Society* 38 (3): 543–567.

Juris, Jeffrey, and Maple Razsa. 2012. "Occupy, Anthropology, and the 2011 Global Uprisings." *Fieldsights – Hot Spots, Cultural Anthropology Online,* July 27. http://culanth.org/fieldsights/63 -occupy-anthropology-and-the -2011-global-uprisings.

Kalb, Don. 2009. "Conversations with a Polish Populist: Tracing Hidden Histories of Globalization, Class, and Dispossession in Postsocialism (and Beyond)." *American Ethnologist* 36 (2): 207–223.

Karmalskaia, Elena. 2008. "'I Am Concerned about the Quality of Reproduction . . .': Russian State Demographic Policy in the Eyes of Youth Movement Activists in Tver'." *Anthropology of East Europe Review* 26 (2): 56–67.

Kelly, Catriona, and Vadim Volkov. 1998. "Directed Desires: *Kulturnost'* and Consumption." In *Constructing Russian Culture in the Age of Revolution: 1881–1940,* edited by Catriona Kelly and David G. Shepherd, 293–313. Oxford: Oxford University Press.

Khabibullina, Lilia. 2009. "International Adoption in Russia: 'Market,' 'Children for Organs,' and 'Precious' or 'Bad' Genes." In *International Adoption: Global Inequalities and the Circulation of Children,* edited by Diana Marre and Laura Briggs, 174–189. New York: NYU Press.

Khasbulatova, Olga. 1994. *Opyt i traditsii zhenskogo dvizheniia v Rossii, 1860–1917* [The experience and tradition of the women's movement in Russia, 1860–1917]. Ivanovo: Ivanovskii Gos Universitet.

Kipnis, Andrew. 2008. "Audit Cultures: Neoliberal Governmentality, Socialist Legacy, or Technologies of Governing?" *American Ethnologist* 35 (2): 275–289.

Klingseis, Katharina. 2011. "The Power of Dress in Contemporary Russian Society: On Glamour Discourse and the Everyday Practice of Getting Dressed in Russian Cities." *Laboratorium: Zhurnal sotsial'nykh issledovanii* 3 (1): 84–115.

Krause, Elizabeth L. 2001. "'Empty Cradles' and the Quiet Revolution: Demographic Discourse and Cultural Struggles of Gender, Race, and Class in Italy." *Cultural Anthropology* 16 (4): 576–611.

——. 2005. *A Crisis of Births: Population Politics and Family-Making in Italy.*

Belmont, CA: Wadsworth/Thomson Learning.

Kurtovic, Larisa. 2012. "Activism in the Times of Impasse." *Anthropology News*, May, 28.

Laruelle, MarleÄne, ed. 2009. *Russian Nationalism and the National Reassertion of Russia*. London: Routledge.

Lassila, Jussi. 2011. "Anticipating Ideal Youth in Putin's Russia: The Web-Texts, Communicative Demands, and Symbolic Capital of the Youth Movements 'Nashi' and 'Idushchie Vmeste.' PhD diss., University of Jyvaskyla and Aleksanteri Institute.

———. 2012. *The Quest for an Ideal Youth in Putin's Russia II: The Search for Distinctive Conformism in the Political Communication of Nashi 2005–2009*. Stuttgart: Ibidem-Verlag.

Lassiter, Luke Eric. 2005. *The Chicago Guide to Collaborative Ethnography*. Chicago: University of Chicago Press.

Ledeneva, Alena V. 1998. *Russia's Economy of Favours: Blat, Networking and Informal Exchange*. Cambridge: Cambridge University Press.

———. 2006. *How Russia Really Works: The Informal Practices That Shaped Post-Soviet Politics and Business*. Ithaca, NY: Cornell University Press.

Lerner, Julia. 2011. "TV Therapy without Psychology: Adapting the Self in Post-Soviet Media." *Laboratorium: Russian Review of Social Research* 3 (1): 116–137.

Lipovetsky, Mark. 2004. "Post-Sots: Transformations of Socialist Realism in the Popular Culture of the Recent Period." *Slavic and East European Journal* 48 (3): 356–377.

Lucas, Edward. 2008. *The New Cold War: How the Kremlin Menaces Both Russia and the West*. London: Bloomsbury.

Lukose, Ritty A. 2009. *Liberalization's Children: Gender, Youth, and Consumer Citizenship in Globalizing India*. Durham, NC: Duke University Press.

Lyon-Callo, Vincent. 2004. *Inequality, Poverty, and Neoliberal Governance: Activist Ethnography in the Homeless Sheltering Industry*. Orchard Park, NY: Broadview.

Manning, Paul. 2007. "Rose-Colored Glasses? Color Revolutions and Cartoon Chaos in Postsocialist Georgia." *Cultural Anthropology* 22 (2): 171–213.

Marchesi, Milena. 2013. "Contested Subjects: Biopolitics and the Moral Stakes of Social Cohesion in Post-Welfare Italy." PhD diss., University of Massachusetts Amherst.

Marx, Karl, and Friedrich Engels. (1848) 1978. "Manifesto of the Communist Party." In *The Marx-Engels Reader*, edited by Robert C. Tucker, 473–500. New York: W. W. Norton.

Matza, Tomas. 2009. "Moscow's Echo: Technologies of the Self, Publics, and Politics on the Russian Talk Show." *Cultural Anthropology* 24 (3): 489–522.

———. 2012. "'Good Individualism'? Psychology, Ethics, and Neoliberalism in Postsocialist Russia." *American Ethnologist* 39 (4): 804–818.

Menzel, Birgit. 2008. "Russian Discourse on Glamour." *Kultura* 6 (December): 4–8.

Mijnssen, Ivo. 2014. *The Quest for an Ideal Youth in Putin's Russia I: Back to Our Future! History, Modernity, and Patriotism according to Nashi, 2005–2013*. New York: Columbia University Press.

Mikhailova, Tat'iana. 2008. "In'ektsiia glamura: Politika prozy Oksany Robski" [An injection of glamour: The politics of the prose of Oksana Robski]. *Neprikosnovennyi zapas* 62. http://magazines.russ.ru/nz/2008/6/mi5.html.

———. 2013. "Putin as the Father of the Nation: His Family and Other Animals."

In Goscilo, *Putin as Celebrity and Cultural Icon*, 65–81.

Ministerstvo Obrazovaniia, Rossiiskoi Federatsii. 2002. *Prikaz: O Kontseptsii modernizatsii rossiiskogo obrazovaniia na period do 2010 goda* [Order: On the concept of modernization in Russian education through the year 2010]. Electronic document, no. 393, February 11.

Mohanty, Chandra Talpade. 1984. "Under Western Eyes: Feminist Scholarship and Colonial Discourses." *Boundary 2* 12/13 (3/1): 333–358.

Morton, Keith. 1996. "Issues Related to Integrating Service-Learning into the Curriculum." In *Service-Learning in Higher Education: Concepts and Practices*, edited by Barbara Jacoby and Associates, 276–296. San Francisco: Jossey-Bass.

Muehlebach, Andrea. 2012. *The Moral Neoliberal*. Chicago: University of Chicago Press.

Myers, Steven Lee. 2007. "Youth Groups Created by Kremlin Serve Putin's Cause." *New York Times*, July 8.

Nadkarni, Maya, and Olga Shevchenko. 2004. "The Politics of Nostalgia: A Case for Comparative Analysis of Post-Socialist Practices." *Ab Imperio* 2: 487–519.

Network of Concerned Anthropologists. 2009. *The Counter-Counterinsurgency Manual*. Chicago: Prickly Paradigm.

Nonini, D. M. 2008. "Is China Becoming Neoliberal?" *Critique of Anthropology* 28 (2): 145–176.

Norris, Stephen. 2012. *Blockbuster History in the New Russia: Movies, Memory, and Patriotism*. Bloomington: Indiana University Press.

Nugent, David. 2008. "Democracy Otherwise: Struggles over Popular Rule in the Northern Peruvian Andes." In Paley, *Democracy: Anthropological Approaches*, 21–62.

Omel'chenko, Elena L. 2000. *Molodezhnye kul'tury i subkul'tury* [Youth cultures and subcultures]. Moscow: Institut Sotsiologii RAN.

——. 2006. "Molodezh dlya politikov vs. molodezh dlya sebya? Razmyshleniya o cennostyakh n fobiakh rossiiskoy molodezhi" [Youth for politics vs. youth for themselves? Reflections on the values and phobias of Russian youth]. *Molodezh i politika* 17: 253–276.

——. 2007. *Pokoleniia net: Khroniki sobytii* [The internet generation: A chronicle of events]. Ulyanovsk: Izdatel'skii Tsentr Ulianovskogo Gosudarstvennogo Universiteta.

Ong, Aihwa. 2003. *Buddha Is Hiding: Refugees, Citizenship, the New America*. Berkeley: University of California Press.

——. 2006. *Neoliberalism as Exception: Mutations in Citizenship and Sovereignty*. Durham, NC: Duke University Press.

Ong, Aihwa, and Stephen J. Collier. 2005. *Global Assemblages: Technology, Politics, and Ethics as Anthropological Problems*. Malden, MA: Blackwell.

Ortner, Sherry B. 1997. "Thick Resistance: Death and the Cultural Construction of Agency in Himalayan Mountaineering." *Representations* 59 (1): 135–162.

——. 2014. "Too Soon for Post-Feminism: The Ongoing Life of Patriarchy in Neoliberal America." *History and Anthropology* 25 (4): 530–549.

Ost, David. 1990. *Solidarity and the Politics of Anti-Politics: Opposition and Reform in Poland since 1968*. Philadelphia: Temple University Press.

——. 2006. *The Defeat of Solidarity: Anger and Politics in Postcommunist Europe*. Ithaca, NY: Cornell University Press.

Oushakine, Serguei Alex. 2009. *The Patriotism of Despair: Nation, War, and Loss in*

Russia. Ithaca, NY: Cornell University Press.

Packer, George. 2013. "Change the World." *New Yorker,* May 27.

Paley, Julia. 2001. *Marketing Democracy: Power and Social Movements in Post-Dictatorship Chile.* Berkeley: University of California Press.

———. 2002. "Toward an Anthropology of Democracy." *Annual Review of Anthropology* 31: 469–496.

———, ed. 2008. *Democracy: Anthropological Approaches.* Santa Fe, NM: SAR Press.

Patico, Jennifer. 2008. *Consumption and Social Change in a Post-Soviet Middle Class.* Washington, DC: Woodrow Wilson Center Press.

———. 2009. "Spinning the Market: The Moral Alchemy of Everyday Talk in Postsocialist Russia." *Critique of Anthropology* 29 (2): 205–224.

Phillips, Sarah D. 2000. "NGOs in Ukraine: The Making of a 'Women's Sphere.'" *Anthropology of East Europe Review* 18 (2): 23–29.

Pilkington, Hilary. 1994. *Russia's Youth and Its Culture.* London: Routledge.

Pilkington, Hilary, Elena Omel'chenko, Moya Flynn, Ul'iana Bliudina, and Elena Starkova. 2002. *Looking West? Cultural Globalization and Russian Youth Cultures.* University Park: Pennsylvania State University Press.

Pisano, Jessica. 2014. "The Tug of War: Notes from the Battlefield of Reflexivity." *Fieldsights – Hot Spots, Cultural Anthropology Online,* October 28. http://www.culanth.org/fieldsights/609-the-tug-of-war-notes-from-the-battlefield-of-reflexivity.

Price, David H. 2011. *Weaponizing Anthropology: Social Science in Service of the Militarized State.* Petrolia: CounterPunch.

Ratilainen, Saara. 2012. "Business for Pleasure: Elite Women in the Russian Popular Media." In Salmenniemi, *Rethinking Class in Russia,* 45–66.

Razsa, Maple. 2013. "Occupy Slovenia and the Radical Political Imaginary." Paper presented at the Annual Meeting of the Association for Slavic, East European, and Eurasian Studies, Boston, November 23.

Razsa, Maple, and Andrej Kurnik. 2012. "The Occupy Movement in Žižek's Hometown: Direct Democracy and a Politics of Becoming." *American Ethnologist* 39 (2): 238–258.

Read, Rosie. 2010. "Creating Reflexive Volunteers? Young People's Participation in Czech Hospital Volunteer Programs." *Journal of Youth Studies* 13 (5): 549–563.

Richter, James. 2002. "Evaluating Western Assistance to Russian Women's Organizations." In *The Power and Limits of NGOs,* edited by Sarah E. Mendelson and John K. Glenn, 54–90. New York: Columbia University Press.

———. 2009a. "The Ministry of Civil Society?" *Problems of Post-Communism* 56 (6): 7–20.

———. 2009b. "Putin and the Public Chamber." *Post-Soviet Affairs* 25 (1): 39–65.

Richter, James, and Walter F. Hatch. 2013. "Organizing Civil Society in Russia and China: A Comparative Approach." *International Journal of Politics, Culture, and Society* 26 (4): 323–347.

Ries, Nancy, ed. 2014. "Ukraine and Russia: The Agency of War." *Fieldsights – Hot Spots, Cultural Anthropology Online,* October 28. http://www.culanth.org/fieldsights/610-ukraine-and-russia-the-agency-of-war.

Riordan, Jim. 1989. *Soviet Youth Culture.* London: Macmillan.

Rivkin-Fish, Michele. 1999. "Sexuality Education in Russia: Defining Pleasure and Danger for a Fledgling Democratic Society." *Social Science & Medicine* 49 (6): 801–814.

———. 2003. "Anthropology, Demography, and the Search for a Critical Analysis of Fertility: Insights from Russia." *American Anthropologist* 105 (2): 289–301.

———. 2004. "'Change Yourself and the Whole World Will Become Kinder': Russian Activists for Reproductive Health and the Limits of Claims Making for Women." *Medical Anthropology Quarterly* 18 (3): 281–304.

———. 2005. *Women's Health in Post-Soviet Russia: The Politics of Intervention.* Bloomington: Indiana University Press.

———. 2006. "From 'Demographic Crisis' to 'Dying Nation': The Politics of Language and Reproduction in Russia." In *Gender and National Identity in Twentieth-Century Russian Culture,* edited by Helena Goscilo and Andrea Lanoux, 151–173. DeKalb: Northern Illinois University Press.

———. 2009. "Tracing Landscapes of the Past in Class Subjectivity: Practices of Memory and Distinction in Marketizing Russia." *American Ethnologist* 36 (1): 79–95.

———. 2010. "Pronatalism, Gender Politics, and the Renewal of Family Support in Russia: Toward a Feminist Anthropology of Maternity Capital." *Slavic Review* 69 (3): 701–724.

Rivkin-Fish, Michele, and Cassandra Hartblay. 2014. "When Global LGBTQ Advocacy Became Entangled with New Cold War Sentiment: A Call for Examining Russian Queer Experience." *Brown Journal of World Affairs* 21 (1): 95–111.

Robertson, Graeme B. 2009. "Managing Society: Protest, Civil Society, and Regime in Putin's Russia." *Slavic Review* 68 (3): 528–547.

Robinson, Mark. 1994. "Governance, Democracy and Conditionality: NGOs and the New Policy Agenda." In *Governance, Democracy and Conditionality: What Role for NGOs?,* edited by Andrew Clayton, 35–52. Oxford: INTRAC.

Rogers, Douglas. 2010. "Postsocialisms Unbound: Connections, Critiques, Comparisons." *Slavic Review* 69 (1): 1–15.

———. 2015. *The Depths of Russia: Oil, Power, and Culture after Socialism.* Ithaca, NY: Cornell University Press.

Rose, Nikolas. 1996. "The Death of the Social? Re-Figuring the Territory of Government." *Economy and Society* 3: 327–356.

———. (1996) 2006. "Governing 'Advanced' Liberal Democracies." In *The Anthropology of the State: A Reader,* edited by Aradhana Sharma and Akhil Gupta, 144–162. Malden, MA: Wiley-Blackwell.

Rose, Nikolas, Pat O'Malley, and Mariana Valverde. 2006. "Governmentality." *Annual Review of Law and Social Science* 2 (December): 83–104.

Riabov, Oleg, and Tat'iana Riabova. 2014a. "The Decline of Gayropa? How Russia Intends to Save the World." *Eurozine,* February 5. http://www .eurozine.com/pdf/2014-02-05 -riabova-en.pdf.

———. 2014b. "The Remasculinization of Russia?" *Problems of Post-Communism* 61 (2): 23–35.

Riabova, Tat'iana, and Oleg Riabov. 2010. "Nastoiashchii muzhchina Rossiiskoi politiki? (K voprosu o gendernom diskurse kak resurse vlasti)" [The real man of Russian politics? On gender discourse as a resource for the authorities]. *POLIS: Politicheskie issledovaniia,* no. 5: 48–63.

——. 2013. "'Geiropa': Gendernoe iz-
merenie obraza Evropy v praktikakh
politicheskoi mobilizatsii" ["Gayropa":
Gendered changes in the image of
Europe in the practice of political mo-
bilization]. Zhenshchina v rossiiskom
obshchestve 3: 31–39.

Rudova, Larissa. 2008. "The Glamorous
Heroines of Oksana Robski." Kultura,
December 6. http://www.kultura-rus
.uni-bremen.de/kultura_dokumente
/artikel/englisch/k6_2008_EN
_Rudova_Menzel_GE.pdf.

Russian Federation. 2004. Educational System in Russia: The National Report of the
Russian Federation. Geneva: UNESCO.

Salmenniemi, Suvi. 2008. Democratization
and Gender in Contemporary Russia.
London: Routledge.

——. 2010. "Struggling for Citizenship."
Demokratizatsiya: The Journal of Post-
Soviet Democratization 18 (4): 309–328.

——. 2012a. "Introduction." In Salmenniemi, Rethinking Class in Russia, 1–22.

——. 2012b. "Post-Soviet Khoziain: Class,
Self and Morality in Russian Self-Help
Literature." In Salmenniemi, Rethinking
Class in Russia, 67–84.

——, ed. 2012c. Rethinking Class in Russia.
Farnham, UK: Ashgate.

Salmenniemi, Suvi, and Maria Adamson.
2015. "New Heroines of Labour: Domes-
ticating Post-Feminism and Neoliberal
Capitalism in Russia." Sociology 49 (1):
88–105.

Sampson, Steven. 1996. "The Social Life of
Projects: Importing Civil Society to Al-
bania." In Hann and Dunn, Civil Society,
121–142.

Seligman, Adam. 1998. "Between Public
and Private: Towards a Sociology of
Civil Society." In Democratic Civility:
The History and Cross-Cultural Possibility of a Modern Political Ideal, edited by

Robert W. Hefner, 79–111. New Bruns-
wick, NJ: Transaction.

Shevchenko, Olga. 2009. Crisis and the
Everyday in Postsocialist Moscow. Bloomington: Indiana University Press.

Smith, Kathleen E. 2002. Mythmaking in
the New Russia: Politics and Memory during the Yeltsin Era. Ithaca, NY: Cornell
University Press.

Snitow, Ann. 1999. "Cautionary Tales." In
Proceedings of the 93rd Annual Meetings
of the American Society of International
Law, 35–42.

Song, Jesook. 2009. "Between Flexible Life
and Flexible Labor: The Inadvertent
Convergence of Socialism and Neoliberalism in South Korea." Critique of
Anthropology 29 (2): 139–159.

Sperling, Valerie. 1999. Organizing Women
in Contemporary Russia: Engendering
Transition. Cambridge: Cambridge University Press.

——. 2003. "The Last Refuge of a Scoun-
drel: Patriotism, Militarism, and the
Russian National Idea." Nations and
Nationalism 9 (2): 235–253.

——. 2009. "Making the Public Patriotic:
Militarism and Anti-Militarism in Russia." In Laruelle, Russian Nationalism
and the National Reassertion of Russia,
218–271.

——. 2012. "Nashi Devushki: Gender and
Political Youth Activism in Putin's and
Medvedev's Russia." Post-Soviet Affairs
28 (2): 232–261.

——. 2014. Sex, Politics, and Putin: Political
Legitimacy in Russia. New York: Oxford
University Press, 2014.

Standing, Guy. 2011. The Precariat: A New
Dangerous Class. New York: Bloomsbury Academic.

Stanton, Timothy K., Dwight E. Giles
Jr., and Nadinne I. Cruz. 1999. Service-
Learning: A Movement's Pioneers Reflect

on Its Origins, Practice, and Future. San Francisco: Jossey-Bass.

Stites, Richard. 1989. *Revolutionary Dreams: Utopian Vision and Experimental Life in the Russian Revolution.* New York: Oxford University Press.

Strand, Kerry. 2000. "Community-Based Research as Pedagogy." *Michigan Journal of Service Learning,* Fall, 85–96.

Temkina, Anna, and Elena Zdravomyslova. 2003. "Gender Studies in Post-Soviet Society: Western Frames and Cultural Differences." *Studies in East European Thought* 55 (1): 51–61.

Tolz, Vera. 1990. *The USSR's Emerging Multiparty System.* Westport, CT: Greenwood.

Topalova, Viktoriya. 2006. "In Search of Heroes: Cultural Politics and Political Mobilization of Youths in Contemporary Russia and Ukraine." *Demotratizatsiya* 14 (1): 23–41.

Trubina, Elena. 2012. "Class Differences and Social Mobility amongst College-Educated Young People in Russia." In Salmenniemi, *Rethinking Class in Russia,* 203–219.

Tumarkin, Nina. 1994. *The Living and the Dead: The Rise and Fall of the Cult of World War II in Russia.* New York: Basic Books.

Urla, Jacqueline, and Justin Helepololei. 2014. "The Ethnography of Resistance Then and Now: On Thickness and Activist Engagement in the Twenty-First Century." *History and Anthropology* 25 (4): 431–451.

Uspenskaya, V. I., ed. 2003. Aleksandra Kollotai: Teoriia Zhenskoi Emansipatsii v Kontekste Rossiiskoe Gendernoi Politiki [Alexandra Kollonati: Theories of women's emancipation in the context of Russian gender politics]. Tver'. Tver' gos. universitet.

Verdery, Katherine. 1996. *What Was Socialism, and What Comes Next?* Princeton, NJ: Princeton University Press.

———. 2001. "Socialist Societies: Anthropological Aspects." In *International Encyclopedia of the Social and Behavioral Sciences,* edited by Neil Smelser and Paul Baltes, 14,496–14,500. New York: Elsevier.

Volkov, Vadim. 2002. *Violent Entrepreneurs: The Use of Force in the Making of Russian Capitalism.* Ithaca, NY: Cornell University Press.

Wedel, Janine. 1998. *Collision and Collusion: The Strange Case of Western Aid to Eastern Europe 1989–1998.* New York: St. Martin's.

Wengle, Susanne, and Michael Rasell. 2008. "The Monetisation of L'goty: Changing Patterns of Welfare Politics and Provision in Russia." *Europe-Asia Studies* 60 (5): 739–756.

Wilson, Andrew. 2005. *Virtual Politics: Faking Democracy in the Post-Soviet World.* New Haven, CT: Yale University Press.

Wood, Elizabeth. "Putin: Masculinity and Hypermasculinity." Lecture, Center for Russian, East European, and Eurasian Studies, University of Michigan, Ann Arbor, January 19, 2011.

Yngvesson, Barbara. 2010. *Belonging in an Adopted World: Race, Identity, and Transnational Adoption.* Chicago: Chicago University Press.

Yurchak, Alexei. 1999. "Gagarin and the Rave Kids: Transforming Power, Identity and Aesthetics in Post-Soviet Nightlife." In *Consuming Russia: Popular Culture, Sex, and Society since Gorbachev,* edited by Adele Marie Barker, 76–109. Durham, NC: Duke University Press.

———. 2002. "Entrepreneurial Governmentality in Post-Socialist Russia: A Cultural Investigation of Business

Practices." In *The New Entrepreneurs of Europe and Asia: Patterns of Business Development in Russia, Eastern Europe and China,* edited by Victoria E. Bonnell and Thomas B. Gold, 278–324. New York: M. E. Sharpe.

———. 2003. "Russian Neoliberal: The Entrepreneurial Ethic and the Spirit of 'True Careerism.'" *Russian Review* 62 (1): 72–90.

———. 2006. *Everything Was Forever, until It Was No More: The Last Soviet Generation.* Princeton, NJ: Princeton University Press.

———. 2008. "Post-Post-Soviet Sincerity: Young Pioneers, Cosmonauts and Other Soviet Heroes Born Today." In *What Is Soviet Now? Identities, Legacies, Memories,* edited by Thomas Lahusen and Peter H. Solomon, 257–276. Berlin: LIT Verlag.

———. 2014. "Revolutions and Their Translators: Maidan, the Conflict in Ukraine, and the Russian New Left." *Fieldsights – Hot Spots, Cultural Anthropology Online,* October 28. http://www.culanth .org/fieldsights/619-revolutions-and -their-translators-maidan-the-conflict -in-ukraine-and-the-russian-new-left.

Zhurzhenko, Tatiana. 2008. *Gendernye rynki Ukrainy: Politicheskaia ekonomiia natsional'nogo stroitel'stva* [Gendered markets of Ukraine: The political economy of nation building]. Vilnius, Lithuania: Evropeiskii Gumanitarnyi Universitet.

Zibbell, Jon E. 2009. "'To Promote, Encourage or Condone': Science, Activism and the Political Role of Moralism in the Formation of Needle Exchange Policy in Springfield, Massachusetts, 1998–2005." PhD diss., University of Massachusetts Amherst.

Zigon, Jarrett. 2010. "Moral and Ethical Assemblages: A Response to Fassin and Stoczkowski." *Anthropological Theory* 10 (1–2): 3–15.

———. 2011. "Working on the Self in Russian Orthodox Church Drug Rehabilitation: A Moral and Ethical Assemblage." *Ethnos* 39 (1): 30–50.

INDEX

Page numbers in italics refer to illustrations.

abortion, 202, 203, 204, 209, 237n38
adoptions policy, 163, 234n15
agency, 15, 68, 69, 76, 103, 132; individual
    agency inhibited by state projects, 158;
    in Komsomol work, 24; of Nashi komis-
    sars, 101
anarchists, 58, 74
Another Russia, 230n27
anthropology, 18, 215, 218, 220, 228n22; of
    postsocialism, 14, 15, 34–35, 37, 57, 237n1;
    reflexive imperative of, 33, 181, 213; of
    resistance, lessons from, 16, 68, 218–219,
    224n15. *See also* ethnography
antifascism, 72, 73
antiglobalization/alter-globalization, 38,
    68, 87, 224n11
anti-Semitism, 95, 119, 200, 232n12
apoliticism, 28, 32, 108; of educated youth,
    226n32; of Millennial generation, 8;
    Nashi's effort to mobilize apolitical
    youth, 74, 229n3; nationalist turn of
    2000s and, 52–53; students' cynicism
    about politics, 92; youth left vulnerable
    to political manipulation by, 85
Arab Spring, 8, 13
asset-based development, 114, 154–155,
    232n9
authoritarianism, 2, 7, 37, 62, 73, 134, 189,
    217; civil-society concept and resur-

gence of, 34–36, 76, 80; "color" revolutions and, 80; liberal youth projects as
antidote to, 9; politics of representation
and, 16, 37, 181, 212; problematic binary
with liberal democracy, 7, 49, 237n3;
sexualized politics as manifestation of,
181, 212

bespredel ("boundlessness" of 1990s), 28,
    225n25
binary socialism, 7, 33, 67, 218
birthrates, low, 8, 28
Bologna Process, 46, 227n7
Bolshevik period, 7, 99, 185, 186, 197; civil
    war, 78, 119; institutions of, 224n19. *See
    also* Soviet Union (USSR)
Bush, George W., 17, 36, 38, 46, 81

capitalism, 24–25, 29, 67; utopian elements
    of, 25
"careerism," 26, 225n22
CEDAW (UN Convention on the Elimi-
    nation of All Forms of Discrimination
    against Women), 197, 236n31
celebrity culture, 30, 129, 189, 199
Chapman, Anna, 191–192, 235n20
Chechens and Chechnya, 78, 95, 230n29
children, 97, 98, 164, 171; adoption of
    orphans, 163, 172, 234n15; child care,
    203; Children First campaign, 165–167,
    170, 173

Chubais, Anatoly, 110, 231n4

citizenship, 10, 14, 16, 18, 55; gendered redrawing of, 178; global and pan-European, 38; Nashi's agentive mode of, 88; Soviet, 56; youth voluntarism and, 142

civil society, 8, 10, 12, 14, 90; as changing concept, 33–36, 76–80, 214–215; "functioning," 81, 87, 95; Medvedev and, 109–110, 231n2; militarized version of, 215; Nashi activists and, 78–81, 88; neoliberalism and, 34, 108, 214; Putinera rendition of, 81, 88, 102, 144; as soft power, 36, 80; university as, 54; youth voluntarism and, 142, 145

Clinton, Bill, 80

Cold War, 17, 37, 62, 218; binary logic of, 214, 237n3; espionage terminology derived from, 43; gender relations during, 39; mutual constitution of "East" and "West," 224n21; "new Cold War," 17, 49; nostalgia for, 192; Ukraine conflict (2014) and, 237n3

collaboration/collaborative projects, 42–43, 51, 64, 76, 221; collaborative ethnography, 10–18, 221; geopolitics and, 182, 221; "politics of possibility" and, 44, 67, 221; push and pull of relationships in, 66, 228n24; second-generation East-West feminist collaboration, 17, 43–49, 55, 201–213; stance and, 67, 68; uncertain effects of, 68, 217–218

"color" revolutions, 76, 80, 82, 224n11

Communist Party, 57, 58, 158

community service learning (CSL) methodologies, 48–49

conspiracy thinking, 85

consumerism, 26, 190

contraception, 202, 203

corruption, 88, 94, 98

cultural intimacy, 63

deconstructionist sensibility, 85, 96, 102

"defeatists," 76, 83, 89, 94

democracy, 7, 8, 34, 73; "American democracy" as threat, 95; civil society and, 80;

"democratization" of 1990s, 27–28; disillusionment in, 10, 27, 214–215; feminism and, 213; narrowing of liberal democracy, 218; Nashi's critique of, 86. *See also* sovereign democracy

democracy promotion, 11, 27, 33; anthropology of, 13, 33–34, 224n11, 229n16; civil-society concept and, 78, 229n16; commonality with Putin-era civil-society projects, 33; militarization of aid under Bush (George W.) administration, 36, 38, 80, 81, 88; Nashi as response to, 74; retort to, 12, 83; transnational governmentality and, 34; voluntarism and, 145

Democratic Union, 58, 228n20

demographic crisis, 28, 32, 186, 208–209

difference, 33, 55, 56–69

DIY (do it yourself) culture, 74, 81, 87

economic crisis, 10, 111; of 1998, 26, 55; of 2008, 8, 9, 39, 109

Edinaia Rossiia ("Party of Power"), 86, 191

education, 46–47, 57, 106, 151, 227n7; "academic nationalism," 84; "modernization" of, 46, 110; "patriotic," 29, 234n9; "psychology renaissance" of 2000s and, 145; scientific work extinguished in universities, 66; Seliger as alternative venue for, 107, 125–129; sociality in Russian education, 165, 170; women employed in, 205

Election Day (satirical film), 177

Eliasoph, Nina, 9, 36, 139, 147–148, 175, 223n7

empowerment, 34, 36, 114, 127, 131; experience of volunteers at Seliger and, 170–176; global "empowerment projects," 7, 11, 36, 120, 150, 175, 218, 223n7; as theme at Seliger, 107–108, 109, 113, 120; voluntarism and, 147, 148; of women in postsocialist society, 35

entrepreneurship, 2, 31, 109, 120, 141, 217

Estonia, Bronze Soldier incident in, 89, 230n27

ethics, 17, 59, 62
ethnography, 17, 51, 53, 221; collaborative, 10–18; pace and rhythm of research methodology, 37; paraethnographers, 52, 227n12; in Putin era, 53–69. *See also* anthropology
Europe, Western, 27, 40, 54, 162, 181, 213; civil-society discourse in, 218; feminism in, 200; sexualized images in public space, 196. *See also* West, the
European Union (EU), 8, 9, 54, 194, 218, 228n21
European University (St. Petersburg), 54, 228n16
Evening School for Gender Studies, 47

families, 40, 187, 197, 205. *See also* children; pronatalism
fascism, 73, 89, 93; political opponents discredited as "fascists," 219; sexualized "cult" of Putin compared with, 189; simplistic use as term, 90; Ukraine conflict (2014) and, 237n3
Federal Youth Affairs Agency (Rosmolodezh), 2, 19, 20, 56, 59, 138, 223n2; education and, 232n18; "forbidden video" and, 105, 121–122; founding of, 111, 231n7; innovation and, 175; "new youth policies" and, 31, 111; "project design" technology and, 115, 217, 232n10; Russia 2020 project, 141; Seliger organized by, 104; Vazhnoe Delo (Important Business) and, 149; voluntarism and, 144. *See also* Year of Youth (2009)
feminism, 14, 17, 34, 37, 41, 66; 1990s-era international feminist exchanges, 35, 37, 43, 45; popular hostility towards, 193–196, 197–198, 236n29; postsocialist inequality associated with, 35; Pussy Riot controversy and, 193, 236n26; satire (*stiob*) directed at, 182, 192–193, 224n13; second-generation postsocialist (East-West) exchange, 17, 43–49, 55, 201–213; sexualized "cult" of Putin criticized by,

180, 189; stereotypes of, 200. *See also* postfeminism
Ford Foundation, 35, 37, 46
"foreign agents" legislation, 43, 61, 63, 228n21
"Freedom Agenda," 36, 46

Gagarin, Yuri, 22, 118
Gapova, Elena, 35, 236n26
gender, 25, 35, 39, 177; contradictory incitements concerning, 178–180; as "dissident term," 195; "geopolitical performances" and, 179–185; liberal gender regime, resistance to, 193–195; public sector employment and, 205–206; shifting regimes of gender in Soviet/Russian history, 185–189; Soviet-era claims of egalitarianism, 196; "technologies of kindness" and, 164
gender studies, 41, 47, 65, 196
Gender Studies Center, Tver', 47, 93, 227n8
generation, last Soviet, 11, 16, 122, 215, 223n9; Millenial, 8, 11
geopolitics, 17, 44, 83; essentialist construction of, 84; feminism and, 199; "geopolitical performances," 40, 180, 182, 192, 211; reconfigured terrain of, 43, 61; Westernness as liability, 55
Gibson-Graham, J. K., 44, 67, 226n2, 228n24
glamour (*glamur*), 29, 107, 181, 190, 212, 226n31; feminism and, 199, 200; state-run youth projects and, 208. *See also* "oil-and-gas glamour"
"global war on terror" discourse, 193
globalization, 84–85, 180, 211, 212
Goscilo, Helena, 225n29
Greenberg, Jessica, 224n11, 229n16

homophobia, 195, 234n3, 236n25
homosexuality, 186, 193–194, 237n4
housing crisis, 29
human rights, 35, 73, 88, 197

identity, national, 180, 229n15
independent Russian women's movement, 34, 36
indifference (*bezrazlichie*), 32, 226n33
innovation, 12, 32, 111; as theme at Seliger, 105, 118, 139, 173; Zvorykinsky Project and, 119, 128, 175
International Monetary Fund, 27
Iraq, U.S.-led war in, 80

Kasparov, Garry, 83
Khakamada, Irina, 191
Khodorkovsky, Mikhail, 81, 229n14
Kirill, Patriarch, 188, 235n15
Kollontai, Aleksandra, 200
Kommersant (liberal newspaper), 87–88, 103
komissars (Nashi activists), 19, 27, 31, 51–52, 59, 68, 92; elite society of, 175; motivations of, 216; portraits of individual komissars, 93–103; Seliger run by, 125, 129
Komsomol (Communist Youth League), 1, 7, 16, 23–24, 37, 56, 92; *dobrovol'tsy* (volunteers) of, 146, 149; entrepreneurial voluntarism and, 176; establishment of, 224n19; gender equality in, 208; knowledge management and, 122; moral education and, 25; Nashi compared with, 30; peak membership of, 224n20; post-Soviet voluntarism and, 142; as predecessor of Nashi, 81, 97; Vazhnoe Delo compared with, 152

League of Equality (*Liga Spravedlivosti*), 96
leftists, 74, 77
LGBT rights, 193, 195, 236n29
Liberal Democratic Party of Russia, 224n16
liberalism, 14, 74, 224n21; disappointment with, 13; discredited after 1990s, 26, 27; "geopolitical performances" as critique of, 180, 211; liberal intelligentsia, 33; "political correctness" associated with, 193;

satire (*stiob*) directed at, 182; suspicion of, 22
Limonov, Eduard, 83
Lipovetsky, Mark, 232n14
"loyalty," as key word of Putin era, 45, 226n6

"Man Like Putin, A" (pop song), 190–191, 203, 235n17
marriage, low rates of, 29, 32
Marxism-Leninism, 24, 38
masculinity: crisis of, 187, 209; "Men with Children in their Arms, Not Weapons" (feminist art exhibition), 201–202; militarized forms of, 219
"mass actions," 99, 100
Medvedev, Dmitry, 106, 107, 187; civil-society concept and, 109–110, 231n2; innovation awards announced by, 110, 231n3; on possible collapse of Russian state, 77–78; presidency of, 2, 5, 202
memory, 15
methodologies, 15, 44, 220; community service learning (CSL), 48–49; ethics and, 17; participatory action research (PAR), 42–43, 226n1; of political technologists, 145; politics of representation and, 37; of state-run projects, 149, 151, 157; voluntarism and, 155–156
Ministry of Education and Science, 28, 46, 225n27
Ministry of Sports, Tourism, and Youth Policy, 2, 19, 144
modernization, 22, 27, 31–33, 81, 111, 149; as buzzword, 109; "patriotic education" and, 120; Skolkovo as flagship of, 110; youth voluntarism as central plank of, 142
Molodaia Gvardiia, 191
mortality rates, 35
Moscow State University (MGU), 54, 179; erotic calendar produced by journalism students, 178–179, 192, 235n18; Political Science Department, 121
movie industry, Russian, 29, 225n28

Moving Together (*Idushchiye Vmeste*), 29
multiculturalism, 98
muzhik (macho man), 188, 219

Nashi (Ours), 2, 12, 49, 89–93, 114, 162,
223n2; agency of participants, 139–140;
campus activism of, 89–93; civil society
and, 76–81, 215, 216; end of, 103, 104, 202,
231n34; founding of, 30; gender in political discourse of, 178–179, 234n3; Kremlin backers alienated by, 74, 229n4;
Kremlin support for, 73, 229n2; at Lake
Seliger youth camp, 30, 39, 86, 104,
105; liberal gender politics opposed by,
194–195; "nashisty" as pejorative term
for, 1–2, 10, 76; as political technology
project, 38–39, 72–76, 103; pronatalism
of, 202–205; Stal' (Steel) offshoot of,
103, 140; *stiob* deployed for pro-regime
purposes, 192–193, 236n23; welfare section, 97, 163; Western media accounts
of, 62, 181; Yakemenko as founder of, 31,
224n10, 229n2
National Bolshevik Party (Nats Boly), 39,
51, 74, 83, 90–91, 191
nationalism, 9, 11, 14, 53, 84; "academic
nationalism," 84; demographic, 213;
neoliberal rationality fused with, 143;
reasserted in post-Soviet Russia, 40;
right-wing, 38; Soviet-era, 36; ultranationalists, 83, 95, 230n29, 231n32; universities and "academic nationalism," 45
NEETS ("not in employment, education,
or training"), 8, 223n4
neoliberalism, 9, 10, 14, 27, 38, 214; civil
activism and, 117; democratization and,
33–34, 80; disparaged by Putin administration, 143; global empowerment projects and, 11; nationalist-nativist critique
of, 120; repoliticization of youth under,
18; "resonance" with socialism, 175,
224n21; technologies of neoliberal governmentality, 11, 25, 34, 145, 175; youth
voluntarism and, 49, 159
Neschastnyi Sluchai (pop band), 177, 181

Network of East-West Women (NEWW),
45, 226n4
New Policy Agenda, 33, 35, 80
NGOs (nongovernmental organizations),
12, 38, 46; civil society and, 214; disparaged by Nashi, 76; feminists and, 196;
professional and bureaucratic nature of,
35; Putin-era NGO "boom," 79, 225n23;
Putin-era restrictions on, 79, 229n11;
required to register as "foreign agents,"
43, 61, 228n21; Russian popular suspicion of, 80
nostalgia, 13, 15, 146, 215, 225n25; for Cold
War culture, 192; for imperial Russian
past, 29; for late socialism, 144; for
Soviet Union, 22, 57–58, 191, 224n18; in
Western societies, 218

Occupy movement, 219, 224n11
"oil-and-gas glamour" (*neftegazovy glamur*), 30, 33, 74–75, 139, 180; celebrity
culture and, 199; gender politics in era
of, 198; satire (*stiob*) and, 181; sexualized
patriotic performances and, 212
oligarchs, 81, 85, 107, 129; emergence in
Yeltsin era, 28; gender relations and, 198
Omel'chenko, Elena, 54
Open Russia Foundation, 229n14
Orange Revolution, in Ukraine, 38, 76–77,
86, 99; "anti-Orange" elements of Nashi
and, 97; Russia's sovereignty and, 97,
109
Organization for Security and Co-operation in Europe (OSCE), 83
orphans, 31, 97, 163, 164, 165
Orthodox Church, Russian, 14, 73, 84,
185; abortion rights and, 204; growing
influence of, 180, 184–185; liberal gender
politics opposed by, 193, 236n27; Nilova
Pustyn monastery, 184, 188; pronatalist
values associated with, 177–178, 186, 188;
sexualized "cult" of Putin and, 189; as
trusted institution, 235n11
Oushakine, Serguei, 28, 83, 119, 230n20

participatory action research (PAR) methodology, 42–43, 56, 226n1

patriotism, 1, 30–32, 88, 141; fashion line associated with, 178, 189, 234n5; "New Russian Patriotism," 14, 29, 30, 32, 187; "patriotic education," 120; "patriotism of despair," 28, 37; "patriot"/"traitor" binary, 219; pronatalism and, 182, 189; sexualized patriotic performances, 39, 181, 189, 194–195, 207–208, 211–213

personhood, 26, 225n22

philanthropy, 144, 167

"political communication," 81, 82

"political correctness," 193, 236n24

political technologists, 7, 86, 143, 155, 194, 215; ex-Komsomol, 158; gender and, 164; global awareness of, 12–13; "patriotism of despair" and, 37; "revolution" rebranded by, 78; Soviet past used by, 14; Surkov as chief political technologist, 27; voluntarism project and, 145

postfeminism, 189, 190, 195, 212

postsocialism, 34, 68, 83, 145, 196. *See also* anthropology

Potanin Foundation, 128, 169, 170, 234n16

Projects: project design at Seliger, 115–117, 128, 130, 167, 173, 232n10

pronatalism, 51, 177–178, 182; church-state relations and, 187–188; demographic nationalism and, 208–209, 213; "I Want Three" campaign, 178, 202; as Soviet state policy, 186, 189

protests, 229n7; against 2005 social welfare reform, 47, 77, 188; antiglobalization, 68, 87; December 2011 opposition protests, 140, 233nn20, 21;

Public Chamber (Obshchetvennaia Palata), 79, 80

public opinion research, 145, 158

public relations, 31, 82, 144, 152, 173; ironic view of, 176; *pafos* (pathos, pomp), 159, 234n13; political PR, 42, 81, 85; sexualized patriotic performances and, 207

Pussy Riot controversy, 193, 236n26

Putin, Vladimir, 12, 17, 85, 171, 201; approval ratings of, 74; on civil society, 78–79; on collapse of Soviet Union as catastrophe, 78; democracy promotion and, 27, 225nn23–24; gender politics and, 186–187; on innovation and national security, 120; macho images of, 29; modernization of education and, 110; public persona of, 29, 188–189, 225n29; "Putin" as commercial brand, 190–191; rise to power, 26, 28; at Seliger, 113, 117; sexualized "cult" of, 62, 87, 176, 177, 178–180; third presidency (2012), 61, 219; urban liberal opposition to, 194

Putin-Medvedev tandemocracy, 31, 39, 103; economic crisis (2008) and, 109; gender politics of, 178; "modernization" theme of, 106

Putin's Kiss (documentary film, 2013), 88, 230n24

revolution, "color," 76–81, 124; "rebranding" of, 81–89, 229n9; "velvet" (1989), 76. *See also* Orange Revolution

Rivkin-Fish, Michele, 186, 213, 226n36, 237n4

Rogers, Douglas, 79, 229n12

Salmenniemi, Suvi, 190, 234n18, 235n16

satire, 181, 182, 192. See also *stiob*

self, individuated, 25

self-work, 11, 25

Seliger youth camps, 1–3, 12, 23, 59, 171, 182; activities in, 5, 207; application procedure to participate in, 168; commodification projects at, 14, 106, 200; education at, 125–129; marriages and sex at, 178, 182–185, 183, 203; Nashi participation in, 1, 30, 39, 86, 104, 105; portraits of participants at, 129–140; "projects" and "project design" at, 115–117, 128, 130, 167; promotional materials for, 105–106, 110–112, 112, 114, 118–119, 141, 162–163; Putin administration in relation to, 216–217;

qualities encouraged at, 106–109; as rare chance for vacation, 32; Russian Orthodox Church and, 188; Silicon Valley boot camps compared with, 127, 232n11; situated in Russian politics, 109–115; state funding of, 7, 223n2; talent and leadership at, 117–120, 123–125, 232n15; Tolerance session, 136; VIP lectures at, 64–66, 65, 112, 155, 156; Year of Youth (2009) and, 104. *See also* Technologies of Kindness

Serbia, 35, 80, 229n16

sex education, 186

sexism, 191, 208, 234n3

sexualization, 51, 62, 177–178, 203, 213

Shevchenko, Olga, 102

"shock therapy," economic, 12, 34

Silicon Valley, 110, 127, 232n11

Singing Together (girl band), 190

Sochi Olympics (2014), 160, 237n4

social mobility, 111, 117, 210; gendered strategies for, 198, 211; "oil-and-gas glamour" as simulacrum of, 30; pledge of career ladder, 151–154, 174–175; "project design" associated with, 116; Seliger and, 105, 139

social science, 47; political constraints on, 54, 61, 228n16, 228nn21–22

social welfare, 47, 77, 205, 212

socialism, 13, 14, 57, 84–85; changing post-Soviet views of, 27–28; Komsomol and, 24; neoliberal rationality fused with, 143, 175; nostalgia for, 144; self-help discourses of 1990s and, 25–26; "third way" and, 80

societal movement: of early 1990s, 170

"sovereign democracy," 27, 102, 225n24

sovereignty, 79, 81, 87, 97, 144, 218

Soviet Union (USSR), 6, 22, 53; bureaucracy associated with, 140; dissolution of, 11, 24, 33, 116, 187, 214; feminized status of medical profession in, 211, 237n35; gender equality as legitimacy claim of, 185, 196, 235n14; *nomenklatura* (bureaucratic elite) of, 124; nostalgia for,

22, 57–58, 191, 224n18; post-Soviet state projects in relation to, 10, 11; revival of Soviet past, 14; social welfare in, 233n6; voluntarism institutionalized in, 146, 233n4. *See also* Bolshevik period; Komsomol (Communist Youth League)

spectacle, politics and culture as, 29, 74–75, 182, 190

Sperling, Valerie, 191, 234n3, 236n33

stance, 67, 68

State Department, U.S., 55, 61

stiob (parody or ironic aesthetic), 13–14, 39–40, 213, 224n13; deployed for pro-regime purposes, 230n23; directed at liberals and feminists, 192–193, 236n23; sexualized politics and, 181–182

"street," political discourses of the, 76–77, 81–82, 91–92, 229n16; technologies, 39, 74, 212

subbotnik (voluntary day's labor), 24, 146, 233n4

subjectivity, 14, 24, 38, 171; alternative political subjectivities, 56; commodifying logics and, 39; neoliberal, 134; shifts in, 40, 103, 109

Surkov, Vladislav, 27, 73, 106, 216, 224n10; dismissal from post, 140, 233n20; as Kremlin's chief ideologist, 188; on Russian national identity, 229n15

"Sveta from Ivanovo" (Sveta Kuritsina), 199

talent, 32, 39, 105, 109; capitalism and, 12; "Commodify your Talent!" slogan, 11, 106, 200; education and, 125; repatriation of, 117–120

technologies, 38, 40, 143; flash mob, 96; Nashi as political technology project, 38, 72–76, 103; "project design," 115, 129; social-networking, 100; "soft," 85; talent and, 105. *See also* political technologists

Technologies of Kindness (Seliger session, 2009), 64, 126, 136, 141–144, 148, 166; entrepreneurship of self and, 175; gender and, 207–208; "Kind advice" (Dobrye sovety) motivational text, 153–159; organizers and coordinators of, 160, 162; Soviet voluntarism contrasted with, 163, 176

television: disinformation about the West on, 220; NTV (federal channel), 199; reality TV shows, 107, 174, 187, 190, 198

"thick description," 16, 215, 224n15

tolerance: critique of liberal project of, 119, 236n28; in Nashi discourse, 31, 73, 97, 98; as theme at Seliger, 31, 99, 105, 119, 136; as Western political concept, 194

"transition" paradigm, 24, 28, 32, 109, 145–146

Tver' State University, 48, 49, 69, 183; Center for Women's History and Gender Studies, 36–37, 46, 52, 200; methodological center for volunteers at, 155–156; Nashi at, 89–90; political posters at, 50; Sociology Department, 2

Ukraine, 39, 76, 80, 109, 195, 219, 237nn2–3

unemployment, youth, 8, 29, 35

United Nations (UN), 147, 186, 233nn7–8; CEDAW (Convention on the Elimination of All Forms of Discrimination against Women), 197, 236n31; International Year of Volunteers (IYV), 147, 233n7; UNESCO, 9

United Russia party, 179, 199

United States, 17, 18, 27, 181, 192, 220; adoptions of Russian children, 234n15; Christian Evangelicals' influence in Russia, 213, 237n38; civil-society discourse in, 218; "color" revolutions funded from, 76; criticized in nationalist propaganda, 84; feminism in, 200; higher education in, 46; regime-change policies of, 215; relations with Russia, 60; Russian students in, 119; sexualized images in public space, 196; skeptics of voluntarism in, 159; social welfare in,

233n4, 233n6; youth voluntarism in, 49, 64–65, 143, 227n11. *See also* West, the

Uspenskaya, Valentina, 15, 32, 63–64; feminist publishing house of, 134; liberal feminist orientation of, 66, 182; perspective on feminism in Russia, 195–201; projects founded by, 36–37; Zhenskii Svet (Women's Light) group of, 43, 45

Vazhnoe Delo (Important Business), 42, 52, 144, 160, 169; as pilot state-run voluntarism project, 148–153, 234n10

veterans, of World War II, 70, 75, 97, 99, 149

voluntarism, 2, 14, 31, 51, 64–65, 157; activation of youth through, 39; citizenship and, 142; gender and, 207–208; and neoliberalism, 146–148; portraits of volunteers, 160–170; professionalized, 161, 164; in the Soviet context, 146–148; as technology of the self, 144; as theme at Seliger, 105, 141; "true" and "false," 160, 161, 162, 234n14; Vazhnoe Delo as pilot project, 148–153; Western conception of, 161, 174; youth voluntarism, 49, 227n11

Walking Together, 111

West, the, 3, 24, 32, 66, 219, 231n33; demographic crisis of Russia blamed on, 187; disaffection with, 13, 21; Imaginary West, 143, 233n2; liberal democratic pieties of, 192; liberal gender regime of, 193–194; materialism of, 84; mutual constitution of "East" and "West," 24–25, 224n21; reaction to Putin's nationalism, 17; Russia's relations with, 2, 7, 219, 220; seen as rapacious force, 83, 101; Soviet Union and, 23, 25

Women's Council (Zhenotdel), 224n19

Women's rights: draft legislation (Russia), 193–194; international protection for, 197

World War II, 5, 76, 83; "antifascism" as invocation of Soviet heroism in, 73;

Bronze Soldier war memorial in Estonia, 89, 230n27; sacred symbol of Great
Patriotic War, 14; veterans of, 70, 75, 97,
99, 149; Victory Day (Den' Pobedy),
72–73

xenophobia, 9, 22, 182, 200

Yabloko (opposition party), 32
Yakemenko, Vasily, 31, 86, 216, 224n10,
229n2, 231n7; controversies over relations with women at Seliger, 208; dismissal from post, 140; modernization
projects and, 111; political party founded
by, 233n20
Year of Youth (2009), 15, 19, 21, 31, 51; "forbidden video" and, 122; methodological
works on voluntarism and, 156; networking opportunities and, 169; Seliger
youth camp and, 104, 118; voluntarism
and, 143, 152–153
Yeltsin, Boris, 26, 28, 44, 85, 191; sexualized
"cult" of Putin and, 188; unpopularity of
regime of, 77
Young Pioneers, 56, 92, 149

youth: ambivalent positioning of, 21; "empowerment" of, 9, 18; global anxieties
about, 7–9; in the Soviet context, 23–24;
policy, federal, 28, 79, 85, 111, 225n26,
229n13, 234n9; precarity/precariousness
of, 8, 108, 111, 135; rebellion and protest
movements of, 9
youth projects, state-run, 15, 30, 32, 49, 162;
Conception on Youth policies, 28, 111,
225n26, 234n9; empowerment projects
and, 175; former activists in, 207–213;
gender politics of, 51; global youth
culture and, 73; "new youth policies,"
31, 111, 120–123; patriotic recruitment efforts, 18–23; self-realization for girls in,
208; *Strategy* policy document, 28, 79,
85, 225n26, 229n13, 234n9
Yurchak, Alexei, 7, 223n9, 224n18, 237n3;
on the Imaginary West, 233n2; on "last
Soviet generation," 122; on *stiob,* 14,
224n13

Zhenskii Svet (Women's Light), 36, 43, 45,
47, 55, 197
Zhirinovsky, Vladimir, 19, 224n16
Zvorykinsky Project, 119, 128, 175

JULIE HEMMENT is Associate Professor of Anthropology
at the University of Massachusetts Amherst and author
of *Empowering Women in Russia: Activism, Aid, and
NGOs* (Indiana University Press, 2007).